TEACHING TIPS

TEACHING
TIPS SEVENTH EDITION

*A Guidebook for
the Beginning
College Teacher*

Wilbert J. McKeachie
University of Michigan

D. C. HEATH AND COMPANY
Lexington, Massachusetts / Toronto

*To my earliest teachers in the classroom and out,
my parents,
Bert and Edith McKeachie*

Preface

Teaching Tips was written to answer the multitude of questions posed by new college teachers, to place them at ease in their jobs, and to get them started effectively in the classroom.

This edition follows the general plan of earlier editions, but gives more of the theory and research relevant to each of the teaching methods discussed than did earlier editions. Because the book is still oriented toward the beginning teacher who faces a number of immediate practical problems, chapters usually begin with "tips," but these are now usually followed by a more serious discussion of the topic. New chapters have been added on the personalized system of instruction, roles of teachers, using students to teach other students, and instructional games and simulations. The chapter on motivation, learning, and cognition has been completely rewritten in order to bring the coverage in line with recent developments in cognitive psychology. The treatment of student rating of faculty has been substantially expanded.

I am pleased that so many copies of previous editions of this guide have been used outside the United States. My increasing interactions with colleagues in other countries who are concerned about improving teaching make me aware of the cultural bias of much of what I say. I trust that *Teaching Tips* will nevertheless have value for everyone concerned about student learning.

The first edition of this book was prepared in collaboration with Gregory Kimble. His wit and wisdom are still evident at many points in this seventh edition.

WILBERT J. McKEACHIE

Contents

1

Introduction

This is not a textbook in the Educational Psychology of College Teaching. It is merely a compilation of useful (occasionally mechanical) tricks of the trade which I, as a teacher, have found helpful in running classes. What is contained in this discussion will not make you a Great Teacher. It may be that Great Teachers are born and not made, but anyone with ability enough to get a job as a college teacher can be a *good* teacher. Many of us get bogged down in the details of running the classroom. In this book I have tried to suggest ways of making things go more smoothly. It is quite possible that teaching benefits from varied, but planned, routine.

The techniques of teaching that one uses will undoubtedly reflect one's philosophy of teaching. Thus, it might be a good idea for me to state my views here and now. These are some of the considerations that have guided me in making the recommendations in this book:

1. Education should be guided by a democratic philosophy. This has nothing to do with politico-social doctrine, but is simply a statement of my belief that education is a cooperative enterprise that works best when the student is allowed to contribute to it—when teachers listen and respond.
2. Students are adults. I feel strongly on this point. One of the severest criticisms that can be leveled against American higher education is that it perpetuates adolescence for another four years. It seems clear that adult behavior is *learned*. If no opportunity to practice adult behavior is allowed, such behavior will not be learned.
3. Instructors can occasionally be wrong. If they are wrong too often, they should not be teaching. If they are never wrong, they belong in heaven, not a college classroom.
4. There are many important goals of college teaching. Not the least of these is that of increasing the student's motivation and ability to *continue* learning after leaving college.

The College Culture

A college course cannot be divorced from the total college culture.

First of all, the college makes certain requirements of instructors. In most colleges you must submit grades for the students' work. You probably must give a final course examination. You may have to report on attendance. A classroom is usually assigned for the class, and the class usually meets in this assigned place. Frequently, smoking in the classroom is prohibited. Usually the class meets at certain regularly scheduled periods. It is not implied that these regulations are harmful, but they do provide boundaries within which instructors must work.

There are, in addition, areas not covered by the formal rules of the college in which instructors must tread lightly. For example, there may be certain limitations upon the instructor's social relationships with the students. In many college cultures unmarried instructors who become socially involved with their students are overstepping the bounds of propriety. In some colleges it would be deemed improper for instructors to convene classes in taverns. Certain limits upon class discussion of religion, sex, or politics may exist. Instructors must learn not only to operate within the fences of college regulations, but also to skirt the pitfalls of the college mores.

But instructors who consider only college mores in plans for their courses are ignoring a far more important limitation upon teaching, for the college culture has not only placed limitations upon instructors, but has also pretty much hobbled the students. Most important are the students' needs for success in college. To stay in college they must show evidence of achievement. With law, medical, and other graduate and professional schools overcrowded, they must present evidence of outstanding achievement in college courses to gain admission to these schools.

Average college students have already been rewarded year after year for superior achievement in elementary and high school classrooms. In many colleges they have had experience in their previous college classes with instructors who, in a more or less fatherly way, gave information and rewarded those students who could best give it back. Not only has the role of the teacher been similar in these classes, but teaching procedures were probably much the same. Depending upon the college, the method used may have been lecture, questions and answer, discussion, or something else. The sort of tests, frequency of tests, and methods of grading may also have conformed closely to certain college norms. As a result instructors who attempt to revolutionize teaching with new methods or techniques may find that they are only frustrating the needs and expectations imposed upon their students by the college culture.

One of the most important areas neglected in reports of research in varying methods of teaching is the relationship of the methods used in one class to the methods used in other classes in the same college. A method that may be greeted enthusiastically by students in one college may encounter open rebellion in another. Hence, one of the major considerations that must guide beginning teachers in their classroom procedures is the relationship of these procedures to the college culture. Thus, each reader will need to adapt my suggestions to the college culture of which he or she is a part.

Research vs. Teaching?

One aspect of the local culture critical for new teachers is the definition of the proper role of a faculty member. In many universities, for example, formal definitions of the criteria for promotion give research and teaching equal weight, but it is not uncommon to find that research is "more equal." This may come about not because of any attempt to hide the truth but because many faculty members serving on promotions committees honestly believe that you cannot be an effective teacher unless you are doing research.

While research in this area is difficult to conduct, there seems to be evidence that research and teaching are not necessarily in conflict. Many faculty members are excellent researchers and excellent teachers as well. Some excellent researchers are poor teachers; some excellent teachers do not publish research. The point here is not that you should choose one emphasis at the expense of the other. Rather, I advocate finding out what the local norms are, and if you feel a conflict, choosing the balance that suits your own talents and interests with an informed awareness of the likelihood of support for that self-definition.

Whatever your choice, it is likely that teaching will be a part of your role. Teaching well is more fun than teaching poorly. Thus, some investment of time and attention to developing skill in teaching is likely to have substantial pay-off in self-satisfaction over a career.

Research in Teaching

Some of you will disagree with me, at least at certain points. This is your perfect right since my ideas are only partly based on objective evidence, experimental or otherwise. But I believe that my ideas as well as your ideas should be experimentally tested. I hope that this book will not be accepted as infallible, but as the background for research that will give us an experimentally tested foundation for our teaching practice.

What I have tried to set down here is simply a set of hints that have seemed to me to be useful. I hope that you can use some of them too and that they add to the enjoyment and progress of your students. If they contribute to your joy in teaching, my purpose will have been fulfilled.

2

Countdown for
Course Preparation

For teachers, courses do not start on the first day of classes. Rather, a course begins well before they meet their students.

Time: Three Months Before the First Class*

Write Objectives

The first step in preparing for a course is the working out of course objectives, because the choice of text, the selection of the type and order of assignments, the choice of teaching techniques, and all the decisions involved in course planning should derive from your objectives. In Appendix A I have suggested a sample list of course

---

* The idea of three months, six weeks, and so on, I have borrowed from P. G. Zimbardo and J. W. Newton, *Instructor's resource book to accompany psychology and life* (Glenview, Ill.: Scott, Foresman, 1975).

objectives for the first course in psychology. At this point your list of goals should be taken only as a rough reminder to be revised as you develop other aspects of the course plan, and to be further revised in interaction with students.

Some of you have heard of behavioral objectives and may wish to phrase your objectives in behavioral terms. If so, do so. But don't omit important objectives simply because you can't think of good ways to convert them to behavioral language. The purpose of phrasing objectives behaviorally is to encourage you to be specific, but usually the behavior specified in a behavioral objective is an indicator of a more general objective you want to achieve. Don't get trapped into thinking that the behavior you list is all you should aim for—and don't become so obsessed with writing objectives that you neglect other parts of planning. The purpose of working out objectives is to facilitate planning, not inhibit it. The clearer you can become about what you're trying to do, the better. Behavioral objectives may help, but there is no evidence that they are better for student learning than other statements of objectives—in fact, there is little evidence that teachers who develop behavioral objectives are more effective than those who don't develop any list of objectives.* Whether behavioral objectives facilitate or interfere with student learning seems to depend upon the students' abilities, cognitive styles and previous backgrounds, the nature of the subject matter, and the teaching method used.

It seems logical that course planning should start with thinking about goals or objectives. I think it's likely to be helpful. But it is neither necessary nor sufficient for good teaching.

So begin by thinking about your objectives. What should they be? The answer obviously depends upon the course and discipline, but it is important to begin with the note that the objectives involve educating students; the objectives are not to cover a certain set of

---

* Duchastel and Merrill (1973) have reviewed empirical studies of the effects of behavioral objectives. Amidst the plethora of nonsignificant results are some studies indicating that sharing behavioral objectives with students may sometimes help focus their attention or assist them organizing material. So if you've worked out objectives, let your students know what they are, and if possible, give them a chance to help revise them. (This study and others mentioned in the text, as well as supplementary works, are found in the **References** at the back of the book. In addition, some chapters are followed by brief lists of supplementary reading from the **References** that are specifically applicable to those chapters).

topics, but rather to facilitate student learning. Typically, too, we are not concerned simply with the learning of a set of facts, but rather with the learning that can be applied and used in situations outside the course examinations. In fact, in most courses we are concerned about helping our students begin a lifelong learning process; that is, we want to develop interest in further learning and provide a base of knowledge and skills that will facilitate further learning. Similarly, each course contributes to other general goals of a university education that transcend specific subject matter, such as being willing to explore ideas contrary to one's own beliefs and knowing when information or data are relevant to an issue and how to find them.

In addition to this general perspective you need to keep in mind characteristics of the setting in which you teach. What is the role of this course in your department? Are other instructors depending upon this course to provide specific kinds of background knowledge or skill? What are your students like? What are their current concerns? Self-discovery? Social action? Getting a job?

A committee of college and university examiners developed two books to assist faculty members in thinking about their objectives. The two books, entitled *Taxonomy of Educational Objectives, Handbook I: Cognitive Domain* (Bloom et al., 1956) and *Handbook II: Affective Domain* (Krathwohl et al., 1964) will help point your objective writing in the right direction.

Draft a Syllabus for the Course

The syllabus will force you to begin thinking about the practicalities of what you must give up in order to fit within the constraints of time, place, students, available resources, and your own limitations.

As you begin to block out activities in relation to the college calendar, you will begin to note when you will want films, guest lecturers, field work, or other things that require scheduling ahead.

Order Textbooks or Other Resources Students May Need

● *Should you use a text?*   The revolution in teaching media has not been the advent of television, teaching machines, or computers, but rather the readier availability of a variety of printed materials.

With paperback books, reprint series, and a Xerox* machine in the library, young instructors are immediately beguiled by the thought that they can do a much better job in compiling a set of required readings than any previous author or editor.

There is much to be said for such a procedure. It provides flexibility, a variety of points of view, and an opportunity to maintain maximum interest. Even the difficulty of providing an integrated point of view may, in fact, be a virtue if it challenges students to provide their own integration. Moreover, since no single text covers every topic equally well, the use of a variety of sources enables the teacher to provide more uniformly excellent materials and to range over a variety of sources from theoretical papers and research reports to cases.

The "cons" of not using a textbook are apparent. Without a text the task of integration may be so overwhelming that great pressure is placed on instructors to provide integration. This may limit their freedom to use the class period for problem solving, applications, or other purposes. With a well-chosen textbook, they may rely upon the students to obtain the basic content and structure of the subject matter through reading and thus be freer to vary procedures in the classroom. Moreover, the managerial task of determining appropriate readings and arranging to have them available for students is not to be taken lightly. One is torn between potential student complaints about the cost of buying several sources and complaints from the librarian about the cost of multiple copies along with student complaints about their inability to get a reading assignment in the library.

A final consideration is the extent to which you want to use required vs. free reading, as in my use of a "reading log" (see Chapter 10). I use a text as a base to provide structure and then require students to write a log on readings they choose. To assign diverse required readings and additional free reading seems to me to require too much integration even for well-prepared, bright students.

● *Choosing a text or reading materials.* In choosing reading materials the most important thing is that they fit your objectives. One of the most annoying and confusing of practices to students is instructor disagreement with the textbook. It is doubtful that any

---

* Check the new copyright law before making copies.

book will satisfy you completely, but if you use a text, choose one that is as much in line with your view as possible.

Your library facilities will probably help you decide whether you choose a book that omits materials you would like to cover or a book that contains extra material you consider unimportant. Generally speaking I have found that students prefer to have additional material presented in lecture or by supplementary reading assignments. They dislike reading material the instructor later says isn't important, and, surprisingly enough, they also dislike omitting material in the textbook. (Somehow they feel that they're missing something.) This student need for continuity and closure also should influence the instructor's outline of assignments. Students don't like to jump around. They prefer going through a book as it was written. If the author also wrote the book in a systematic way, building one concept on another, using learning from early chapters to go more deeply into later topics, there may be good pedagogical reasons for following the author's order. Since I know of no text that completely suits many teachers, however, I can only recommend that you keep the skipping around to a minimum.

There is no substitute for detailed review of the competing texts for the course you are teaching. As introductory texts multiply, it becomes increasingly tempting to throw up your hands in frustration over the time required for a conscientious review and to choose the book primarily on the basis of appearance, the personality of the book sales representative, or the inclusion of your name as author of one of the studies cited. Yet the research on teaching methods suggests that the major influence on what students learn is not the teaching method but the textbook. Moreover, some of the superficially most attractive textbooks today are "managed books," written in the offices of the publisher rather than by persons who know the field. Managed books vary a great deal in the degree to which scholars are involved, and in some cases the person to whom the book is attributed may have exercised close supervision over the content so that it is equally as sound as one actually written by a scholar. The most egregious cases of plagiarism and errors in content are now disappearing, and the newer managed books may be worthy of consideration. The point is, however, that one cannot adopt a textbook on the basis of the sales representative's description anymore than physicians should prescribe drugs on the advice of the drug company's detail men.

Time: Two Months Before the First Class

Work Out a Tentative Set of Assignments for the Students

The next point at which course objectives influence preparation for the course is in terms of the kind, length, and content distribution of assignments. Two instructors who have chosen the same text-books will probably stress different materials. Since no one but the person teaching from his or her own text is probably well satisfied with the relative weightings of materials in available texts, it will almost always be necessary to assign chapters on some topics which, from your point of view, are incomplete and to assign others that treat a topic more extensively than you would desire. For the former situation, additional readings may partially solve the problem. For the latter, no very satisfactory solution is availa' le.

To summarize the argument so far in this section, the following schedule suggests the way in which a course may be planned in a preliminary way.

1. Decide what you want the students to gain from the course.
2. Choose one or more texts or other sources that make the points you want made.
3. Plan the course for the whole semester or year in such a way as to allot appropriate amounts of time to various topics.

It is on this third point that elaboration appears to be necessary. In making plans for the term you need to consult (in addition to textbooks and your conscience) the college catalogue or bulletin in order to anticipate some or all of the following circumstances:

1. For a given term you are allowed a certain number of class periods (about 40–50 for a 3-hour course in a typical semester.) Your wisdom must, therefore, be compressed into a period of some-what less than two clock days. You will want to decide ahead of time approximately the number of sessions to be allotted to each of the topics you want to cover.
2. My estimate of 40–50 days includes:
   a. one day for orientation (which we recommend).
   b. one day for a final summing up (upon which the students will probably insist).

    c. one or more class periods devoted to examinations.
This, of course, reduces the students' time at your disposal to 35–45 hours.

3. Students (unlike the faculty) get holidays. One must consider them in planning a course in order, insofar as is possible, to avoid:
   a. tests or important class sessions just before or just after holidays or major college events, such as homecoming.
   b. having closely related materials presented partly before and partly after a recess.

Midterm or other preliminary grades may be due at specified times. Such estimates of student achievement should be based upon at least one, and perferably more, examinations or other evidence of achievement.

From what I have said in the preceding paragraphs it is evident by now that the easy accomplishment of course objectives is frustrated in two ways: by lack of satisfactory text material and by the college schedule.

Compromising as little as possible with course objectives, if you have followed recommendations to this point you now have a rough course outline completed. You have decided what you want to cover in your course and how to distribute available time. You may even make a schedule of where in the course you expect to be at any given date. My suggestion now is that you make such a schedule and have it mimeographed for distribution to the class. If you wish, you may delay the final steps until you have met with the class and obtained their expectations. This is a good way of getting structure and indicates the value you attach to the students' needs.

How complete, detailed, and precise should your schedule be? My answer is "not very" for three reasons:

1. Like most of us, you are apt to change your mind about the details you will cover before you come to a specific topic. There is little point in committing yourself in print to a course of action you will later regard as ill advised.
2. Inevitably, circumstances arise that make it advisable to deviate slightly from the schedule.
3. The students themselves are important variables in determining the pace and structure of the course. Some classes gallop along at a fine pace; others are slow to move. Some classes develop

great interest in one topic; others in another. Your schedule should be sufficiently flexible to take advantage of the students' own awarenesses of how they can best learn.

But if an instructor is really student centered, isn't preparation of a course outline a cue that the course is really instructor centered and that student needs are really not going to be considered? Not necessarily so. Research by Richard Mann and his associates at the University of Michigan (1970) suggests that students see the teacher who takes a nondirective, student-centered role as not interested in the class.

Decide What Should Be in the Course Outline or Syllabus

Such an outline should at least contain the assignments for the semester. One very satisfactory way to prepare such an outline is to provide the students with a topic outline of the course. Under the various topic headings, assignments and the dates when they are due can be easily scheduled. This method has the special advantage of relieving the instructor of the task of making assignments every few days and of repeating the assignment two or three times for the benefit of students who have been absent when the assignment was first announced.

Other items that may be appropriate to include in such an outline are the dates when examinations, quizzes, or laboratory exercises are scheduled, announcements of films to be shown in connection with various topics, and the particular libraries in which collateral reading materials have been placed on reserve if the library facilities in your college or university are decentralized. Including the call numbers of the books required for library use will save a good deal of student time. Finally, you may include any special rules of classroom behavior you may want to emphasize. In this latter category are rules of attendance (if they are left to the instructor's discretion). A timesaving feature is to include a statement to the effect that the assignments for the course are included in the course outline, without any special additional prodding. In fact it is generally helpful to list the responsibilities of the student and those of the instructor. All of these considerations, of course, help set the stage for the course—they structure the situation, help the students discover at the outset what their responsibilities are going to be, and give them the security of seeing where they are going.

Choose Appropriate Teaching Methods

A third and final point at which your preparation for a course is determined by your objectives is in the type of instruction you will use. For some goals and for some materials an orthodox lecture presentation is as good as or better than any other. For others, discussion may be preferable. For the accomplishment of still other ends the "buzz session" or "role playing" techniques described later in the book may be useful. Probably most successful teachers vary their methods to suit their objectives. Thus you may wish one day to present some new material in a lecture. You may then follow this with a class discussion on implications of this material. Since your choice in the matter is determined as much by your own personality as by your course objectives, I shall not dwell on it here. From the description of these techniques in later sections of the book, you may be able to decide which techniques are suited to your philosophy of teaching, your abilities, the class you are teaching, and the particular goals you are emphasizing at a particular time.

Check Resources Needing Advance Work

Order films, make arrangements for field work, guest lecturers, slides, demonstrations or other resources needing advance work.

Begin Preparing Lectures (If You Plan to Lecture)

Time: Two Weeks Before the First Class

Check on Textbooks and Library Resources

Check to see that the textbooks are in and the library has books, records, or videotapes you have asked for.

Check on Enrollment Projections

If your college has preregistration, check to see if enrollment projections are out of line with your expectations.

Visit Your Classroom

Prepare for the First Class Period

SUPPLEMENTARY READING

A good brief source on how to define objectives is Chapter 3 in S. C. Ericksen, *Motivation for learning* (Ann Arbor: University of Michigan Press, 1974).

The classic source is B. S. Bloom et al., *Taxonomy of educational objectives, Handbook 1: cognitive domain* (New York: Longmans, Green, 1956).

3

Meeting a Class for the First Time

The first class meeting, like any other situation in which you are meeting a group of strangers who will affect your well being, is at the same time exciting and anxiety producing for both students and teacher. Some teachers handle their anxiety by postponing it, simply handing out the syllabus and leaving. This does not convey the idea that class time is valuable, nor does it capitalize on the fact that first day excitement can be constructive.

Other things being equal, anxiety is less disruptive in situations where stimulus events are clear and unambiguous. When the students know what to expect they can direct their energy more productively. An important function of the first day's meeting in any class is to provide this structure; that is, to present the classroom situation clearly, so that the students will know from the date of this meeting what is expected of them and how they should behave in the classroom situation. They come to the first class wanting to know what the course is all about and what kind of person the teacher is. To this end, the following concrete suggestions are offered.

One point to keep in mind both the first day and throughout the term is that yours is not the students' only class. They come to you from classes in chemistry, music, English, physical education, or rushing from their dormitory beds or from parking lots. The first few minutes need to help this varied group shift their thoughts and feelings to you and your subject.

You can ease them into the course gradually or you can grab their attention by something dramatically different, but in either case you need to think consciously about how you set the stage to facilitate achieving the course objectives.

Since the instructor is inevitably an important aspect of the classroom situation, one of your tasks in meeting a class for the first time is introducing yourself. It takes but a moment to write your name on the blackboard. Trivial as this may seem, it precludes the ego-dissolving experience of having taught a student for a whole year who never found out your name.

Breaking the Ice

If the class is small enough for using the discussion method, you may want to use the first period for getting acquainted and establishing goals. You might begin by informally asking freshmen to raise their hands, then sophomores, juniors, seniors, or out-of-staters. This gives you some idea of the composition of the class and gets students started participating. Sometimes you may pass around seating charts and ask all class members (including yourself) to introduce themselves, tell where they're from, mention their field of concentration, and answer any questions the group has. This may seem artificial for some classes, but the information still turns out to facilitate quicker development of rapport.

In any case, having established a degree of freedom of communication, the class can discuss the objectives of the course. It seems helpful to list these on the board as class members suggest them or react to your suggestions. After class record them so that the class may periodically refer to them and check progress, although it should be clear to the class that these are only a first approximation that will be altered and rephrased as the class becomes aware of new needs during the course.

*Problem Posting**

The technique of posting problems is not only a useful icebreaker, but one of value whenever it is useful to stimulate interest and assist students in communicating their problems to one another. This may be the case not only at the beginning of the course, but also after a lecture or other classroom method has aroused anxiety or defensiveness. The technique may also be useful to you when you wish to avoid answering questions immediately yourself. This might be because you don't wish to be placed on the defensive, because you wish to lay more groundwork, or because you don't wish to reinforce or to engage in a colloquy with a particular questioner whose concerns are not likely to contribute toward achievement of the goals of the class as a whole.

Do these potentialities intrigue you? All the discussion leader need do is to say something like, "Let's see if we can get all the questions out so that we can see what they are and how to handle them."

If it is the first class meeting, you might say, "Let's see what problems you'd like to have us tackle during the course. What sorts of concerns do you think that we might deal with?"

The instructor's task then becomes that of understanding and recording briefly on the blackboard the problems contributed by the group. This means that you must be ready to accept all contributions whether or not you yourself feel they are important. To test your understanding of the problem it is useful to restate the problem in different words, although this technique may lead participants to feel that you are critical of the way they stated the problem. Thus it may be helpful to tell the group in the beginning that you will be restating questions to test your own understanding, not because you state the problems better than anyone else. Restatement may also be useful in removing emotional loading or in bringing out implicit feelings. When you feel that a question is ambiguous or too general, it is helpful to ask for an illustration or to ask other group members to help you understand.

As contributions begin to slow down, it is often helpful to suggest stopping after a few more. But, if possible, the posting should

---

* This technique is one I learned from Norman R. F. Maier, described in his book, *Problem-solving discussions and conferences: leadership methods and skills* (New York: McGraw-Hill, 1963).

not be ended before there has been a good pause, since some of the most deeply felt problems will not come out until the student has seen that the teacher is really accepting and noncritical of the problems raised. This is a point where sensitivity is particularly important, for one can often see the visible signs of conflict about whether or not to raise an emotion-laden problem. If such a problem does come out and elicits a new batch of problems, forget about the suggested ending and get the problems out.

It is important in problem posting to maintain an accepting, non-evaluative atmosphere. Thus, if other members of the group argue that someone's contribution is not really a problem or that the real problem is different from that stated, the leader needs to make it clear that even though not everyone agrees about a given problem, anything that is a problem for any member of the group is entitled to be listed. Disagreement should be used to get additional problems out rather than to persuade a group member to withdraw his contribution.

Inevitably some discussion will come out about solutions. While this should not be abruptly censored, if it becomes involved or lengthy the teacher may point out that the task of dealing with the problems comes later.

By the end of the problem posting the class normally has become better acquainted, has become used to active participation, has taken the first step toward developing an attitude of attempting to understand rather than compete with one another, has reduced the attitude that everything must come from the teacher, has learned that the teacher can listen as well as talk and is not going to reject ideas different from their own, and, I hope, has begun to feel some responsibility for solving its own problems rather than waiting for them to be answered by the instructor.

The Course Outline

From problem posting it is a natural transition to an introduction of ways to tackle the problems. The instructor here faces a dilemma. You need to give students some notion of what to expect. You need to give them a sense that you have worked to prepare for the course and will continue to work to help them learn, but you also want to leave students with a sense of their own responsibility for achieving course goals. Thus, in presenting a course outline, a summary of your evaluation and grading plans and other aspects of the course structure, you need to communicate their relevance to the problems raised by the students, your responsiveness to them, and a sense of willingness to change as the course develops.

It is tempting to avoid the dilemma with verbal ambiguities about the course evolving from the students' needs as they manifest themselves from day to day. Such ambiguity may excite some students, but for most it simply arouses anxiety. As we saw in Chapter 2, a simple way to reduce some of that anxiety is to distribute a mimeographed course schedule.

Introducing the Teacher

In presenting the course outline and mechanics you also give the students some notion of the kind of person that you are. Although I am not recommending a complete personality change in the instructor without benefit of at least short-term psychotherapy, three characteristics seem to be especially appreciated by the student: 1) enthusiasm and willingness to work to make the course worthwhile, 2) objectivity (the students will call it "fairness"), 3) a sympathetic attitude toward the problems of the students. If these characteristics apply to you at all, or if you think they do, let the students know it.

Presenting a syllabus is one demonstration that you have made an investment in the course. Obviously you want to be open to student input, but in my experience students resent much more than an authoritarian teacher the teacher who says, "This is your class," and leaves completely to the student the organization and structure of the course. As we shall see in Chapter 6, student-centered discussion is an effective teaching method, but students often interpret a student-centered beginning as evidence that the instructor is lazy and uninterested in the course.

Promoting the notion that you are objective or fair can best be handled in connection with marks and the assignment of grades. For this reason, we will postpone direct discussion of the topic until later. But it cannot be pointed out too strongly that a large part of the students' motivation in the classroom situation is (perhaps unfortunately) directed toward the mark they hope to get from the course. The very least that students can expect of you is that this mark will be arrived at on some impartial basis. The simplest way to show students that you are objective and fair is to let the students know that you are willing to meet and advise them. At the same time, as a protection for yourself, suggest that such problems be discussed during your office hours unless the problem is insistent or unless the student has no time available during your regularly scheduled conference hours. In addition to this, students appreciate it if you are willing (and have the time) to spend a few minutes in the classroom after each class answering specific questions. Such queries most often concern questions of fact that can be answered briefly and would hardly warrant a trip to your office at a later time in another building, even if the student could be counted on to remember the question for that long. If your time permits, adjournment to a convenient snack bar or lounge may give students with special interests a chance to pursue them and get to know you better.

The first class is not the time to make sure the students understand your inadequacies and limitations. Frankly admitting that you don't know something is fine after the course is underway, but apologies in advance for lack of experience or expertise simply increase student insecurity.

Introducing the Textbook

To continue with the discussion of this situation-structuring procedure that I feel should be accomplished at the first meeting of the class, we turn now to the presentation of the textbook(s). Here the most serious question that arises concerns possible disagreement between the textbook and the materials you intend to present in your lectures. Unfortunately this is a matter that cannot always be solved simply by judicious selection of text materials. In some cases, there is simply no book available that presents certain material as you would like to have it presented. In others, the textbook is decided upon by someone other than yourself, and you have to make the best of it. In the case where disagreement is inevitable, the students have a right to know which version to accept as TRUTH and what they are supposed to do about such discrepancies on examinations. By facing the situation squarely, you can not only escape from the horns of this dilemma, but also turn it to your advantage. If you are philosophically minded (some of you would want to call it scientifically minded), you will be able to point out that truth is never absolute except in logic and religion. Give the

notion that rival interpretations stand or fall on the basis of perti-
nent evidence and plan to give your reasons for disagreeing with
the textbook. This procedure will accomplish two things: 1) it will
give the student the notion that your opinions are based upon evidence, and 2) it will frequently point up current problems in theory
that often have great appeal for the serious student.

To be avoided is the tirade against the author. This may serve as
an emotional catharsis for the instructor. But for the student, any
severe criticism you raise may generalize to the textbook as a whole.
Or, if the student is not convinced by your argument, it may generalize to much of what you have to say.

Questions

Even in a large lecture it seems well to interrupt these first descriptions of the course for questions. Some of the questions will be
designed as much to test you as to get information. Often the underlying questions are such things as:

—"Are you rigid?"

—"Will you really try to help students?"

—"Are you easily rattled?"

—"Are you a person as well as a teacher?"

—"Can you handle criticism?"

In general, it is good to respond to the surface content and not
to the indirect one in this first class before trust has been built up.
Nevertheless, an awareness of the feelings behind the questions may
help temper your responses.

SUPPLEMENTARY READING

Kenneth E. Eble, *The craft of teaching* (San Francisco: Jossey-Bass,
1976), Chapter 9.

4

Lecturing

One of the problems of the lecturer is that students in a lecture are usually passive and sometimes asleep—a condition not conducive to maximum learning.*

One method I have used to increase the students' feeling of participation in the lecture, while keeping the lectures closely related to student needs, was to choose a student lecture committee. Lecture notes were duplicated a week in advance, then a committee was chosen from volunteers to read over the next week's assignment and lectures. The members of the committee also interviewed other members of the class to obtain their reactions to past lectures. They then met with me to suggest revisions of the forthcoming lectures. Since they could cloak their criticisms by saying, "Some of the students I interviewed said . . . ," they were usually quite frank.

---

* Probably not all sleeping and inattention is the fault of the lecture. Classrooms are frequently hot, stuffy, and malodorous. Airing out the room before a lecture may make the lecture seem much less soporific.

Some of the special techniques favored by such lecture committees are:

1. Placing a brief outline on the blackboard during the lecture. (Perhaps students pay more attention to an outline they copy than one given to them printed.)
2. Summarizing important points at the end of the lecture.
3. Using demonstrations or movies to break up the lecture.
4. Breaking the lecture group into small buzz sessions to discuss particular problems. This technique seems to secure much greater student acceptance of some lecture materials. I've broken lecture sections of 500 students into groups of six. These groups discuss a problem for ten minutes, after which I call upon some of the groups to report. After each idea or suggestion other groups that had the same idea are asked to raise their hands so that they too are involved and rewarded. I place the main points of the reports on the blackboard and then try to incorporate them into the lecture or at least discuss the problems involved.

All four of these points are related to a general problem faced by the lecturer—the lecture is not learner controlled. Students cannot reread, slow down, or meditate a few minutes before resuming in a lecture as they can with a book. This means that if you write out a lecture, you need to put in more redundancy and more helps to let the students know what you've said and are going to say than if you were writing an article. Every student's mind will wander at some points during the lecture—in fact one criterion of a good lecture is that it stimulates students to think about examples in their own experiences. But when a student has been thinking for a few moments, you need to provide a chance for the student to tune back in and understand what you're now discussing. Moreover, you need to provide enough attention-getting cues to keep students from drifting completely out of the situation.

Every student in a freshman speech course is taught the importance of vocal variety. Yet it is appalling to note the number of college lecturers whose voices are monotones. Lack of variety in pitch and volume may sometimes cause students to fall asleep in lectures that are otherwise interesting. A little practice will work wonders, particularly if you are able to record your lecture and listen to yourself. Of a similar fundamental nature is the simple matter of looking at the audience. Remember that you're talking to the students, not the windows.

No matter how well you have planned the content of the lecture, it will be of no avail if you are inaudible. Ask a couple of students in the back row to give you a sign if they can't hear you. It will help keep their attention on the lecture as well as give you an awareness of the need to reach them. Don't be reluctant to ask for a microphone. Most colleges can provide microphones that can be worn around the neck without inhibiting movement. You cannot be spontaneous about the material if you are having to devote your attention to speaking more loudly than is comfortable.

Vocal variety, audibility, and movement are overt cues to your own enthusiasm, and if there is any teacher characteristic related to learning, it is enthusiasm (Coats and Smidchens, 1966; Isaacson, McKeachie, and Milholland, 1963; Ware and Williams, 1975; Perry, Abrami, and Leventhal, 1976). Enthusiasm probably cannot be successfully faked, but it is possible to influence the degree to which your enthusiasm shows. Moreover, my enthusiasm about a lecture topic seems to be a function of the degree to which I've prepared for it. I find it hard to be enthusiastic about most lectures I've given before, but if I've reworked a lecture, learned some new things, and come up with some new ideas, I approach the lecture with much more enthusiasm.

It's probably unnecessary to emphasize that any nervous or habitual behavior is disruptive to communication, whether it is pacing the floor, twisting the chalk, removing glasses, or standing firmly in one spot.

Not only words but voice, eyes, facial expression, and movement communicate your security or lack of it to your students. It is well to admit frankly that you don't know the answers to some questions. In general, you should remember that the students begin the course in a dependent relationship to the instructor. It isn't likely that they will feel secure enough to become independent if you do not give them the feeling that you are secure. Admitting errors is more likely to communicate security than trying to cover them up.

Possibly one way in which your own security may be communicated to the students is through use of humor at your own expense. Spontaneous, such humor seems to create a warmer atmosphere and improve student-teacher relationships.

Petrie (1963), reviewing research on informative speaking, lists meaningfulness, informality, verbal emphasis, visible action, eye contact, and *student expectation of a test* as factors leading toward greater learning.

Lecture Organization

Most teachers try to arouse an attitude of expectancy in their students. The ideal student is one who comes to each class with the feeling, "Something worthwhile is going to come out of this hour." Obviously the best way to build up this attitude is to make sure that each period does leave students with the feeling that they have gained something significant. But you may also arouse it by the statement of a problem such as, "Here is a case of a ———. What could cause such a condition?"

Katona's experiments on learning (1940) suggest to us that the ideal lecture would start with a problem—one that is meaningful to the students—presented in such a way that the students feel a need for problem solution. Then the lecturer would interweave the evidence and examples leading to a conclusion in such a manner that the average student would discover the solution before the instructor pointed it out. Sometimes, the lecturer might even ask the class to verbalize the conclusion. I recommend that the lecturer organize the lecture so as to permit the students to solve the problem, rather than requiring them to follow a dreary set of facts justifying a statement the instructor has made or hear a rehash of the textbook. The problem-centered approach seems, to me, to aid learning whether in lecture or discussion.

I shall say more about lecture organization later, but at this point it is worth noting that a high degree of organization does *not* seem to contribute to student learning (Petrie, 1963; Thompson, 1967).

Theoretical Notes

College teaching and lecturing have been so long associated that when you picture a college professor in a classroom, you almost inevitably picture the professor lecturing. The popularity of the lecture method probably derives from a conception of the instructor's primary goal as being the transmission of knowledge and from the effectiveness of the lecture in summarizing content in a form understandable by a particular group of students. Moreover, the lecture can be more up-to-date than a book and more personal than technology, providing a living person as a model of scholarship and problem solving.

Since lectures typically provide few opportunities for students to respond, there is little opportunity for them to receive knowledge of their progress (feedback) except through periodic tests. However, delay of feedback may not be a major detriment in learning knowledge if the learner is motivated and the material is not too difficult. We would, however, expect lack of feedback to be a greater handicap if the lecturer's goal is to develop concepts or to teach problem-solving skills. With these goals, there is experimental evidence that active participation on the part of the learner is more effective than passive listening or observing. Consequently, a passive role for the student in the lecture would be expected to be a handicap.

Lecture has often been compared in effectiveness with discussion. Since discussion offers the opportunity for a good deal of student activity and feedback, it could, according to theory, be more effective than lecture in developing concepts and problem-solving skills. However, because the rate of transmission of information is slow in discussion classes, I would expect lecture classes to be superior in attaining the objective of teaching knowledge.

Research on Lecture vs. Discussion

Unfortunately, although there have been many research studies of the lecture method as compared to discussion or other methods, few have used independent measures of the different types of outcomes suggested above. The results of experiments are generally in line with my hypotheses. For example, using tests of information, Remmers (1933) found slight but nonsignificant differences favoring learning in large lecture groups as compared with that in small (35–40 student) recitation sections. Spence (1928) obtained similar results comparing lecture and discussion technique in classes of over one hundred students. Ruja (1954) found that the lecture was superior to discussion as measured by a test of subject-matter mastery in a general psychology course. In the other two courses in his experiment there were no significant differences in achievement, nor were there differences in changes in adjustment in any of the courses. Similarly, Solomon, Rosenberg, and Bezdek (1964) found that among 24 teachers of evening college courses in American Government those who stressed lectures tended to produce higher achievement on a factual test but not on a test of comprehension. Eglash (1954) found no difference between a discussion class and lecture class, not only in scores on the final examination in the course, but also in scores on an achievement test administered several weeks after the course had ended and in scores on a measure of tolerance. Husband (1951) also found no significant difference in achievement of students in large (200 student) lectures versus those in small (50 student) recitation classes, but in five out of six semesters, the lecture group was non-significantly superior. In these and other experiments, the information measured by the examination could be obtained from a textbook; in only one was a discussion group smaller than 35 students used.

When we turn to measures of more complex outcomes, the results favor discussion. In one of the earliest comparisons of lecture and discussion, Bane (1925) found little difference between the methods on measures of immediate recall, but a significant superiority for discussion on a measure of delayed recall. Hirschman (1952) compared the effectiveness of presenting written materials followed by discussion and rereading using a measure of concept learning. The reading-discussion method resulted in superior ability to identify examples of the concepts presented.

In quite a different type of experiment Barnard (1942) compared the effectiveness of a lecture-demonstration teaching method with that of a problem-solving developmental discussion in a college science course. The lecture-demonstration method proved superior on a test of specific information, but the discussion method proved to be superior on measures of problem solving and scientific attitude. Likewise Dawson (1956) found problem-solving recitation and lecture-demonstration methods to be equally effective in a course in elementary soil science as measured by a test of recall of specific information, but the problem-solving method was significantly superior as measured by tests of problem-solving abilities.

Other evidence favoring discussion was the experiment of Elliott (Beardslee, Birney, and McKeachie, 1951), which found that students in his discussion groups in elementary psychology became interested in electing more additional courses in psychology than did students in a large lecture. Similarly, Casey and Weaver (1956) found no differences in knowledge of content but superiority in attitudinal outcomes (as measured by the Minnesota Teacher Attitude Inventory) for small group discussions as compared to lectures. Results of studies comparing lecture and discussion are summarized in Table 4–1.

TABLE 4–1 *Lecture vs. Discussion*

REFERENCE	COURSE	CRITERIA		
		Factual Exam	*Higher Level Cognitive*	*Attitude, Motivation*
Spence (1928)	Educ. Psych	*L		
Remmers (1933)	Elem. Psych	L		
Husband (1951)	Gen. Psych	L (5 classes)		
Lifson et al. (1956)	Gen. Psych	L = D		*D
Ruja (1954)	Gen. Psych	*L (4 classes)		
	Philosophy	D (2 classes)		
Elliott (1951)	Elem. Psych			D
Casey & Weaver (1956)	Human Devel. & Behavior			D
Beach (1960)	Social Psych	D		*D
Hill (1960)	Anthropology (15 classes)	D		D
Bane (1925)	Education (5 experiments)	L(3) D(2)	*D(5)	
Solomon et al. (1964)	Government (24 classes)	L	D	
Gerberich & Warner (1936)	Government	L		
Barnard (1942)	Science (6 classes)	L	*D	*D
Barnard (1936)	(2 classes)	L = D		
Dawson (1956)	Elem. Soil Sci. (6 classes)	L	D	
Lancaster et al. (1961)	Physics	D		
Warren (1954)	Physics	D		

L = Lecture Superior
D = Discussion Superior
* = Difference significant at .05 level or better. All other results indicate only the direction of difference in the experiment.

Distribution of Lecture and Discussion Time

Many universities and large colleges use a method of distributing class meetings between lectures and discussions. This administrative arrangement is supported by a study in the teaching of psychology in which discussion meetings were substituted for one-third of the lectures (Lifson et al., 1956). There were no significant differences in achievement. However, the partial discussion method, as compared with the all lecture method, resulted in more favorable student attitudes that persisted in a follow-up study two years later.

Warren (1954) compared the effectiveness of one lecture and four recitations to two lectures and three demonstrations per week. In one out of five comparisons the four-recitations plan was superior while the other comparisons found nonsignificant differences. Superior students tended to prefer the two-lecture plan while poorer students did not. On the other hand, in Remmers's comparison (1933) of two lectures and one recitation vs. three recitations, the poorer students tended to do better in the lecture-recitation combination. Students preferred the all-recitation classes. In Klapper's study (1958), most NYU students preferred a combination lecture-discussion method to all lectures or all discussions. Iowa students preferred all group discussion or a combination of lecture and discussion to lectures alone (Becker et al., 1958).

In a course in which the instructors must not only give information but also develop concepts, the use of both lectures and discussions would thus seem to be a logical and popular choice.

The Lecturer vs. Automation

Since I have hypothesized that the lecturer is particularly effective in transmitting information, it seems in order to ask how the lecturer in the ordinary classroom compares with other means of transmitting information. I have already suggested that if the learner is motivated, a good deal of communication of knowledge apparently can take place with relatively infrequent checks on the progress of the learner. In fact, Harlow's research with primates (1950) suggests that there may be some inherent satisfaction simply in learning new things or solving new problems. Hebbian theory (Hebb, 1949) would predict that relatively fresh ideas would be motivating, but that experiences too far removed from the student's past experience would produce anxiety. This suggests that the organization of materials should be of great importance in learning.

Skinner (1958) and his students popularized programmed materials that presented course materials in well-organized, step-by-step fashion with questions. When a student misses a question in such a program, the question may be repeated, but when the correct response is made, the learner proceeds. It would seem that the teaching machine or program should have advantages over the lecturer, for the sequence can be carefully planned to utilize the best research on the method of successive approximations, concrete-to-abstract sequences in problem-solving, and building up generalizations from varying specifics. The research evidence, however, has not revealed superiority of programmed materials over lectures in most college-level courses. A more promising variant is the Keller-Plan, or Personalized System of Instruction, which will be discussed in Chapter 11.

Actually, the chief competitor of the lecturer is not the program, teaching machine, television, film, or the computer, but rather a much older invention—writing. If rate of transmission of knowledge is important, a good book is hard to beat. Not only can readers control their own rates, but motivated, skilled readers can traverse the printed page much more rapidly than even the fastest lecturers can deliver the material. Over a generation ago, Greene (1928) conducted an experiment demonstrating that college students learned as much from reading a passage as from hearing the same material in a lecture.

Although printed materials have been almost as popular as television and have existed a much longer time, lectures have survived. Even the advent of picture-book textbooks did not dislodge the lecturer. If we had stopped to think about this, we probably would not have been surprised that dozens of research studies have not had much impact upon lecturers' attitudes toward television.

Perhaps the lecturer's arguments are rationalizations, for there is little research to support them. Nevertheless, psychologists may have underestimated important factors in their usual analyses of the learning situation. Because of the need to maintain good experimental controls, rate and sequence of presentation are carefully controlled in most of their experiments. The materials used are meaningless to the learner. The results lead us to stress the importance of feedback to the learner.

Lecturing, however, is largely devoted to communicating meaningful materials to somewhat motivated learners. Such learning can take place with relatively infrequent checks on the progress of the learner. With experimental controls, researchers miss the important fact that when knowledge is presented by teachers, they are able to respond to feedback from the learners. This may be an important asset of the instructor. While films and television present material at a relatively fixed rate, instructors can go faster or slower when they get clues of inattention, glares, or blank confusion from their classes.

Readers, too, can pace themselves, but inexperienced students may not be able to separate the meat of a book from the fat. Even though lecturers are slower than books, good lecturers may be able to give their students all they need from a book in much less time than it would take them to read it.

Moreover, lecturers can be effective guides to reading. By indicating the most important points, by posing questions with which students can approach their reading, by their own appreciation and interpretation of what has been assigned, instructors can help students develop ability to read. Presumably this role of the instructor is particularly important early in a student's entrance into a field. As the student gains experience, the lecturer can rely more and more upon the student to get needed information from reading.

As reading materials carry an increasing portion of the task of communication of knowledge, the lecturer's role becomes that of presenting new materials that are not yet in print. Thus, it may be particularly appropriate for a professor to lecture about new research.

Textbooks, films, and teaching machines must be organized to fit average students if they are to be economically feasible. Lecturers can not only plan their lectures for their own classes, but they can also respond to feedback from the classes as they deliver it. This responsiveness to cues from the class is probably the reason that material can be covered less rapidly in "live" classes than in television classes. Because instructors respond to feedback, their presentation may appear to be unorganized. Yet I would hypothesize that this very responsiveness may be more effective than a carefully organized, inflexible presentation.

Thus, live lecturing is likely to be most effective in situations where there is considerable variation between groups in ability, relevant background, or motivation and where flexible adjustment to the group is consequently important. You should ordinarily not lecture when the same material can be made available in printed form. Mimeographed materials, for example, may be a more efficient substitute for lecturing. Lectures should be revised from year to year in order that material now in print can be dropped from the lecture and new research included. The lecture is the newspaper or journal of teaching; it, more than any other teaching, must be up-to-date.

Methods of Lecturing

Few experiments have compared the effectiveness of classroom lectures with other teaching methods in achieving attitude change, but in turning from classroom experiments to other research dealing with change of attitudes, we find a substantial and growing literature relevant to differing techniques of lecturing.

The research of Hovland and his associates (1953) at Yale University indicates that such variables as credibility of the lecturer, order of presentation of one side vs. presenting both sides of an issue, and emotionality of argument are important in determining the effect of a lecture. For example, the Hovland group found that a group of college students were more likely to change their opinions (at least temporarily) when they received a persuasive communication from a source they considered highly credible than when the same communication came from a less credible source. Although we assume that students perceive their instructors as credible sources, faculty rating scales which include an item "knowledge of subject matter" have revealed that students do discriminate among professors on this dimension. I have argued against inclusion of this item on the grounds that students are not competent judges of the instructor's knowledge. Regardless of their validity, however, ratings on this item may be a good indication of the students' credence in the instructor's statements and thus of her effectiveness in bringing about attitude change.

Sometimes even college professors try to reinforce their points by waving the flag or preaching academic hellfire and brimstone. The Yale studies are reassuring to those who feel this type of teaching is inappropriate, for they report that the greatest change in reported behavior occurred in those groups that heard a minimally fear-arousing lecture. This difference persisted at least a year, even though all presentations resulted in equal factual learning.

In presenting controversial points lecturers often wonder whether they should present the evidence on both sides of the issue or simply present that evidence favoring the position they accept. This is basically an ethical problem, but even leaving aside the ethical problems involved, the results of Yale and Army research studies indicate the greater effectiveness of presenting both sides to 1) an intelligent audience, 2) those initially disagreeing with the lecturer's position, and 3) those who come into contact with the opposing arguments.

If the lecturer chooses to present two sides of an issue, he faces the problem of choosing the order in which they are presented. An extensive series of studies illuminated the effects of differing orders. The results most relevant have been summarized by Hovland et al. (1953). They found that those points presented first dominated the learner's impression even though both sides of a controversial issue are presented.

Research on organization of materials is also relevant to lecturing aimed at cognitive changes. In organizing a lecture the professor frequently is guided by the maxim "Tell them what you're going to tell them. Tell them. Then tell them what you've told them." In a classroom experiment in a course in physics (Lahti, 1956), the instructor started with a statement of a principle and then illustrated and applied the principle. He compared this with a technique in which he developed principles by demonstration and analysis of application situations before the principles were stated. For students with poor backgrounds the results showed the latter (inductive) method to be superior to the former method on tests of ability to apply the principles. On the other hand, Hovland and Mandell (1952) found that opinions were more likely to change in the direction advocated by the speaker if he drew the appropriate conclusion rather than leaving it to the students. As I shall show again in a consideration of laboratory teaching, research on this topic is not clear cut. Probably it is important for instructors to point out the conclusion if most students would not arrive at it by themselves. On the other hand, discovery of a conclusion by themselves may have considerable motivational value for students.

As I said earlier, the classic studies of college-student learning by Katona (1940) support the importance of organization in learning and retention and also point toward the importance of the learner's own organization. Katona found that learning by organization results both in superior retention and in superior application when compared to learning by rote memorization. More recent research by Marton and Säljö (1976) supports the same conclusion. In the light of such findings it is apparent that many professors do not lecture as effectively as they might. I shall say more about the theoretical aspects of lectures and instructional materials in Chapter 20.

The Lecturer: A Summary

What is the role of the lecturer in higher education? The research results I have cited provide little basis for an answer. Nevertheless, they do not contradict, and sometimes they support, my earlier notions that the lecture is sometimes an effective way of communicating information, particularly in classes where variations in student background, ability, or interest make feedback to the lecturer important. We have also shown that the organization and presentation of lectures may influence their effectiveness in achieving application of knowledge or in influencing attitudes. Other methods of teaching, however, may be more effective than lecturing in achieving some of the higher level cognitive and attitudinal objectives.

SUPPLEMENTARY READING

An excellent down-to-earth source of help in lecturing is Donald A. Bligh, *What's the use of lectures?* 3rd ed., (Hertfordshire, England: Penguin Books, 1972).

A good review of research is Frank Costin. Lecturing versus other methods of teaching: a review of research, *British Journal of Educational Technology*, 1972, *3*, 4–31.

5

Organizing Effective Discussion

Discussion is probably not effective for presenting new information the student is already motivated to learn, but discussion techniques seem particularly appropriate when the instructor wants to do the following:

1. Use the resources of members of the group.
2. Give students opportunities to formulate applications of principles.
3. Get prompt feedback on how well objectives are being attained.
4. Help students learn to think in terms of the subject matter by giving them practice in thinking.
5. Help students learn to evaluate the logic of, and evidence for, their own and others' positions.
6. Help students become aware of and formulate problems using information to be gained from readings or lectures.

7. Gain acceptance for information or theories counter to folklore or previous beliefs of students.
8. Develop motivation for further learning.

Why should discussion be the method of choice for achieving such objectives? The first justification is a very simple extrapolation of the old adage, "Practice makes perfect." If instructors expect students to learn how to integrate, apply, and problem solve, it seems reasonable that students should have an opportunity to do so. Most important, learning should be facilitated if this practice is accompanied by feedback the students can utilize to identify their errors and successes. Further, I would expect learning to be most effective if there is sufficient guidance to insure some successes. Experiments on learning motor skills reveal that guidance is most helpful in the early stages of learning, suggesting that the instructor should play a more directive role at the beginning of a course than at its end.

In discussion groups the instructor is faced with several problems:

1. Getting participation in the discussion.
2. Making progress (or making the student aware of the progress) toward course objectives.
3. Handling emotional reactions of students, which are less likely to be expressed verbally in lecture classes.

The type of discussion method used will determine the extent to which particular roles are dominant. Discussion methods range from recitation, in which the instructor asks specific questions in an oral quiz, to nondirective methods, in which the instructor says very little and students determine the topic and content of discussion. A little later I shall review some of the evidence on the relative effectiveness of these types of discussions, but first I will describe a middle-of-the-road discussion method particularly useful in developing skills in the use of content in problem solving.

Developmental Discussion

The term "developmental discussion" was coined by Professor Norman R. F. Maier (1952) to describe a problem-solving discussion technique in which the teacher breaks problems into parts so that all group members are working on the same part of the problem at the same time.* One of the reasons discussion often seems ineffective and disorganized is that different members of the group are working on different aspects of the problem and are thus often frustrated by what they perceive as irrelevant comments by other students. In developmental discussion the teacher tries to keep the students aware of the step of discussion that is the current focus. Typical steps might be:

1. formulating the problem
2. suggesting hypotheses
3. getting relevant data
4. evaluating alternative solutions.

Typically, an early step in developmental discussion is to get information relevant to the problem for discussion. Such information can be supplied by a lecture, reading, or group members. In this technique teachers should feel free to give information or raise questions. They do not ask questions to which they already know the answers. Often an appropriate problem for developmental discussion is the application or implications of particular principles or findings presented by lectures or reading.

Like other discussion methods, developmental discussion implies active participation of group members. In developmental discussion, participation is directed to a definite goal. However, this does not imply a type of discussion leadership in which the leader manipulates the group to follow the steps and reach a predetermined goal. Rather the leader helps the group progress by dividing the problem up into parts that can be solved in steps. In short, developmental discussion is not nondirective, but neither is it autocratic.

Skills in Leading Discussion

In a developmental discussion the teacher attempts to guide a discussion along a certain line, but not to push it beyond the group's interest and acceptance. Obviously this requires skill in initiating

---

* I've learned most of what I know about discussion from my colleague, Professor N. R. F. Maier. An excellent source on techniques of discussion leadership is his book, *Problem-solving discussions and conferences: leadership methods and skills* (New York: McGraw-Hill, 1963).

discussion, getting student participation, appraising group progress, asking questions, and overcoming resistance.

Starting Discussion

After a class has been meeting and discussing problems successfully, there is little problem in initiating discussion, for it will develop almost spontaneously from problems encountered in outside reading or experiences or from continuation of discussion of unresolved problems from the previous meeting. But during the first meetings of new groups, the instructor may need to assume the initiative in beginning the discussion.

● *Starting discussion with a common experience.*   One of the best ways of starting a discussion is to provide a concrete, common experience through presentation of a demonstration, film, or role playing. Following such a presentation it's easy to ask, "Why did ———?"

Such an opening has a number of advantages. Since everyone in the group has seen it, everyone knows something about the topic under discussion. In addition, by focusing the discussion on the demonstration, the instructor takes some of the pressure off anxious or threatened students who are afraid to reveal their own opinions or feelings.

However, you will not always be able to find the demonstration you need to introduce each discussion; thus you may be forced to turn to other techniques of initiating discussion. One such technique is Problem Posting, which was discussed in Chapter 3. But the most commonly used technique is the question.

● *Starting discussion with a question.*   There are times when it is appropriate to check student background knowledge with a series of brief factual questions, but more frequently you want to stimulate problem solving. One common error in question-phrasing for this purpose is to ask a question in a form conveying to students the message, "I know something you don't know and you'll look stupid if you don't guess right." Rather than dealing with factual questions, discussions need to be formulated so as to get at relationships, applications, or analyses of facts and materials. Solomon, Rosenberg, and Bezdek (1964) found that teachers who used interpretation questions were effective as measured by gains in student comprehension.

A question of the type, "How does the idea that ———— apply to
————?" is much more likely to stimulate discussion than the question, "What is the definition of ————?" The problem may arise from a case; it may be a hypothetical problem. It may be a problem whose solution the instructor knows; it may be a problem which he has not solved himself. In any case it should be a problem that is meaningful to the students and, for the sake of morale, it should be a problem the students can make some progress on. And even if the teacher knows an answer or has a preferred solution, the students should have a chance to come up with new solutions. The teacher's job usually is not to sell students on a particular solution, but rather to teach them how to solve problems themselves. As Maier has shown in his studies of group leadership, one barrier to problem solving is presenting an issue in such a way that participants take sides arguing the apparent solution rather than attempting to solve the problem by considering data and devising alternative solutions. Maier suggests the following principles for group problem solving.*

1. Success in problem solving requires that effort be directed toward overcoming surmountable obstacles.
2. Available facts should be used even when they are inadequate.
3. The starting point of the problem is richest in solution possibilities.
4. Problem-mindedness should be increased while solution-mindedness should be delayed.
5. Disagreement can lead either to hard feelings or to innovation depending on the discussion leadership.
6. The "idea-getting" process should be separated from the "idea-evaluation" process because the latter inhibits the former.

A second common error in question-phrasing is to frame the question at a level of abstraction inappropriate for the class. Students are most likely to participate in discussion when they feel that they have an experience or idea that will contribute to the discussion. This means that the discussion questions need to be phrased as problems that are meaningful to the students as well as the instructor. Such questions can be devised more easily if you know something of the students' background. An experiment by Sturgis (1958) showed that

---

* N. R. F. Maier, *Problem-solving discussions and conferences* (New York: McGraw-Hill, 1963).

knowledge of student background makes a significant difference in a teacher's effectiveness as measured by students' learning.

A third error in raising questions is to ask your question before finding out about the students' problems. Often a good question fails to elicit responses because students are hung up on some prior problem.

Suppose you ask a question and no one answers, or the student simply says, "I don't know." Discouraging as this may be, it should not necessarily be the end of the interaction. Usually the student can respond if the question is rephrased. Perhaps you need to give an example of the problem first; perhaps you need to suggest some alternative answer; perhaps you need to reformulate a prior question. More often than not you can help the students discover that they are more competent than they thought.

● *Starting discussion with a controversy.*   A third technique of stimulating discussion is to cause disagreement. Experimental evidence is accumulating to indicate that a certain degree of surprise or uncertainty arouses curiosity, a basic motive for learning (Berlyne, 1960). Some teachers effectively play the role of devil's advocate; others are effective in pointing up differences in point of view.

I have some concerns about the devil's advocate role. I believe that it can be an effective device in getting students to think actively rather than accept passively the instructor's every sentence as "Truth." Yet it has its risks, the most important of which is that it may create lack of trust in the instructor. Of course, instructors want students to challenge their ideas, but few want their students to feel they are untrustworthy, lying about their own beliefs.

A second danger in the "devil's advocate" role is that it will be perceived as manipulative. Students may feel (with justification) that the instructor "is just playing games with us—trying to show how smart he is and how easily he can fool us."

A third danger is that the devil's advocate role will be used as a screen to prevent students from ever successfully challenging the instructor. In this use the instructor, whenever the student wins an argument, simply says, "Well I just presented that position to see if you could see its weakness."

Not only are all of these possible problems infuriating for the student, but they maintain a superior-subordinate relationship antithetical to the sort of learning environment that this book is plugging for. If the best classroom is one in which both students and teacher are learning, a role that provides armor against the instructor's learning is bad. Yet the devil's advocate role can be effective. Its success depends a good deal upon the spirit with which it is played. My own compromise solution is to make it clear when I'm taking such a role by saying, "Suppose I take the position that ———" or, "Let me play the role of devil's advocate for a bit."

In any case the instructor should realize that disagreement is not a sign of failure but may be used constructively. When rigid dogmatism interfers with constructive problem solving following a disagreement, the instructor may ask the disagreeing students to switch sides and argue the opposing point of view. Such a technique seems to be effective in developing awareness of the strengths of other positions.

What Can I Do About Nonparticipants?

In most classes some students talk too much and others never volunteer a sentence. What can the teacher do?

Unfortunately, most students are used to being passive recipients in class. To help them become participants I try to create an expectation of participation in the discussion section. You can start to do this in the first meeting of the course by defining the functions of various aspects of the course and explaining why discussion is valuable. In addition to this initial structuring, however, you must continually work to increase the students' awareness of the values of participation. Wise instructors realize that participation is not an end in itself. For many purposes wide-spread participation may be vital; for others it may be detrimental. But they must try to create a climate in which an important contribution is not lost because the person with the necessary idea did not feel free to express it.

Even superficial techniques can help. Rewarding infrequent contributors at least by a smile helps encourage participation even if the contribution has to be developed or corrected. Calling students by name seems to encourage freer communication. Seating is important too. Rooms with seats in a circle help tremendously.

Getting to know the nonparticipant is also helpful. For example, I have found that it is sometimes helpful to make the first assignment to write a brief life history indicating the student's interests and experiences. These autobiographies help me to gain a better knowledge of each student as an individual, to know what problems or illustrations will be of particular interest to a number of students, and to know whom I can call on for special information. One of the best ways of getting nonparticipants into the discussion is to ask them to contribute in a problem area in which they have special knowledge.

The technique of asking for a student's special knowledge deals directly with one of the major barriers to class discussion—fear of being wrong. No one likes to look foolish, especially in a situation where mistakes may be pounced upon by a teacher or other students. One of the major reasons for the deadliness of a question in which the teacher asks a student to fill in the one right word—such as, "This is an example of what?"—is that it puts the students on the spot. There is an infinity of wrong answers, and obviously the teacher knows the one right answer; so why should the student risk making a mistake when the odds are so much against the student? And even if the answer is obvious, why look like a stooge to the other students for the teacher?

One way of putting the student in a more favorable position is to ask general questions that have no wrong answers. For example, you can ask, "How do you feel about this?" or, "How does this look to you?" as a first step in analysis of a problem. The student's feelings or perceptions may not be the same as yours, but as a reporter of his own feelings, he can't be challenged as being inaccurate. While such an approach by no means eliminates anxiety about participation (for an answer involves revealing oneself as a person), it will more often open up discussion that involves the student than questions of fact will.

Another technique for reducing the risk of participation for students is to ask a question a class period before the discussion and ask students to write out answers involving an example from their own experience.

All of these techniques will still not make every student into an active, verbal participant. Two group techniques can help. One is "buzz groups," which will be discussed later in this chapter; the other is the "inner circle" technique. In using this technique I announce that at the next class meeting we are going to have a class within a class, with half the students acting as the discussion group and the other half as observers. If the classroom has moveable chairs, I arrange the seating in the form of two concentric circles for the next class meeting. I may explain that I want to give some of the quieter members of the class a chance to express their ideas. In any case, I am impressed that students who are normally silent will, when they feel an increased sense of responsibility, talk.

The Discussion Monopolizer

If you have worked on nonparticipation effectively, the discussion monopolizer is less likely to be a problem, but there will still be classes in which one student talks so much that you and the other students become annoyed. As with nonparticipation one solution is to raise with the class the question of participation in discussion— "Would the class be more effective if participation were more evenly distributed?"

A second technique is to have one or more members of the class act as observers for one or more class periods, reporting back to the class their observations. Whether assigning the dominant member to the observer role would help his sensitivity is questionable.

A direct approach should not be ruled out. Talking to the student individually outside class may be the simplest and most effective solution.

Breaking a Problem into Subproblems

One of Maier's important contributions to effective group problem solving as well as to teaching is to point out that groups are likely to be more effective if they tackle one aspect of a problem at a time rather than skipping from formulation of the problem, to solutions, to evidence, to "what-have-you," as different members of the group toss in their own ideas. In developmental discussion the group tackles one thing at a time.

One of the first tasks is likely to be a clarification of the problem. Often groups are ineffective because different participants have different ideas of what the problem is, and group members may feel frustrated at the end of the discussion because "the group never got to the real problem." A second task is likely to be, "What do we know?" or, "What data are relevant?" A third task may be, "What are the characteristics of an acceptable solution?"—for example, "What is needed?" A fourth step could be, "What are possible solutions?", and a fifth step may be to evaluate these solutions against the criteria for a solution determined in the previous step.

The developmental discussion technique can be used even in large groups, since there are a limited number of points to be made at each step regardless of the number of participants. Maier and Maier (1957) have shown that developmental discussion techniques improve the quality of decisions as compared with freer, more nondirective discussion methods, but unfortunately no research has compared this technique with others as an educational device.

Patience

You should not expect an immediate response to every question. If your question is intended to stimulate thinking, give the students time to think. A few seconds of silence may seem an eternity, but a pause for thought may result in better discussion than a quick answer generated out of a desire to avoid silence. In some cases you may plan for such a thoughtful silence by asking the students to think about the question a few seconds and then write down one element that might help answer the question. Such a technique increases the chance that the shyer or slower students will participate, since they know what they want to say when the discussion begins. In fact you may even draw one in by saying, "You were writing vigorously, Ronnie, what's your suggestion?"

Appraising Progress

One of the important skills of discussion leaders is the ability to appraise the group's progress and to be aware of barriers or resistances that are blocking learning. This skill depends upon attention to such clues as inattention, hostility, or diversionary questions.

Skill at appraising is of little avail if instructors don't respond to the feedback they receive. In some cases they may need to respond only by interposing a guiding question or by emphasizing a significant contribution. In other cases they may need to summarize progress and restate the current issue or point out the stumbling block or diversion that has stopped progress. In extreme cases, they may have to stop the discussion to begin a discussion of the reasons for lack of progress.

Barriers to Discussion

As I showed earlier, one barrier to effective discussion may be inadequate information. Your role then may be to refer students to necessary sources of information, or you may provide the information yourself.

Another barrier is fuzziness and ambiguity. When a student's contribution is unclear, the instructor may restate it and have the restatement confirmed or rejected by the student. However, this device should not be used so much that the students begin to feel that they are ventriloquist's dummies.

Occasional summaries during the hour not only help students chart their progress, but also help smooth out communication problems. A summary need not be a statement of conclusions. In many cases the most effective summary is a restatement of the problem in terms of the issues resolved and those remaining.

Probably one of the most common barriers to good discussion is the instructor's tendency to tell the students the answer or to put the solution in abstract or general terms before the students have developed an answer or meaning for themselves. Of course, teachers can sometimes save time by tying things together or stating a generalization that is emerging. But all too often they do this before the class is ready for it.

Another barrier to discussion is agreement. Usually instructors are so eager to reach agreement in groups that they are likely to be happy when the students are agreeing. But agreement is not the objective of most educational discussions. Students come to class with certain common naive attitudes and values. While the attitudes they hold may be "good" ones, they may be so stereotyped that the students fail to develop an understanding of the complex phenomena to which their attitudes apply. The teacher's task is often directed not so much toward attitude change as toward increased sensitivity to other points of view and increased understanding of the phenomena to which the attitude applies. As I suggested earlier, the instructors may sometimes need to assume a role of opposition.

When the instructor opposes a student's opinion, he must be careful not to overwhelm the student with the force of his criticism. His objective is to start discussion, not smother it. Thus he must give students an opportunity to take hold and respond to his criticisms, examining the point of view that was opposed. Above all, the instructor should avoid personal criticism of students.

Handling Arguments

In any good discussion conflicts will arise. If such conflicts are left ambiguous and uncertain, they, like repressed conflicts in the individual, may cause continuing trouble. One of the leader's functions is to help focus these conflicts so that they may contribute to learning. Reference to the text or other authority may be one method of resolution, if the solution depends upon certain facts. Using the conflict as the basis for a library assignment for the class or a delegated group is another solution. If there is no experimentally verified answer, this is a good opportunity to review the method by which the answer could be determined. If the question is one of values, probably the teacher's goal will be to help students become aware of the values involved. In any case it should be clear that conflict may be an aid to learning, and the instructor need not frantically seek to smother it.

Sometimes students will dispute statements or decisions by instructors. Such disagreements may sometimes be resolved by a comparison of the evidence for both points of view, but since teachers are human, they are all too likely to become drawn into an argument in which they finally rest upon their own authority. To give yourself time to think as well as to indicate understanding and acceptance of the students' point, I suggest listing the objections on the blackboard. (Incidentally, listing evidence or arguments is also a good technique when the conflict is between two members of the class.) Such listing tends to prevent repetition of the same arguments.

The Two-Column Method

Another of Maier's techniques, the two-column method, is a particularly effective use of the blackboard in a situation where there is a conflict or where a strong bias prevents full consideration of alternate points of view. Experimental studies (Hovland, 1957) suggest that when people hear arguments against their point of view, they become involved in attempting to refute the arguments rather than listening and understanding. Disagreement thus often tends to push the debaters into opposite corners in which every idea is right or wrong, good or bad, or black or white. The truth is often more complex and not in either extreme.

The two-column method is designed to permit consideration of complications and alternatives. As in problem posting, leaders using this technique suggest that before debating the issues before the group, all the arguments on each side be listed on the board. The leader then heads two columns, "Favorable to A" and "Favorable to B" or "For" and "Against," and then asks for the facts or arguments group members wish to present. The instructor's task is to understand and record in brief the arguments presented. If someone wishes to debate an argument presented for the other side, the instructor simply tries to reformulate the point so that it can be listed as a positive point in the debater's own column. But even though an argument is countered or protested it should not be erased, for the rules of the game are that the two columns are to include all ideas that members consider relevant. Evaluation can come later.

When the arguments have been exhausted, discussion can turn to the next step in problem solving. At this point the group can usually identify areas of agreement and disagreement and in many cases it is already clear that the situation is neither black nor white. Now the issue becomes one of relative values rather than good vs. bad. By directing discussion toward arguments, some of the personal animosities have been avoided, and some underlying feelings may have been brought to light. The next stages of the discussion are thus more likely to be directed toward constructive problem solving.

Challenges and disagreements may be an indication of an alert, involved class. But the instructor should also be aware of the possibility that they may be symptoms of frustration arising because the students are uncertain of what the problem is or how to go about solving it.

Teaching Students How to Learn Through Discussion

I have already implied that classes don't automatically carry on effective discussions. To a large extent students have to learn how to learn from discussions just as they have to learn how to learn from reading. How can this occur? *

---

* A helpful manual is Ida S. Hill and W. F. Hill, *Learning and teaching through discussion,* Center for the Study of Liberal Education for Adults (4819 Greenwood Avenue, Chicago, Illinois, 1958).

Some of the attributes are already apparent. For example, one skill is clarification of what it is the group is trying to do. Developmental discussion carries this to the extent of specifying subgoals for each stage of the discussion. One of the skills in learning through discussion is developing sensitivity to confusion about what the group is working on and asking for clarification. For teachers this implies presenting their own goals for the discussion and encouraging students to participate in formulating the group's goals.

A second attribute is the students' development of a willingness to talk about their own ideas openly and to listen and respond to others' ideas. It is important for students to realize that it is easy to deceive themselves about their own insights or understandings and that verbalizing an idea is one way of getting checks upon and extensions of it. Teachers can encourage development of listening skills by asking one group member to repeat or paraphrase what another said before responding to it.

A third skill is planning. Discussions are sometimes frustrating because they are only getting underway when the end of the class period comes. If this results in continuation of the discussion outside the class, so much the better, but often learning is facilitated if students learn to formulate the issues and determine what out-of-class study or follow-up is necessary before the group breaks up.

A fourth skill is building on others' ideas in such a way as to increase their motivation rather than make them feel punished or forgotten. Often students see discussion as a competitive situation in which they win by tearing down other students' ideas. As Haines and McKeachie (1967) have shown, cooperative discussion methods encourage more effective work and better morale than competitive methods. This implies rewarding group performance rather than individual performance in discussion.

A fifth attribute is sensitivity to feelings of other group members. Students need to become aware of the possibility that feelings of rejection, frustration, dependence, and so on, may influence group members' participation in discussion. Sometimes it is more productive to recognize the underlying feeling than to focus on the content of an individual's statement.

A sixth attribute is skill in evaluation. If classes are to learn how to discuss effectively, they need to review periodically what aspects of their discussion are proving to be worthwhile and what barriers, gaps, or difficulties have occurred. Some classes reserve the last five minutes of the period for a review of the discussion's effectiveness.

Leadership Functions

While I advocate the sharing of leadership responsibilities with other members of the group, I have already indicated some of the duties I believe the teacher should perform when necessary. These include:

1. Calling the meeting to order and introducing the topic for discussion.
2. Clarification of goals during the discussion.
3. Summarization.
4. Mediation and clarification of differences.

In addition, the teacher needs to be particularly aware of two leadership functions discussed in the previous section: 1) agenda setting, and 2) evaluation.

If the agenda is set at the preceding meeting, the group can be better prepared for the current meeting. Agenda setting, like other leadership functions, can be shared with the group, and should be flexible enough so that it can be changed when the group wishes. Keeping the agenda a secret may spare the instructor the embarrassment of having students complain that only half the day's agenda was completed, but if students understand the agenda, their cooperation can be of much value to the struggling teacher.

Evaluation of the group by its own members may occasionally be threatening to the leader, but it seems to help solve many of the problems I have already discussed. Many instructors have found it helpful to choose a volunteer at each class meeting to observe the class, reporting at the end of the period on the functioning of the class as a group and making suggestions for improved functioning at the next meeting. A tape recording of a discussion helps instructors spot opportunities they've missed and makes them aware of their rejection or favoring of a student.

The teachers' own needs are more evident in their conduct of discussion than in a lecture, for skillful discussion leading requires a quick awareness of individual and group needs. Instructors must, at least occasionally, relinquish their spots in the limelight and banish the temptation to make the discussion a little lecture.

In general, if an instructor is enthusiastic, friendly, and obviously interested in the subject, students also will be. Let me emphasize again that both lecture and discussion may have advantages at certain points in a course. Skillful teachers will choose the method best adapted to their objectives rather than rigidly sticking to one method only.

Research on Discussion Methods

I have anticipated my treatment of research on discussion methods in the review of research comparing the effectiveness of lecture and discussion in Chapter 4. I implied there that discussion may be ill adapted for communicating information because the rate of communication from instructor to student is slow. However, not all information is eagerly received. When information encounters intellectual or emotional resistance, discussion methods may be necessary in order to bring the source of resistance to light. If students have misunderstandings or misconceptions, it is important that they come out and be corrected.

Moreover, if students are to achieve application, critical thinking, or some higher cognitive outcomes, it seems reasonable to assume that they should have an opportunity to practice application and critical thinking and to receive feedback on the results. Group discussion provides an opportunity to do this. While computers and simulations may also be programmed to provide prompt and realistic feedback, a group discussion permits presentation of a variety of problems and enables a number of people to gain experience in integrating facts, formulating hypotheses, amassing relevant evidence, and evaluating conclusions. In fact, the prompt feedback provided by the computer may actually be less effective than a method in which students are encouraged to discover solutions for themselves with less step-by-step guidance (Della-Piana, 1956). Since problem solving ordinarily requires information, instructors might expect discussion to be more effective for groups with more information than for those lacking in background. Some support for this hypothesis is provided by a study on the learning of children in visiting a museum. Melton, Feldman, and Mason (1936) found that lectures were more effective than discussions for children in grades five, six, and seven, but discussions were more effective for eighth graders.

In discussing the liabilities of lecturing, I mentioned that lectures usually place the learner in a passive role, and passive learning is less efficient than active. We would expect discussions to promote more active learning, and there is some relevant evidence. Bloom and his colleagues at Chicago used recordings of classes to stimulate students to recall their thoughts during class (1953). As predicted, they found that discussion did stimulate more active thinking than lecture classes did. Krauskopf (1960) substituted written for oral responses to the tape recordings and found that rated relevance of thoughts was positively correlated to achievement, accounting for variance in achievement beyond that accounted for by ability.

The idea that discussion methods should help overcome resistance to learning is difficult to verify. Essentially, the argument is that some desired learning encounters emotional barriers preventing it from affecting behavior. For example, psychology students may learn that distributed practice is effective, but not change their study methods because their anxiety about grades is so great that they don't dare try anything different. In such circumstances experiments on attitude change suggest that instructors must either bring about changes in underlying attitude and motivation, or they must change students' perceptions of the instrumental relationship between their beliefs and their motives. Psychotherapists believe that expressing one's attitude in a nonthreatening situation is one of the steps in the process of change. A group discussion may provide such opportunities for expression as well as give opportunities for other group members to point out other instrumental relationships.

In addition, most attitudes influencing learning have some interpersonal antecedents and are stabilized by a person's perception of the attitudes of other liked persons. Group discussion may facilitate a high degree of liking for the instructor and for other group members. It also permits more accurate assessment of group norms than is likely in other techniques of instruction. Consequently change may follow.

In fact, while individual instruction would be advantageous for many teaching purposes, group processes can provide a real advantage in bringing about changes in motivation and attitudes. Lewin (1952) showed in his classic experiments on group decision that it is sometimes easier to change a group than an individual.

Whether or not discussions actually are superior in these respects cannot be easily determined, for discussions range from monologues in which occasional questions are interposed to bull sessions in which the instructor is an interested (or bored!) observer. Nevertheless, a good deal of research has attempted to compare the effectiveness of differing discussion techniques.

Student-Centered vs. Instructor-Centered Teaching

A wide variety of teaching methods are described by the labels "student-centered," "nondirective," "group-centered," or "democratic" discussion. Proponents of these various methods have in common the desire to break away from the traditional instructor-dominated classroom and to encourage greater student participation and responsibility. Table 5-1 lists some of the ways in which the student-centered method has been supposed to differ from the traditional "instructor-centered" class.*

From the standpoint of theory, student-centered teaching in its more extreme forms might be expected to have some serious weaknesses, at least in achieving lower level cognitive goals. With the instructors' role as information giver reduced, their role as source of feedback virtually eliminated, and their opportunity to provide organization and structure curtailed, it is apparent that a heavy burden falls upon the group members to carry out any of these functions. These functions can best be assumed by groups that not only have some background in the academic discipline involved but which also have had experience in "democratic" groups.

Since student-centered teaching attempts to reduce dependence upon the instructor, it would be expected to diminish his influence as a prestige figure, and possibly to reduce his power to bring about attitudinal changes. However, this may be more than compensated for by increased freedom of expression and increased potency of group norms as sources of influence. Participation in discussion gives students an opportunity to gain recognition and praise that should, according to learning theory, strengthen motivation. Thistlethwaite (1960) found that National Merit Scholars check "allowing time for classroom discussion" as one of the outstanding characteristics of the teachers who contributed most to their desire to learn. Other characteristics mentioned included "modifying course content to meet students' needs and interests," "treating students as colleagues," and

---

* A good summary and critical evaluation of studies in this area may be found in R. C. Anderson (1959).

TABLE 5–1   *Dimensions Upon Which Student-Centered and Instructor-Centered Methods May Differ*

STUDENT-CENTERED	INSTRUCTOR-CENTERED
Goals	
Determined by group (Faw, 1949)	Determined by instructor
Emphasis upon affective and attitudinal changes (Faw, 1949)	Emphasis upon intellectual changes
Attempts to develop group cohesiveness (Bovard, 1951)	No attempt to develop group cohesiveness
Classroom Activities	
Much student participation (Faw, 1949)	Much instructor participation
Student-student interaction (McKeachie, 1951)	Instructor-student interaction
Instructor accepts erroneous or irrelevant student contributions (Faw, 1949)	Instructor corrects, criticizes, or rejects erroneous or irrelevant student contributions
Group decides upon own activities (McKeachie, 1951)	Instructor determines activities
Discussion of students' personal experiences encouraged (Faw, 1949)	Discussion kept on course materials
De-emphasis of tests and grades (Asch, 1951)	Traditional use of tests and grades
Students share responsibility for evaluation (Ashmus and Haigh, 1952)	Instructor evaluates
Instructor interprets feelings and ideas of class member when necessary for class progress (Axelrod, 1955)	Instructor avoids interpretation of feelings
Reaction reports (Asch, 1951)	No reaction reports

"taking a personal interest in students." However, in line with my earlier discussion of feedback, another trait mentioned was "providing evaluations reassuring the student of his creative or productive potentialities."

The advocates of student-centered or group-centered teaching also introduced another category of objectives, not usually considered in traditional classes—the goal of developing skills in group membership and leadership. The group-centered teacher might argue that even if group-centered teaching were no more effective than traditional methods in achieving the usual course objectives, it is so important that students learn to work effectively in groups that it may even be worth sacrificing some other objectives in order to promote this kind of growth.

Since student-centered teachers often stress group cohesiveness, a possible explanation for the contradictory results in the experiments to follow may be found in the studies of group cohesiveness and productivity in industry (for example, Seashore, 1954). These studies indicate that it is not safe to assume that a cohesive group will be a productive one. Cohesive groups are effective in maintaining group standards, but may set either high or low standards of productivity. Since cohesive groups feel less threatened by management than less cohesive groups, it may be difficult to change their standards. Thus, in creating "groupy" classes instructors may sometimes be helping their students develop strength to set low standards of achievement and maintain them against instructor pressures, or at least to develop group goals different from their normal academic goals.

Another factor may account for the fact that some researchers report student enthusiasm for student-centered teaching while others report hostility. Horwitz (1958) found that aggression toward the teacher increased when the teacher exercised his authority arbitrarily; for example, refused to abide by the students' decision about teaching methods after telling them that their vote would count. The same method was not resented when the instructor indicated that he would make the final decision. This is important because the limits of student power are often ambiguous in student-centered classes. Also of relevance was Horwitz's finding that the more inhibition of hostility, the less learning (on a type-setting task).

Three Early Experiments on Student-Centered Teaching

The previous section serves as an introduction to a review of the experimental attempts to demonstrate the effectiveness of student-centered teaching.

One of the best known comparisons of student-centered and instructor-centered instruction is that made by Faw (1949). Faw's class of 102 students met 2 hours a week to listen to lectures and 2 hours a week in 3 discussion groups of 34 students each. One discussion group was taught by a student-centered method, one by an instructor-centered method, and one group alternated between the two methods. Faw was the instructor for all of the classes.

As compared with the instructor-centered class, the student-centered class was characterized by more student participation, no instructor correction of inaccurate statements, lack of instructor direction, and more discussion of ideas related to personal experiences.

Faw's major measure of attainment of objectives was in the intellectual area. Scores on the objective course examination based on the textbook showed small but significant differences favoring the student-centered method. In the area of major interest, emotional growth, Faw's method of evaluation was to ask students in the student-centered and alternating classes to write anonymous comments about the class. Generally Faw thought that these comments indicated that the students felt that they received greater social and emotional value from the student-centered discussion groups than they would have from an instructor-centered class.

A very similar experiment was carried out by Asch (1951). Like Faw, Asch taught all the groups involved in his experiment. Three sections of about 30–35 students were taught by an instructor-centered method—half lecture and half discussion. One section of 23 students was taught by a nondirective method, quite similar to that of Faw. However, there were certain differences between Faw's and Asch's experiments. In Faw's experiment both student-centered and instructor-centered classes also spent 2 hours a week listening to lectures. While Faw did not mention grading, one assumes that grades were determined by the instructor on the basis of the course-wide examination. In Asch's experiment, students in the student-centered class were allowed to determine their own grades.

Asch's results do not completely agree with Faw's. On the final examination in the course, students in the instructor-centered class scored significantly higher than members of the student-centered class, both on the objective and essay portions of the test. Note, however, that the student-centered class was specifically told that this examination would in no way affect their grades in the course; therefore, the two groups were probably not equivalent in motivation. Haigh and Schmidt (1956) found no significant differences in a similar comparison.

As measured by the Bogardus Social Distance scale, attitude change in the two sections of Asch's course was not significantly different. Yet as compared with the instructor-centered class, a greater percentage of members of the student-centered class improved in adjustment as measured by the Minnesota Multi-Phasic Inventory.

Asch's students, like Faw's, had a different perception of their achievement from that shown by the course examination. Faw's student-centered class did better on the course examination than the instructor-centered class section, but thought they would have learned more if they had been in an instructor-centered class. Asch's students, however, rated the student-centered class higher than the instructor-centered class in helping them to learn the subject matter of the course even though they actually scored lower than the instructor-centered class.

Following the model of Lewin, Lippitt, and White's study (1939) of authoritarian, democratic, and laissez-faire group climates, the staff of the University of Michigan's general psychology course set up an experiment using three styles of teaching: recitation, discussion, and group tutorial (Guetzkow, Kelly, and McKeachie, 1954). As compared to discussion and tutorial methods, the more autocratic recitation method proved not only to produce superior performance on the final examination, but also to produce greater interest in psychology, as measured by the election of advanced courses in psychology. Furthermore, students liked the recitation method better than the other methods. The greater gains in knowledge produced by the recitation method fit in with the general principle that feedback aids learning, for students in the recitation sections had weekly or semi-weekly quizzes. I have suggested (McKeachie, 1951) that the popularity of this method is related to student anxiety about grades, which is most easily handled when students are in familiar, highly structured situations. Another factor in these results may be the inexperience of the instructors involved, most of whom had had less than a year of previous teaching experience. It is possible that skillful discussion or tutorial teaching requires greater skill than more highly structured methods.

Despite the immediate superiority of the recitation method, two results in motivational outcomes favored the discussion and tutorial methods: 1) the discussion sections were significantly more favorable than the other groups in their attitude toward psychology, and 2) a follow-up of the students three years later revealed that seven men each from the tutorial and discussion groups majored in psychology, while none of those in the recitation sections did so. Women majoring in psychology came about equally from all three groups.

These three experiments thus point toward the more structured discussion as being superior for knowledge objectives. This is supported by the results of Burke (1956). In a freshman orientation course Burke found student performance in classes of 125 to be superior to that of students in cooperative groups of 4 to 7 students. But on the basis of these early studies, the more unstructured methods tend to be superior for attitudinal and motivational outcomes.

Other Experiments on Student-Centered Teaching

One of the most comprehensive experiments on student-centered teaching was that of Landsman (1950). Landsman contrasted a student-centered type of teaching with a more directive type of democratic discussion organized around a syllabus. His experimental design involved eight classes in a course sequence of "Human Development," "Adjustment," and "Learning." Three instructors took part in the experiment, and each instructor used both methods. Outcome measures included the Horrocks-Troyer test (an analysis of case histories), a local case history analysis test, the group Rorschach, the MMPI, autobiographies, and students' reactions. His results showed no significant difference between methods on any of the measures.

Other experiments have also been carried out with negative results. For example, Johnson and Smith (1953) also found no significant difference between small democratic and large lecture classes in achievement test scores. An interesting sidelight of their experiment was that one democratic class gave the course extremely favorable evaluations, while the other democratic class tended to be less satisfied than lecture classes.

The Johnson and Smith study is one of the few to provide support for my earlier suggestion that the success of student-centered teaching depends upon the previous group experience of the students. Johnson and Smith suggest that the critical factor in making their successful democratic class go was the enthusiastic participation of a member of a student cooperative.

Bills (1952), too, found no difference in achievement between psychology classes taught by lecture-discussion vs. student-centered methods, but did find that the students in the student-centered class were significantly more favorable in attitude toward psychology. Maloney (1956) also found no differences in achievement between two types of discussion groups but did find gains in group cohesiveness, participation, and other indices of effectiveness in groups in which the leader specifically aimed at establishing acceptance and other characteristics of the student-centered group.

In a graduate course in counseling, Slomowitz (1955) found no significant differences between nondirective and problem-oriented discussions in achievement or application to a case study test. The nondirectively taught students did, however, change in self-concept more (at the 10 percent level of confidence) than did students in the other group. Like Slomowitz, Deignan (1956) was concerned not only with achievement but also with emotional changes. Although there were no other significant differences between the groups on follow-up tests a semester later, the student-centered group evaluated the course higher. Rasmussen (1956) also reported no difference in achievement but did find higher morale among groups of in-service teachers electing student-centered extension courses as compared with students taught by instructor-centered methods. Krumboltz and Farquhar (1957) compared student-centered, instructor-centered, and eclectic teaching methods in a "How to Study" course. There were no significant differences between methods on an achievement test or on self-ratings of study habits.

In an attempt to teach critical thinking Lyle (1958) compared a problem-oriented approach with conventional lecture-discussion-test procedures. Apparently he found that the conventional group was superior to the problem-oriented group in achievement. Gains in critical thinking were not greater in the problem-centered classes. When students were asked to write a question for the final examination, however, the conventional group wrote factual questions and the problem-centered group wrote thought questions.

In an experiment in teaching written and spoken English, Jenkins (1952) found that a teaching role in which the instructor acted as resource person in a democratic class was not significantly superior to traditional methods on three measures of communication skills.

Wispe (1951) carried out an interesting variation of the student-centered vs. instructor-centered experiment. Instead of attempting to control the instructor personality variable by forcing instructors to teach both instructor-centered and student-centered classes, Wispe selected instructors who were rated as naturally permissive or directive. He then compared their sections of the Harvard course in "Social Relations." He found no difference in final examination scores between students taught by different methods. Students preferred the directive method, and the poorer students gained more in directive classes.

As a counterpoint to Wispe's study with teachers using their preferred method, the Springfield College experiment (Ashmus and Haigh, 1952; Haigh and Schmidt, 1956) gave the students their choice of group-centered or instructor-centered teaching. Students choosing either type did not differ significantly in intelligence. The results showed no difference in the achievement of the two groups on a test not counted toward the course grade. Those in the nondirective classes were more highly satisfied with the course.

Moore and Popham (1959) reported that three student-centered interviews produced greater gains on the college Inventory of Academic Adjustment than did three content-centered interviews.

While scores on objective final examinations seem to be little affected by teaching method, there are, in addition to the changes in adjustment reported by Asch, Faw, Zeleny (1940) and Moore and Popham, other indications that student behavior outside the usual testing situation may be influenced in the directions of educational goals by student-centered teaching. The classes compared by Bovard (1951a and b) and McKeachie (1951) differed in the degree to which interaction between students was encouraged and in the degree to which the class made decisions about assignments, examinations, and other matters of classroom procedure. Like other experimenters, Bovard and McKeachie found that the groups did not differ in achievement as measured by the final examination. However, two clinical psychologists evaluated recordings of the class discussions that followed the showing of the film, "The Feeling of Rejection." Both clinicians reported that the "group-centered" class showed much more insight and understanding of the problems of the girl in the film.

Patton (1955) felt that an important variable in group-centered classes was the students' acceptance of responsibility for learning. He compared traditional classes to two classes in which there were no examinations, no lectures, and no assigned readings. Students in the experimental classes decided what reading they would do, what class procedure would be used, what they would hand in, and how they would be graded, so that they had even more power than had previous experimental groups. At the end of the course, these classes, as compared to the control group, 1) felt the course was more valuable, 2) showed greater interest in psychology, and 3) tended to give more dynamic, motivational analyses of a problem of behavior.

But giving students power can't work if students will not accept responsibility; so Patton also obtained individual measures of acceptance of responsibility within the experimental classes. As hypothesized, he found that the degree to which the student accepted responsibility was positively correlated with gain in psychological knowledge, gain in ability to apply psychology, interest in it, and rating of the value of the course.

Although the Bovard, McKeachie, and Patton experiments suggested that student-centered classes promoted transfer of learning, D. E. P. Smith (1954) found no differences between three methods varying in degree of directiveness as to their effects upon students' abilities to make "applicational transfer" of their learning. Wieder (1954), however, found that a nondirectively taught psychology class tended to produce more reduction in prejudice than conventional classes.

Gibb and Gibb (1952) reported that students who were taught by their "participative-action" method were significantly superior to students taught by traditional lecture-discussion methods in role flexibility and self-insight. In the participative-action method class, activities centered around "sub-grouping methods designed to increase effective group participation."

The instructor, who played a constantly diminishing role in the decisions and activities of the group, gave training in role playing, group goal setting, problem centering, distributive leadership, evaluation of individual performance by intra-group ratings, process observing, and group selection, evaluation and revision of class activities.

Gibb and Gibb also provide support for the assumption that group-centered teaching can facilitate development of group membership skills. They found that in nonclassroom groups the participative-action students were rated higher than other students in leadership, likableness, and group membership skills. Di Vesta's results tend to support this (1954), and Anderson and Kelly (1954) report that members of student-centered groups are characterized by positive attitudes toward themselves as participants.

Additional evidence for the effectiveness of small group discussion is cited in Chapter 8, "Project Methods and Independent Study." A number of studies suggest that small group discussion without a teacher present can be an effective educational method.

Another bit of support for less directive teaching is Thistle-thwaite's finding (1959) that there is a significant negative correlation between a college's productivity of Ph.D.'s in natural science and the directiveness of teaching methods used. His finding (1960) of a positive correlation for National Merit Scholars (1960, p. 67) between their desire to learn and the flexibility and permissiveness of their teachers lends additional support to student-centered teaching. Similarly, Solomon, Rosenberg, and Bezdek (1964) found a nonlinear relationship between scores on a test of comprehension and permissiveness. Moderate permissiveness was most effective.

A recently completed and as yet unpublished study by our University of Michigan research group also has shown that psychology instructors whose students do best on achievement tests of critical thinking (with intelligence controlled) tend to be described as follows: "He listened attentively to what class members had to say." "He was friendly." "He was permissive and flexible." "He explained the reason for criticism." "Things are explained clearly." "He is skillful in observing student reactions." Both the Thistlethwaite and Michigan results, then, support the value of student-centered teaching for motivation and critical thinking.

Student-Centered Teaching: Conclusions

The results of the spate of research on student-centered teaching methods support the theory with which this discussion began. I had suggested that student-centered teaching might be ineffective in achieving lower-order cognitive objectives. There seem to be few instances of such a loss. Students apparently can get information from textbooks as well as from the instructor. But I had also predicted that any superiority of student-centered discussion methods would be revealed in higher level incomes. As Table 5–2 indicates, differences in ability to apply concepts, in attitudes, in motivation, or in group membership skills have been found between discussion techniques emphasizing freer student participation compared with discussion with greater instructor dominance. In all but one of these studies, the differences favored the more student-centered method. The other (Guetzkow, Kelly, and McKeachie, 1954) had mixed results.

TABLE 5-2

REFERENCE	COURSE	STUDENT-CENTERED VS. INSTRUCTOR-CENTERED CRITERIA		
		Factual Exam	Higher Exam Cognitive	Attitude, Motivation
Faw (1949)	Psychology	*S		S
Asch (1951)	Psychology	*I		S
Deignan (1956)	Psychology			S
Bovard (1951a & b)	Psychology		S	S
McKeachie (1951)	Psychology		S	S&I
Patton (1955)	Psychology		S	*S
Carpenter (1959 & Davage (1958; 1959)	Psychology	*S	*S	*S
Anderson & Kelly (1954)	Psychology			S
McKeachie (1954a)	Psychology			S
Wieder (1954)	Psychology			S
Guetzkow, Kelly, & McKeachie (1954)	Gen. Psych.	I		S
Bills (1952)	Gen. Psych.	I		*S
Lyle (1958)	Gen. Psych.		I	
Perkins (1950)				S
Gibb & Gibb (1952)	Gen. Psych.			*S
Johnson & Smith (1953)	Intro. Psych.			S (2 classes)
Smith (1954)	Intro. Psych.			
Maloney (1956)	Educ. Psych.			S
Rasmussen (1956)	Educ. Psych.			S
Moore & Popham (1959)	Educ. Psych.			S
Landsman (1950)	Human Development			S
Di Vesta (1954)	Human Relations			S
Slomowitz (1955)	Grad. Counseling			S
Krumboltz & Farquhar (1957)	"How to Study Course"			
Burke	College Freshman Orientation	I		
Jenkins (1952)	English			
Wispe (1951)	Social Relations			
Ashmus & Haigh (1952); Haigh & Schmidt (1956)	Child and Adolescent Psych.			S
Zeleny (1940)	Sociology			S

I = Instructor-Centered Superior
S = Student-Centered Superior
* = Difference significant at .05 level or better. All other results are the actual direction of the difference in the experiment.

The choice of instructor-centered vs. student-centered discussion thus appears to depend upon your goals. The more highly you value outcomes going beyond knowledge acquisition, the more likely you will prefer student-centered methods.

Special Techniques of Discussion Teaching

Buzz Sessions

One of the popular techniques for achieving student participation in groups is the buzz session. In this procedure, classes are split into small subgroups for a brief discussion of a problem. Although many teachers feel that this technique is valuable as a change of pace or as a way of getting active thinking from students, little research has tested its effectiveness. Vinacke (1957) found that, as compared with performance on a pretest, students in two- and three-man groups wrote more new ideas after a five-minute discussion than students did working alone. It is possible, however, that similar changes could have been produced by a general discussion or a lecture.

Leadership

Laboratory and field studies of group processes may shed some light on factors that condition the effectiveness of groups and thus may help account for the lack of effectiveness of many discussion classes.

For example, one problem faced by the discussion leader is the student who dominates discussion or the clique that carries the ball. It may be that in some discussion classes, the instructor's fear of exerting too much control over the class has resulted in failure to insure that minority points of view were given an adequate hearing. Research suggests that effectiveness of group problem solving depends upon the leader's ability to obtain a hearing for minority opinion (Maier and Solem, 1952).

Some student-centered teachers have assumed that all decisions should be made by the group. Hence the instructor should not determine objectives, make assignments, or give tests, but should ask the group to make these decisions. If the group does this, can the time lost from academic work in making decisions be compensated for by the increased motivation of the students? Democratic methods permit the formation of group norms and the more acute perception of group norms, but as in industry these norms may not necessarily be conducive to high productivity or learning. The general question of the areas in which the instructor should make decisions is one that different instructors have answered in different ways, and one well worth further discussion and research. One hunch, based on research on business conferences, is that the instructor should make most procedural decisions, leaving the class time for problems related to the content of the course (Heyns, 1952).

Even in discussion of course content, however, it appears that some instructor direction may be useful if the goals are the learning of relationships and the ability to apply this learning. In an experiment comparing groups given more vs. less instructor direction in discovering the basis of solutions of verbal problems, Craig (1956) found that the directed group not only learned faster, but also retained their learning better than the group given less help. This result is supported by Corman's research on guidance in problem solving (1957).

Studies of business conferences have also found that one of the most common causes of dissatisfaction is the members' failure to understand the purpose of the conference. When students are confused about the purposes of teaching procedures, coupled with the stress involved in getting a good grade, it's little wonder that the student with a high need for achieving success is frustrated and often aggressive in a democratic class. Bloom's studies of student thought processes in Chicago classes show that, on the average, 30 percent of the students' time in discussion classes is spent in thinking about themselves and other people, as compared with 18 percent of the time in lectures. With members of the group thus concerned about their own needs, it is no wonder that discussion groups are not always productive.

Homogeneous vs. Heterogeneous Grouping

One of the common criticisms of discussion classes is that they waste time in discussion of problems raised either by the able students, which are beyond the ken of the other students, or by poor students, which the other students feel are too elementary. One answer to such criticism is to use homogeneous groupings so that students are discussing problems with other students of their own ability.

In the late 1950s, concern about America's resources of high level talent resulted in the proliferation of Honors Programs featuring homogeneous classes for students with high academic aptitude and achievement. Some evidence supports their educational value. Nevertheless, one of the earliest college experiments on ability grouping showed no significant advantages for homogeneous grouping by intelligence and even a trend toward the opposite result in psychology classes (Longstaff, 1932).

Briggs (1947), on the other hand, found that special intensive seminars meeting less often than conventional classes produced greater achievement for superior students than did the conventional class for a control group. Unfortunately, the seminar students volunteered and were selected by interview so that they probably had higher motivation than their controls. The two earliest publications in this area (Burtt, Chassel, and Hatch, 1923; Ullrich, 1926) reported results that seem very reasonable. They both concluded that homogeneous groups were not superior to heterogeneous groups when given standard material, but did superior work when the bright students were pushed with more difficult material. Similarly Tharp (1930) found homogeneous grouping superior in foreign language classes, and Taylor (1931) found it superior in analytic geometry. All in all, then, it seems safe to conclude that homogeneous grouping by ability is profitable if teaching makes use of the known characteristics of the groups.

Homogeneous grouping by personality proved to be ineffective in the experiment in group problem solving reported by Hoffman (1959). Comparing groups of four students who were similar in personality profiles on the Guilford-Zimmerman Temperament survey to groups made up of dissimilar students, he found that the heterogeneous groups produced superior solutions. Hoffman accounts for this difference by suggesting that heterogeneous groups are more likely to propose a variety of alternatives permitting inventive solutions.

On the other hand, in a study by Stern and Cope (Stern, 1960) groups of "authoritarian," "anti-authoritarian," and "rational" students in a citizenship course were segregated into homogeneous groups in which the instructor was unaware of which group he was teaching. Authoritarian students in the experimental group achieved more than comparable authoritarians in conventional classes.

It is apparent that we need further analysis of what kinds of homogeneities or heterogeneities contribute to what objectives. If we omit from consideration general adjustment problems of segregated groups, the idea that one should be able to do a better job of teaching to a group of known homogeneous characteristics than to a heterogeneous group seems so reasonable that it is surprising to find little research support. It may be that the potential advantages of carefully planned grouping have not been realized simply because we haven't yet learned optimal teaching procedures for such groups.

From a theoretical point of view the importance of group size and heterogeneity probably depends upon the purpose of the discussion. If, for example, you are interested in using group members as sources of information or of differing points of view, the larger and more heterogeneous the group, the greater its resources. On the other hand, the degree to which a group uses its resources depends upon communication, and it is not only apparent that a smaller proportion of group members can participate in a large group, but also that members are less likely to feel free to volunteer their contributions in large groups.

A final problem is that of group pressures toward consensus and conformity. As I suggested earlier, one of the barriers to effective group problem solving is the tendency of a group to accept the majority view with insufficient consideration of minority views. Since group members may be less likely to express divergent opinions in large groups than in small groups, perhaps the paradoxical hypothesis is true that the larger the group, the more effect a few outspoken members are likely to have in determining the success of discussion.

SUPPLEMENTARY READING

One of the greatest stimuli to the use of the discussion method in teaching has been the enthusiasm of teachers who have tried what has been variously called nondirective, student-centered, or democratic teaching. One of the earliest and best descriptions of this method is contained in N. Cantor, *The dynamics of learning* (Buffalo: Foster & Steward, 1946).

A source of interesting techniques adaptable for large groups is N. R. F. Maier, *Problem-solving discussions and conferences* (New York: McGraw-Hill, 1963).

A description of the use of group-centered methods in the Harvard "Human Relations" course is R. Mann, *Interpersonal styles and group development* (New York: Wiley, 1967).

6

Six Roles of Teachers

There are many varieties of discussion. Some discussions primarily involve group problem solving; some are gripe sessions; some may be pep meetings; some may provide practice in integrating and applying information gained from textbooks or lectures. The instructor's role will vary depending upon which of these or other functions the discussion is serving. The roles are most apparent in discussion classes, but every class places demands upon teacher behavior which result in role behavior that has much in common whatever teaching method is used.

Solomon Cytrÿnbaum, working with my colleague Richard Mann in our research on college teaching, has suggested the following categorization of teacher roles:*

* The following sections in this chapter are excerpted from W. McKeachie, J. Milholland, and R. Mann et al., *Research on the characteristics of effective teaching.* Final Report to the Bureau of Research, Office of Education, on Project No. 05950, Grant No. OE–4–10–001, Dept. of Psychology, University

1. The teacher as expert.
2. The teacher as formal authority.
3. The teacher as socializing agent.
4. The teacher as facilitator.
5. The teacher as ego ideal.
6. The teacher as person.

He describes them as follows:

The Teacher as Expert

"Looked at from one perspective, the teacher is connected to the students in his classroom because to some extent and in some form or other he stands before them as an expert. The core of his goal is to transmit whatever information, analytic perspectives, or critical viewpoints he wishes the students to acquire in that course. His relevance for that situation flows directly from the fact that he knows something the students do not know yet. Whether his expertise be displayed by means of a lecture, by means of answering questions, or by the act of correcting or validating what a student has said, his interests revolve around the effort to achieve one or more of what Bloom has described as the educational objectives within the cognitive domain.

"To complete the picture, we must ask about the roles and activities of the student while he is connected with the teacher as expert. While the student in the large lecture course relates to the teacher as expert primarily by taking notes, the student's activities are not necessarily passive and accepting. Whether the student is asking a highly technical question or is quarreling with a teacher over how to prove a particular Euclidian theorem, he is operating within the ground rules of this aspect of total task if he is at that moment responding to the teacher in his capacity as expert. The student's response may include uncertainty ("What did you say the three causes of the Peloponnesian War were?") or discouragement ("I just can't get this stuff.") or any of a number of emotions. It is simply a matter of convenience to note first how the classroom interaction might look when all is going relatively smoothly.

---

of Michigan, Ann Arbor, 1968. A more accessible and detailed account may be found in R. D. Mann et al., *The college classroom* (New York: Wiley, 1970).

"Beyond specifying the kinds of goals and activities which characterize this aspect of the total task, it might be useful to note some of the satisfactions and motives which propel and sustain these activities. Perhaps the core of the matter is best approached by way of the concept of competence. For the teacher the issue of competence includes both his ability to comprehend and organize the relevant intellectual material and his capacity to present this material clearly and convincingly. Questions of the teacher's ability to remain well informed on new developments in his area, as well as his ability to make creative and critical judgments concerning the main trends in his field, bear directly upon the teacher's competence as an expert. From the student's perspective the issue of competence is no less relevant. One may wish to refer to the student's curiosity or to his intrinsic love of knowledge, or one may wish, in the line of analysis suggested by McClelland et al. to consider the student's need for achievement, which in this case would center around his concern for meeting his own internal standards of excellence with respect to the mastery of the relevant intellectual material. However, it is well to remember that this and each other aspect of the total task is sustained not only by positive or approach motivation but by negative or avoidance motivation as well. One need only think back to the experience of sitting in a lecture hall listening to words whose meaning seemed totally beyond one's grasp to know that the fear of appearing stupid to others and to oneself makes its contribution to the college classroom. Not only are the students chasing after the goal of confidence and greater knowledge; they are seeking to avoid one of the many disasters inherent in the process of education—the realization that one is over one's head, that certain kinds of information cannot be acquired with a reasonable expenditure of effort. By the same token, it would be misleading to assert that the teacher is driven only by the positive motivation of wishing to be competent in his own eyes. It would seem fair to assume that no teacher can indefinitely reveal his ignorance or his lack of preparation without experiencing shame and discomfort in dealing with his students.

The Teacher as Formal Authority

"The second aspect of the task is defined by a series of activities and functions in which the teacher serves in the capacity of formal authority. Viewed from the perspective of the larger social structure within which the college classroom is located, the teacher is an agent not only of instruction but of control and evaluation. The Registrar's office expects the grade sheet within some number of hours after the final examination. Beyond certain poorly defined limits one class may not disrupt the activities of another, nor may one student disrupt the learning of another student. Assignments, standards of excellence, and deadlines are all matters of concern, however they may be resolved. The pressures upon the teacher to perform the traditional functions of the formal authority come from many sources. Future employers, professional schools, and Deans' offices all express some need for a meaningful and averageable estimate of the student's performance.

"Some educators view the grading system as a deterrent to self-deception regarding one's ability or one's performance; others seem to view it as the ultimate weapon against the students' inherent slothfulness. Beyond noting these functions it may be useful to remember that, given a choice, most people would rather be the evaluator than the evaluated, and would rather be one up than one down. Even if one intends to be "the good guy" and delegate or deny one's power, it is relevant that one enters the situation with one's power clearly established and institutionalized.

"We would not wish to imply by the above remarks that the teacher's activities and his capacity as formal authority serve only the institution and/or the needs of the teacher. Given the traditional institutional structure within which the student operates, it is very much in the students' interest to know what the teacher expects and what the teacher will reward. And even if the traditional educational structure were removed, there may well be sound pedagogical reasons why learning is more effective in an interpersonal situation where the students ascribe legitimacy and power to a teacher, who then would proceed to make clear demands and to distribute objectively based rewards for excellence. However one feels about the latter point, it is at least true that, given the existence and consequences of the grade sheet, many of the students' concerns center around the dual emphasis on the assignment and the evaluation of the students' intellectual activity.

"We would include within the activities relevant to the teacher as formal authority all those instances of moment-by-moment control over the classroom which derive ultimately from the teacher's power to banish the student from the classroom in the interest of maintaining an environment in which the other students could learn. While this ultimate power might never be invoked, the fact remains that it is typically within the teacher's power to define what is relevant for class discussion, who shall speak in class, and what kinds of behavior are unacceptably disruptive. It follows, then, that we would include within the set of activities initiated by students within this definition of the task not only the familiar requests for clarity regarding assignments and grades but also those activities which address the issue of the teacher's control over the classroom interaction. Students may indicate their acceptance of this control by requesting permission to speak or by complaining about the irrelevance of other students' digressions, or by efforts during office hours to have the teacher control a particularly annoying fellow class member.

"We have already discussed several of the pressures which can impel the teacher to take over various functions of the formal authority, and we have implied that among the teacher's fears in the classroom one often finds the fear of "losing control of the class." It does not take much experience with college classrooms to recognize that some students are motivated by their desire for a good grade. While some teachers seem to spurn this source of the students' motivation, referring to it as "extrinsic" motivation or "grade grubbing," their scorn often conveys the impression that they feel capable of making somewhat deeper interpretations regarding the underlying dependency or passivity of the students in their classes. There is little doubt that a lifetime of educational experience has suggested to some students either that the teacher knows best or that it is the better part of wisdom to act as if he does. Be that as it may, it is in our interest here to indicate those other forces which impel students to want the teacher to fulfill his functions as formal authority. These forces vary considerably from student to student. When, for whatever reason, the student has little energy available for a particular course, to have a teacher specify clearly what is expected often seems far preferable to having a teacher create an open-ended situation in which the student feels guilty for anything less than total absorption in the course. Even students who will eventually find other sources of motivation sometimes find it useful to focus initially upon the teacher's demands and standards. To emphasize that there are other motives than dependency which underlie the student's involvement with the teacher as formal authority is not to deny the relevance of dependency needs among college students. Nor would we deny that there are students who stubbornly cling to the notion that the teacher's evaluations constitute the sole criterion of success or failure. Our intention in the above discussion has been simply to indicate that there are many sources for such student activities as attempting to clarify what is expected, attempting to anticipate what will be on the final exam, and attempting to use the teacher as the final arbiter of what is acceptable classroom behavior.

The Teacher as Socializing Agent

"The third aspect of the task facing the classroom can be understood only if one realizes two things about the context in which education takes place. First, the teacher is not only in possession of certain intellectual material; he is also a member of various overlapping collectivities with respect to which the students are either outsiders or marginal members. Furthermore, the goals toward which the students are striving typically extend in time far beyond the particular classroom and the particular course. The teacher is a member of the community of scholars as accredited by a particular professional and academic discipline, and he is, as well, a member of an institution that may be highly relevant to the occupational aspirations of a given student. The teacher resembles in some sense the gatekeeper, the one who does or does not pass the individual student along to the next plateau or the next screening process. It is soon apparent to the students that acceptability within the standards of the discipline or even within the standards of the community of intellectuals involves more than the ability to master the intellectual material.

"If we wish to talk seriously about the actual state of affairs in American education, and not simply about how it should be, we must realize that many students are discouraged from being majors in a given department or from going on to graduate work because individual faculty members operate on the assumption that acceptability involves matters of temperament, value commitment, and many other factors. When the faculty member tells the student that going on in his field does not seem to be that student's "cup of tea," he may be responding every bit as much to the student's conception of the good life as to his capacity for intellectual attainment. In a very real sense a college teacher is a recruiting officer whose job includes encouraging, discouraging, and training students to "go on."

"To the extent that undergraduate programs are adapted to this aspect of college education, they tend to become highly "pre-professional." The student is encouraged to take courses which would be useful to him in graduate school. He is engaged in discussions of the underlying commitment to science or humanism or beauty which seems to the faculty member to be a necessary condition for acceptance into training programs at a higher level. But we should not overlook the socializing activities of the teacher whose relevant reference group is the more broadly defined community of scholars. While a particular teacher may shun the more explicit forms of creating "little graduate students," he may feel very strongly about the extent to which the university is an appropriate place only for those who share their political or social values.

"From the student's perspective, the potential letter of recommendation may be a more salient reward to be obtained from the teacher than the grade in that one course. Some students declare that they would like to get into the world, however broadly or narrowly defined, inhabited by the teacher; that is, students sense that they would like to test out whether they could get in, or whether it would be satisfying if they attempted to move in that direction. For understandable reasons students may have mixed emotions about the fact that the teacher controls access to further training and membership in "the elect." Some may seize eagerly upon any opportunity to join with the faculty member as junior members of the circle while others may resist any attempt on the teacher's part to ensnare them into the pre-professional pathway. In either case they are contending with the issue of the teacher as socializing agent.

"The students make their contribution to the establishment of this aspect of the total task. For many students, to imagine their future in terms of a particular occupational goal is to crystallize their still-developing interests and passions; for others, it makes concrete and reachable a future that assures them the necessities and pleasures of life. And then there are many students who are motivated primarily by their alienation from or rejection of the life style associated with their parents, their community, or their peers.

"Thus the teacher and the students may in various ways be bound together within the socialization process. For the student to try on the discipline or profession which the teacher represents may involve him in the acquisition of sacred artifacts or the awkward mimicry of an accepted intellectual pose. Fortunately for the student most teachers overlook these ungainly beginnings. A faculty member may remark to a colleague that such and such a bright undergraduate seems to be "coming into the field," although he may feel constrained to conceal his sense of pleasure at this indication that his field has proved capable of attracting yet another valuable recruit.

The Teacher as Facilitator

"Different teachers tend to conceive of the most troublesome impediments to learning in different ways. Some view the student as capable of productive intellectual effort only to the extent that such impediments as fear of failure, self-abasement in the face of authority, or discouragement in the face of excessively high standards are removed. Others, who operate more like administrators than like therapists, address themselves to the situational impediments: the students do not know how to use the library system; they find it difficult, without assistance, to gain access to the field experiences which would make their intellectual work more salient; or they need someone to fight for them in their battle for ungraded or more socially relevant courses. In whatever form it takes it is clear that the teacher as facilitator tends to respond primarily to the student's own definition of his goals. The student's goals may be quite divergent from the teacher's goals, but then for one person to facilitate the learning and development of another often involves a recognition of the substantial differences between individuals in terms of what they value and what they are seeking. If we were to capture the pedagogical fervor which often underlies some teachers who strongly emphasize the facilitator functions, we would note the teacher's rejection of any effort to "impose" his answers and even his questions upon the students who need more than anything else to develop questions and answers that are relevant to their own lives. The prototypic behaviors associated with the teacher as facilitator would include a fair amount of listening and efforts on the teacher's part to clarify in everyone's mind what a particular student is trying to say.

"The student, or, more properly, that aspect of all students which connects with the teacher as facilitator may be characterized as one whose personal agenda includes not only finding out more about the course material but also finding out more about himself. Thus the student asks: "What am I interested in? What am I good at? What are my ideas about a particular event or body of knowledge? Why am I in this classroom?" One senses here that the student's performance in class is partly expressive, driven by a need to articulate new ideas and to develop some sense of ownership vis-à-vis old and borrowed knowledge. Probably the most relevant words within this aspect of teaching and learning are creativity and independence. Over and over again the students test out in relation to the teacher whether they can be creative, as opposed to restricted within the teacher's definition of what is appropriate; and independent, as opposed to functioning as the perfect robot. However, the path to functioning creatively and independently turns out to have snares and pitfalls which have nothing to do with the teacher. Some have to do with the inherent difficulty of the material or with the difficulty of gaining access to it; some have to do with the pre-existing limitations or immaturities of the particular learner.

"There are few interpersonal dramas more intricate than the one created by a student who wishes help but only if it entails no loss of independence on his part. The teacher may often sense that the student, hidden among the various efforts to appear supremely confident and self-reliant, is trying to tell him that he is having a hard time getting started on a paper, that he suffers from recurrent perceptions of himself as stupid, or that he is far more anxious than he seems about how the teacher will receive the fruits of his labor. The teacher often feels caught in the cross-currents between wanting to respond to the pleas and wanting to preserve whatever mutual respect had thus far developed. The point we make here is that the pressures on the teacher to perform as facilitator may begin with pressures to remove various constraints, but the situation often moves to the point where to facilitate is to assist a student over the real and imaginary barriers which block him from his goals. But here, as well, the pressures are complex. As the history of man has indicated in numerous arenas, unremitting oppression is sometimes easier to bear than conditional autonomy. Thus many of the pressures on the teacher test either what limits he places upon the students' freedom or whether the teacher, despite his apparent openness, is basically patronizing or manipulating the students. The teachers do not always pass these tests, and one sometimes wonders whether any human being could pass some of the tests constructed by students. It is clear that from the perspective of the student as well as from that of the teacher, it is not unusual to find intense and mixed feelings regarding the desirability of granting or achieving freedom.

The Teacher as Ego Ideal

"Thus far we have described the teacher in his capacities as expert, formal authority, socializing agent, and facilitator. We would turn now to an aspect of the teacher's total function which may or may not overlap with any or all of the previously discussed aspects of teaching. We would point here to the fact that the teacher may play an essentially heroic or charismatic role in the classroom and in so doing may end up serving in the capacity of ego ideal for the student. Some teachers will accomplish this by emphasizing their expertise, and some will accomplish it by emphasizing their high status within the student's chosen field, but clearly it is possible for a teacher to play the role of expert or socializing agent without becoming in any meaningful sense a part of the students' ideal. Perhaps the key attributes of the teacher as ego ideal are his commitment, or, as it is sometimes referred to, his enthusiasm. Some teachers who function primarily as facilitators convey, by their devotion to an underlying educational philosophy and by their capacity to be patient and helpful, certain qualities which cause some students to identify strongly with them. We cite this particular example because it is all too easy to associate the ego ideal with the flamboyant lecturer whose performances amount to an intellectual and interpersonal *tour de force*.

"Viewed from the most general perspective, it would seem that one very important cue to which students respond when they accept their teacher as an ego ideal is any indication that the teacher enjoys what he is doing. Not only does he evidently enjoy teaching, but he seems to find something in that situation which is personally liberating. He seems to have more than enough energy for the task at hand, more than enough self-confidence, and a belief that the activity or the ideas involved are sufficiently worthwhile to care deeply about them. What this suggests is that an important aspect of being a teacher is the extent to which one's values or one's ideals are engaged. Why do some students report that the enthusiasm of a particular teacher was contagious and caused them to work unusually hard in that course? One answer might be that students and teachers alike are striving to make their life and the activities in which they engage congruent with their developing sense of what is important and what is satisfying. The presence of a person who can so unconflictedly involve himself in a particular body of ideas or a particular kind of teaching sets in motion various responses; some students are alienated by the teacher's exuberance, some are envious and resentful, but some find in that teacher at that moment someone with whom they can identify and who can serve for them as an ideal.

"Faculty members tend to be rather uncharitable about those of their colleagues who attract large numbers of students to their lectures and usually they allege that the consequences of the teacher's activities must be integral to the cause of his performance. That is, since he attracts so many students, he must be doing anything and everything to attract students. He must be a showman or an entertainer, he must be driven by a somewhat excessive desire to have students identify with him. The point here is not that these inferences are always wrong, but rather that they are usually quite incomplete. One must ask what the satisfactions are for the teacher who is functioning as ego ideal. Teachers have internal audiences, composed of significant others whose standards of judgment are important to them. One reason why a particular teacher's performance may be in fact so attractive for others is that the performance also satisfies the teacher's own standards of excellence, and thus one part of his entire performance involves the communication of his pleasure with himself. He acts as if he feels brilliant, more fully alive, more patient and sensitive, i.e., capable of satisfying whatever standards of self-judgment are applicable at that moment.

The Teacher as Person

"The sixth and last aspect of the teacher-student relationship which we would like to isolate and discuss involves the development of a mutually validating relationship. Beyond the fact that the teacher knows more about the field than the student, beyond the fact that the teacher has certain rights and duties which flow from his position in the larger system, beyond the fact that the teacher is a gatekeeper to the various collectivities of which he is a part, beyond the fact that the teacher can sometimes be of use to the student who is formulating and pursuing his own goals, and beyond the fact that the teacher can upon occasion find the energy and skill to satisfy his own standards of excellence, beyond all these facts remains the inescapable fact that the teacher is also a person. The array of goals toward which the teacher strives is not completely accounted for by referring to the fact that he is the teacher. Every social role places constraint upon the extent to which personal gratifications may be obtained within that relationship, without at the same time destroying the foundations of the role or relationship itself. If the new teacher takes too seriously the implications of various snide remarks to the effect that teacher X "just wants to be liked by all his students," he might get the impression that wanting to be liked is out of bounds if one wishes at the same time to be a teacher. One might be tempted to conclude that being a good teacher and being liked are incompatible goals, but it would seem more appropriate to conclude that there may be limits beyond which wanting to be liked will impair a teacher's performance. But what about within those limits?

"We would allege that the teacher and the students alike have a fundamental interest in having themselves, and not simply their course-related selves, validated within the relationship that is developing in the classroom. Basic human and interpersonal issues, issues of trust and misperception, created by people who want to be seen as similar in some respects, or who want to be respected although dissimilar, issues of trustworthiness and affection—in short, the full range of human needs—are very much a part of the classroom.

"Consider the efforts by teachers and students to indicate that they continue to exist beyond the classroom. The implication is that each is telling the other that if he continues to be seen solely in terms of his activities within the classroom then the relationship cannot help but remain a highly limited and less than ideal arrangement. Teachers sneak in little anecdotes about their own days as students or their families or their political activities. Students allude to their summer vacations and their weekends and their religion and their skirmishes with the law. Each is involved in a process of asserting that he would like more of himself to be validated than simply that part of him which joins with the others in the pursuit of the course goals.

"The other parts of oneself, for both the teacher and the students, are not simply those parts which are outside the classroom. Equally important are those feelings and reactions which, while not explicitly part of the agenda for class discussion, press upon one's consciousness. Thus an individual in the classroom may be impelled to break through the task-oriented discussion to comment upon an absurdity which has just occurred to him or to express irritation or a sudden burst of pleasure. Each such attempt is a commentary upon the extent to which the speaker wishes to expand the range of legitimate activity to include other more subjective or emotional reactions to what is going on.

"We would not want to leave the impression that these communications of emotion and "outside-the-class" identity are irrelevant to the manifest task of teaching and learning. If one of the latent goals of the teacher as ego ideal is to convey the relevance of the course material to what is worthwhile and exciting in life, the latent function of the teacher as person is to convey that the intellectual matters under discussion are not irrelevant to the conduct of a life that is within the range of the students in the class. To the extent that the teacher can convey how he came to be interested in these matters, or how his interests are sustained by their application to issues of concern to him in his "everyday life," the student can come to understand the relevance of the teacher's career and knowledge to the student's own interests and personal needs. While one can imagine that a passionate and thoroughly admirable professor may inspire students to join the quest for his version of the Holy Grail, one can also imagine that students are affected by hearing of the haphazard route by which some academics found their way into the field. Some of the reasons why a career is chosen or an interest sustained are far from the stylized versions selected for inclusion in the "Lives of Great Men" mythologies. Watson's route to the formulation of a model for the DNA molecule is full of recognizable human motives and chance occurrences: an unwillingness to study certain fields of mathematics, personal friendships, the coincidences of time and place, and so forth. One senses in his narrative, as in the performance of many teachers in their capacity as persons, that even marvelous achievements are attainable when one hears how large a role good fortune and human frailty have played all along the way. One also senses in such performances a real reluctance to convey only the admirable parts of the process, as if the teacher (or Watson) were impelled not to create a myth when in fact reality is far more humorous (and attractive) than the myth of the genius striking directly toward the Nobel

Prize could ever be. Thus the teacher as person is not only addressing his own need to recognize the self he is portraying by his performance. He is also performing a vital task of puncturing the various mythic constructions which students may develop, and the net effect of this is both to decrease the awe in which he is held and to increase the extent to which his interests reveal him to be an ordinary mortal in pursuit of a recognizable and manageable set of goals.

"Furthermore, as the teacher begins to make possible these kinds of information about himself he is also enabling the student to be "all there" and to work on the integration of his disparate elements in an accepting or trust-inducing interpersonal environment.

"Table 6-1 summarizes some of the contrasting goals and prototypic behaviors which characterize each of the six aspects of the teacher's total function."

TABLE 6–1

THE TEACHER'S ROLES	MAJOR GOALS	CHARACTERISTIC SKILLS	MAJOR SOURCES OF STUDENT MOTIVATION (AND FEAR)
Expert	To transmit information, the concepts and perspectives of the field	Listening, scholarly preparation, class organization and presentation of material: answering questions	Curiosity, need for achievement; intrinsic interest in content (fear of being/appearing stupid; fear of being snowed)
Formal authority	To set goals and procedures for reaching goals	Defining structure, and standards of excellence; evaluating performance	Dependency; getting a good grade (fear of flunking, of being lost and pursuing irrelevant activities)
Socializing agent	To clarify goals and career paths beyond the course; to prepare students for these	Clarifying rewards and demands of the major, the field, and academic	Need to clarify one's interests and calling; desire to be "in" (fear of being rejected by field or having options reduced)

TABLE 6–1 (Cont.)

THE TEACHER'S ROLES	MAJOR GOALS	CHARACTERISTIC SKILLS	MAJOR SOURCES OF STUDENT MOTIVATION (AND FEAR)
Facilitator	To promote creativity and growth in student's own terms; to help overcome obstacles to learning	Bringing students out, sharpening their awareness of their interests and skills; to use insight and problem solving to help students reach goals, avoid blocks	Self-discovery and clarification to grow in desired direction (fear of being/becoming a puppet or gradegrubber; fear of not developing a clear and useful identity)
Ego ideal	To convey the excitement and value of intellectual inquiry in a given field of study	Demonstrating the ultimate worthwhileness of, or personal commitment to one's material/educational goals	The desire to be turned on; the desire for a model, a personification of one's ideals (fear of being bored, unmoved, and cynical)
Person	To convey the full range of human needs and skills relevant to and sustained by one's intellectual activity; to be validated as a human being; to validate the student	Being self-revealing in ways which clarify one's totality beyond the task at hand; being trustworthy and warm enough to encourage students to be open as well	The desire to be known as more than a student; the desire to have one's life cohere (the fear of being ignored or treated as a "product")

7

Laboratory Teaching

The laboratory method is now so widely accepted as necessary for scientific education that it may seem heretical to ask whether laboratory experience is an effective way to achieve educational objectives. Fortunately there is evidence that laboratory instruction can be educational. Whether it typically achieves its potential is another question.

Laboratory teaching assumes that first-hand experience in observation and manipulation of the materials of a science is superior to other methods of developing understanding and appreciation of research methods. Laboratory training is also frequently used to develop complex skills necessary for more advanced study or research and to develop familiarity with equipment, measures, and research tools.

From the standpoint of theory, the activity of the student, the sensorimotor nature of the experience, and the individualization of laboratory instruction should contribute positively to learning. However, information cannot usually be obtained by direct experience as rapidly as from abstractions presented orally or by printing. Films, demonstrations, or simulations may also shortcut some of the trial and error of the laboratory. Thus, one would not expect laboratory teaching to have an advantage over other teaching methods in amount of information learned. Rather, one might expect the differences to be revealed in retention, in ability to apply learning, or in actual skill in observation or manipulation of materials. Unfortunately, little research has attempted to tease out these special types of outcomes. If these outcomes are unmeasured, a finding of no difference in effectiveness between laboratory and other methods of instruction is almost meaningless, since there is little reason to expect laboratory teaching to be effective in simple communication of information.

Research on Laboratory Teaching

In an experiment in a course, "Methods of Engineering," White (1945) found that students taught by a group laboratory method achieved more than those taught by a lecture-demonstration method. A study by Balcziak (1954), however, comparing, 1) demonstration, 2) individual laboratory, and 3) combined demonstration and laboratory in a college physical science course, found no significant differences between them as measured by tests of information, scientific attitude, or laboratory performance.

In experiments in physics and engineering, Kruglak (1952) and White (1945) found that students taught by individual or group laboratory methods achieved more than those taught by lecture-demonstration. In studies by Balcziak (1954), Dearden (1960), Trotter (1960), and Bradley (1963), however, laboratory teaching was compared with, 1) lecture-demonstration, 2) combined demonstration and laboratory, 3) workbook, and 4) term paper. The comparisons were in physical science, general biology, and home economics courses. No significant differences were found between methods as measured by tests of information, practical application, scientific attitude, or laboratory performance. Earlier experiments found no significant loss resulting from reduction in laboratory time or assignment of one cadaver to four students rather than two.*

---

* See R. E. Downing, Methods in science teaching, *Journal of Higher Education*, 1913, 2, 316–320; A. W. Hurd, *Problems of science teaching at the*

The foregoing studies point to the conclusion that time spent in the laboratory could be reduced without educational loss. However, the results of research on methods of teaching in the laboratory indicate that the effectiveness of the laboratory depends on the manner in which the work is taught. Novak (1958), for example, used labeled photomicrographs as an aid in teaching a project-centered general botany course and found that they aided achievement in a botany laboratory. Bainter (1955) found that a problem-solving method was superior to traditional laboratory manual methods in teaching students to apply principles of physics in interpreting phenomena. Lahti (1956) also found a problem-solving method to be superior to more conventional procedures in developing students' abilities to design an experiment. Because many laboratory teachers have been interested in teaching problem-solving methods, this may be an appropriate place to note Burkhardt's (1956) finding that students who are taught calculus with an emphasis on the understanding of concepts learn concepts better than students taught with conventional emphasis upon the solving of problems. On the face of it, this might appear to be in opposition to the results of Kruglak, Bainter, and Lahti. Actually all of these studies point to the importance of developing understanding, rather than teaching problem solutions by going through a routine series of steps. Whether the laboratory is superior to the lecture-demonstration in developing understanding and problem-solving skills probably depends upon the extent to which understanding of concepts and general problem-solving procedures are emphasized as opposed to "cookbook" methods.

SUPPLEMENTARY READING

A brief, good review of work on laboratory teaching may be found in Donald Bligh, G. J. Ebrahim, D. Jaques, and D. W. Piper, *Teaching students* (Devon, England: Exeter University Teaching Services, 1975), pp. 174–175.

college level (Minneapolis: University of Minnesota Press, 1929); C. M. Jackson, Experiment in methods of teaching gross human anatomy. In E. Hudelson, ed., *Problems of college education* (Minneapolis: University of Minnesota Press, 1929), pp. 444–449; V. H. Noll, *Laboratory instruction in the field of inorganic chemistry* (Minneapolis: University of Minnesota Press, 1930); V. H. Noll, "The optimum laboratory emphasis in college chemistry," *School and Society*, 1930, *32*, 300–303.

8

Project Methods and
Independent Study

Interest in independent study as a means of utilizing faculty time more efficiently brought to the fore a teaching method that has been used in some form for many years. If one goal of education is to help students develop the ability to continue learning after their formal education is complete, it seems reasonable that they should have supervised experience in learning independently, experience in which the instructor helps students learn how to formulate problems, find answers, and evaluate their progress themselves. One might expect the values of independent study to be greatest for students of high ability with a good deal of background in the area to be covered, since such students should be less likely to be overwhelmed by difficulties encountered. While this expectation contains some truth, motivation and work habits are also important.

The Project Method

Independent study programs frequently involve the execution of projects in which a student, or group of students, undertakes to gather and integrate data relevant to some more or less important problem.

The results of research on the effectiveness of the project method are not particularly encouraging. One of the first "independent study" experiments was that of Seashore (1928). His course consisted primarily of guided individual study with written reports on eight projects, each of which took about a month to complete. Final examination scores, however, were no different for these students than for students taught by the usual lecture-discussion method (Scheidemann, 1929). Similar results were reported by Barnard (1936) for a "group study" method. In a study in a college botany course, Novak (1958) found that students in conventional classes learned more facts than did those taught by the project method. The project method was particularly ineffective for students in the middle third of the group in intelligence. Similarly Goldstein (1956) reports that students taught pharmacology by a project method did not learn more than those taught in a standard laboratory.

Unfortunately, measures of achievement such as those used in the studies just noted are probably not sufficient measures of the purported objectives of project instruction. Presumably the real superiority of the project method should be revealed in measures of motivation and resourcefulness. Novak's experiment was laudable in its inclusion of a measure of scientific attitude, but neither conventional nor project classes made significant gains from the beginning to the end of the semester. Similarly, in a class in mental hygiene Timmel (1955) found no difference in the effectiveness of the lecture and project methods in changing adjustment. One morsel of support comes from Thistlethwaite's (1960) finding that National Merit Scholars checked requirement of a term paper or laboratory project as one characteristic of their most stimulating course.

Research on Independent Study

With the support of the Fund for Advancement of Education, a number of colleges have experimented with large programs of independent study. As with other comparisons of teaching methods, few large differences were found between achievement of students working independently and those taught in conventional classes. Moreover, the expected gains in independence also often failed to materialize. Students taught by independent study did not always seem to develop greater ability or motivation for learning independently. Nevertheless, a number of encouraging results emerged.

One of the most comprehensive research programs on independent study was carried out by Antioch College (Churchill, 1957; Churchill and Baskin, 1958). The Antioch experiment involved courses in humanities, social science, and science. Periods of independent study were varied, and a serious attempt was made not only to measure cognitive and affective achievement, but also to evaluate the effect of independent study upon "learning resourcefulness." In addition, the Antioch staff, recognizing that not all students are ready to work independently, planned programs of training for independent work.

The results of the experiments, however, do not point clearly to any conclusion. For example, in one experiment, independent small groups learned more subject matter in physics than students working independently as individuals. But in art, students working individually learned more than those in independent small groups, which suggests that the requirements of the task may be important in determining whether students can effectively work together. As in most experiments on teaching methods, the predominant results were "no significant difference." An exception to this may be found in various indexes of student satisfaction in which several significant differences favored lecture-discussion over independent study and especially over independent small groups.

In another well-controlled experiment carried out at Oberlin (McCollough and Van Atta, 1958), students in introductory science, psychology, and mathematics courses were required to work independently of the instructor in small groups. This independent work occupied one third of the college year following several weeks of preliminary training. As in the Antioch experiment, no significant differences in learning appeared either as measured by the usual achievement tests or by a test of learning resourcefulness. Generally Oberlin students seem not to have been unhappy about the independent study experience, although they indicated they would have preferred several two-week periods of independent study to the single longer period.

Much more favorable results on independent study were obtained in the experiments carried out at the University of Colorado by

Gruber and Weitman (1960). In a course in freshman English in which the group met only about 90 percent of the regularly scheduled hours and had little formal training on grammar, the self-directed study group was significantly superior to control groups on a test of grammar. In a course in physical optics groups of students who attended class without the instructor but were free to consult him learned fewer facts and simple applications, but were superior to students in conventional classes in difficult applications and learning new material. Moreover, the areas of superiority were maintained in a retest three months later when the difference in factual knowledge had disappeared. In educational psychology an experimental class meeting once a week with the instructor and twice a week in groups of five or six students without the instructor was equal to a conventional three-lecture-a-week class in mastery of content, but tended to be superior on measures of curiosity. In another experiment, students in self-directed study paid more constant attention to a lecture than did students in conventional classes. Beach (1965) reported two studies of self-directed study groups in social psychology classes at Whitworth College. The self-directed groups did more reading and averaged slightly higher in achievement.

The Pyramid Plan

The most impressive findings on the results of student-led discussion come from the research on the Pyramid Plan at Pennsylvania State University (Carpenter, 1959; Davage, 1958, 1959). The basic plan may be represented by a description of their experiments in psychology. Each "Pyramid Group" of psychology majors consisted of six freshmen, six sophomores, two juniors (who were assistant leaders), and a senior (who was group leader). The group leaders were trained by a faculty supervisor. One control group received comparable special attention by being given a special program of lectures, films, and demonstrations equal to the time spent in discussion by the Pyramid Groups. The results on such measures as attitude toward psychology, knowledge of the field of psychology, scientific thinking, use of the library for scholarly reading, intellectual orientation, and resourcefulness in problem solving were significantly favorable to the Pyramid Plan. Moreover a follow-up study showed that more of the Pyramid students continued as majors in psychology. Such an array of positive results is little short of fantastic, and is not only a testimony to the effectiveness of the Pyramid program but also to the resourcefulness of the Pennsylvania research staff.

Independent Study

Independent study experiments have varied greatly in the amount of assistance given students and in the patterning of instructional vs. independent periods. For example, merely excusing students from attending class is one method of stimulating independent study. The results of such a procedure are not uniform but suggest that classroom experience is not essential for learning. However, different kinds of learning may take place out of class than in class.

The experiment reported by McKeachie, Lin, Forrin, and Teevan (1960) involved a fairly high degree of student-instructor contact. In this experiment students normally met with the instructor in small groups weekly or biweekly, but students were free to consult the instructor whenever they wished to. The results of the experiment suggest that the "tutorial" students did not learn as much from the textbook as students taught in conventional lecture periods and discussion sections, but did develop stronger motivation both for course work and for continued learning after the course. This was indicated not only by responses to a questionnaire administered at the end of the course, but also by the number of advanced psychology courses later elected.

Jenson (1951) compared four groups, including one in which students were completely excused from class attendance. The results showed no difference in gains among the four groups, but students who had worked independently were more willing than others to volunteer for further independent study.

The results of the studies in a child development course by Parsons (1957) and Parsons, Ketcham, and Beach (1958) were, in a sense, more favorable to independent study. In the latter experiment four teaching methods were compared—lecture, instructor-led discussions, autonomous groups that did not come to class, and individual independent study in which each student was sent home with the syllabus, returning for the final examination. In both experiments, students working independently made the best scores on the final examination, which measured retention of factual material in the textbook. The instructor-led discussion groups were the lowest group in performance on the final examination. There were no significant differences between groups on a measure of attitudes toward working with children. The authors explain their results in terms of the independent group's freedom from distraction by interesting examples, possible applications, or opposing points of view from those presented in the text.

However, in their latter experiment one group of students was made up of teachers commuting to campus for a Saturday class. The results for these students were quite different from those for resident students. In this case students in independent study performed significantly worse than other groups on the examination. Perhaps these students were less committed to regular study and may also have experienced more frustration in not having class.

Although the Parsons, Ketcham, and Beach results were favorable to independent study, they are not very satisfying to the advocate of this method, for they lead to the conclusion that if students know that they are going to be tested on the factual content of a particular book, it is more advantageous for them to read that book than to participate in other educational activities. In fact even better results could possibly be obtained if the desired facts could be identified by giving the student test questions in advance. But knowledge of specific facts is not the typical major objective of an independent study program. What instructors are hoping for is greater integration, increased purposefulness, and more intense motivation for further study. That independent study can achieve these ends is indicated by the Colorado and Michigan experiments. But the paucity of positive results suggests that we need more research on methods of selecting and training students for independent study, arranging the independent study experience, and measuring outcomes. Note that the Colorado and Penn State results came in courses in which a good deal of contact with the instructor was retained.

Time in Class

The independent study experiments demonstrate that education is not simply a function of time spent in a class with a teacher. Well-planned activities outside teacher-controlled classrooms can be at least as educational as conventional classes. But merely reducing time in class is not independent study. Generally speaking, the more time spent on learning, the greater the learning. Wakely, Marr, Plath, and

Wilkins (1960) compared performance in a traditional four-hour-a-week lecture class with that in a class meeting only once a week to clear up questions on the textbook. In this experiment the traditional classes proved to be superior. Similarly Paul (1932) found 55-minute class periods to be superior to 30-minute periods, as measured by student achievement. Shortening class periods, reducing the number of classes, cutting the length of the academic term may be advisable as part of a planned educational change, but they should not be undertaken with the blithe assumption that the same educational outcomes will be achieved.

SUPPLEMENTARY READING

Bligh et al. (1975), pp. 118–130, gives an interesting British perspective on independent study.

9

How to Have Smaller Classes Despite a Shortage of Faculty: Students Teaching Students

One of the recurring criticisms of higher education is that it hasn't increased its productivity at the same rate as industry. Surprisingly one even hears such statements from administrators who ought to know better. By productivity such critics typically mean that colleges should turn out more students using fewer teachers—as if colleges were factories producing shoes, automobiles, or soap. I once began to try to help a group of legislators develop a more sophisticated understanding by asking if a legislator's productivity should be measured by the number of bills introduced or if a doctor's productivity should be measured by the number of patients seen, regardless of the number who died. Obviously the product of education is learning, not credit hours.

"But aren't professors simply featherbedding when they resist larger classes, television, computers, and other technological aids? After all, there's no significant difference in effectiveness between these and the traditional classes," says the critic.

I have already shown that the "no significant difference" findings actually turn out quite consistently to favor live, small-class discussions if one is concerned about the longer term goals of higher education such as ability to apply knowledge, solve problems, or learn new material. Thus, more "efficient" methods allow professors to teach more students but with a *loss of learning* for the individual students.

The bottleneck in educational efficiency is that learning to think requires thinking and communicating the thinking through talking, writing, or doing, so that others can react to it. Unfortunately a professor can read only one paper at a time, can listen to only one student's comments at a time, and can respond with only one voice.

The problem is not one of communicating knowledge from professors to students more efficiently. Printed materials have done this very well for years, and for most educational purposes are still superior to any of the modern alternatives. The problem is rather one of interaction between the learner and teacher. For better education we need more rather than fewer teachers.

In fact, however, faculty-student ratios are getting worse rather than better. Faculties are shrinking. Is there any hope of improving education without increased cost?

The answer lies in broadening the definition of teacher to include students who teach one another. Highly trained faculty are essential for higher education, but not every question or comment needs to be answered by a full professor. Students can learn from one another.

Using Students as Teachers

Graduate students have been used as group leaders, laboratory supervisors, or tutors for many years, but little evidence has been gathered on their effectiveness.* The one published research study on this topic, conducted at Miami University by Macomber and Siegel (1960), indicated that graduate student teaching assistants leading small sections were at least as effective as professors teaching large lectures, and perhaps more effective. An unpublished study by Lamphear and McConnell found poorer performance of classes taught by graduate students. A more recent trend has been an in-

---

* This section is based on W. J. McKeachie, and J. Kulik, Effective college teaching. In F. Kerlinger, ed. *Review of research in education,* Vol. 3 (Itaska, IL: F. E. Peacock Publisher, 1975), pp. 166–174.

creasing use of undergraduates as teachers of other undergraduates. The use of undergraduates as teachers is often expected to have two favorable outcomes: stimulating additional learning by the students who teach and facilitating learning by those being taught.

Gagne and Rohwer (1969) express skepticism about the value of learning by teaching, but the research evidence supports the value of this practice. Long (1971), for example, presents data indicating that serving as an experimenter in a paired-associate learning experiment has a beneficial effect on later learning of paired associates. Comparable time as an experimenter with a nonresponding subject or as an observer did not produce the beneficial effect. Nelson (1970) found favorable effects of the Keller Plan on the Graduate Record Examination performance of student proctors. Thus, this evidence is on the side of the beneficial effects of teaching on those who teach.

Probably the most convincing demonstration of the effectiveness of undergraduate student-led discussions for the students taught is the "Pyramid Plan" at Pennsylvania State University (Carpenter, 1959; Davage, 1958, 1959). In this project, a faculty member, graduate students, and seniors planned the activities. The seniors, assisted by juniors, led small-group discussions. In courses in sociology and psychology, these small discussions sections led by more advanced undergraduate students supplemented the regular course activities. Compared with supplementary instructor-led lectures, film presentations, demonstrations, or no supplement at all, the small groups led by juniors and seniors read more, were more likely to go on to major in the subject, had more favorable attitudes toward the role of sociologists (or psychologists), accepted more responsibility for their own learning (in psychology), showed a more intellectual (less vocational) attitude toward college, and performed better on tests of scientific thinking, persistence in critical thinking, and resourcefulness in problem solving. A favorable effect of the experience upon the junior and senior group leaders was also reported. Trowbridge (1969) similarly found favorable results with small groups led by advanced undergraduates as a supplement to lecture, reading, and projects. The experimental class was superior to a conventional lecture-discussion class, both on a standardized test of achievement and on change in self-concept.

Even more daring is the use of students enrolled in a course as leaders for their own discussions. In experiments in educational psychology and general psychology, Gruber and Weitman (1962) found that students taught in small discussion groups without a teacher not only did at least as well on a final examination as students who heard the teacher lecture, but they were also superior in curiosity (as measured by question-asking behavior) and in interest in educational psychology. The discussion students reported a larger number of readings during the term, whereas the lecture students reported more attempts at applying their learning. In an experiment in a physical optics course, the lecture students were superior to student-led discussion students on a test of facts and simple problems, but inferior on a test containing complex problems and learning new material. The superiority of student-led discussions was particularly marked for students below the median in ability. Romig (1972) and Beach (1960, 1968) report similar results in English and psychology classes. Beach also reports that on a factual achievement test, sociable students did better if taught by student-led discussion; less sociable students did better if taught by using lecture-discussion.

Webb and Grib (1967) report six studies in which student-led discussions were compared with instructor-led discussions or lectures. In two of the six studies, significant differences in achievement tests favored the student-led discussions. In the other four, differences were not significant. Both students and instructors reported that the student-led discussions increased student motivation; and students who had been exposed to student-led discussions tended to favor them over instructor-led discussions as supplements to lectures. Webb and Grib (1969) note that students report that the sense of freedom to ask questions and express their own opinions is a major advantage of the student-led discussions. This may explain Gruber and Weitman's finding that the poorer students benefited most from student-led discussions. It makes theoretical sense that this opportunity to expose individual conceptions and misconceptions and compare ideas with those of others should contribute to learning if the group contains sufficient resources of knowledge and higher level thinking. The student-led group would most likely not be effective in areas in which students simply reinforced each other's biases.

Structuring Student-Led Discussions

As I noted in discussing independent study in the previous chapter, simply turning students loose to teach other students is not educationally effective. In using this method, the faculty member needs to help prepare and supervise the student-led discussion groups.*

At Colorado State University, Kitchener and Hurst (1974) have developed a highly structured approach based on Hill's work (1969), the Education Through Student Interaction (ETSI), to render student-led discussion groups more effective. A student manual (Kitchener and Hurst, 1972) guides the students through three phases of the discussion: In the *Overview*, the student is asked to define essential terms and state the main theme of the assignment or the lecture to be discussed. The *Discussion* includes the following four steps: content analysis, critique of the material, integration, and application. The last phase is an *Evaluation* of the group discussion with respect to the content (task orientation and understanding material) and the process (responsible participation, climate of relationship, communication of feelings).

For the first two phases, students must do the necessary preparation before the session by completing a study guide, which in fact constitutes their "admission ticket" to the group discussion. The evaluation takes place after every session. For each session, three students are designated as discussion guides; the first is responsible for the overview, the second and third for the discussion and evaluation phases.

A recent study by Arbes and Kitchener (1974) demonstrated the effectiveness of this approach. Groups using the ETSI structure performed better on subsequent tests of content mastery and evaluated the discussion groups more positively than two control groups that discussed course content without a specific procedure. ETSI groups, furthermore, were more effective when they had undergone workshop training on the ETSI method prior to the group sessions and when a specially trained student facilitator participated in the discussion.

A number of other investigations (Churchill and John, 1958; Diamond, 1972; Vattano et al., 1973; Wrigley, 1973; Hockenberry-Boeding and Vattano, 1975) have also concluded that discussion groups led by undergraduates represent a valuable supplement to large lecture courses.

---

* Much of the following section is based on Goldschmid and Goldschmid (1976).

Learning in Pairs: The Learning Cell

While instructors sometimes assume that the ideal learning situation would be one where students might work individually at their own paces, with their own equipment, with individual help, the common practice in laboratory instruction of having students work in pairs has good educational justification as well as the economic one of saving equipment. At the Third International Conference on Improving University Teaching, both Fukuda of Japan and Elton of England reported that in computerized instruction students learned more effectively when two students shared a computer terminal rather than each having a separate terminal. This fits with other research and experience showing that working and studying in pairs can facilitate student learning.

One of the best-developed systems for helping pairs of students to learn more effectively is the Learning Cell, developed by Marcel Goldschmid of the Swiss Federal Institute of Technology in Lausanne. He describes the learning cell as follows:

The "learning cell" or student dyad refers to a cooperative form of learning in pairs, in which students alternate asking and answering questions on commonly read materials (Goldschmid, 1971). Similar to PSI, the learning cell must be highly structured for success (i.e., effective learning) to occur:

—To prepare for the learning cell, students read an assignment and write questions dealing with the major points raised in the reading proper or other related materials.

—At the beginning of each class meeting, students are randomly assigned to pairs and one partner (A) begins by asking his first question.

—After having answered and perhaps having been corrected or given additional information, B puts his first question to A, and so on.

—During this time, the instructor goes from dyad to dyad, giving feedback, asking and answering questions.

A variation of this procedure has each student read (or prepare) different materials. In this case, A "teaches" B the essentials of his readings, then asks his prepared questions, whereupon they switch roles.

The effectiveness of the learning cell was first explored in a large (250 students) psychology course (Goldschmid, 1970) where four learning options were compared: Seminar, discussion, independent study (essay), and learning cell. Students in the learning-cell option performed significantly better on an unannounced examination and rated their ongoing learning experience significantly higher.

A more extensive "field test" in a number of other disciplines at the university (Goldschmid and Shore, 1974) demonstrated the learning cell's effectiveness and revealed no apparent restriction on the size of the class, its level, or the nature of the subject matter.

A third, more experimental, investigation served to evaluate the learning cell across three age groups (Schirmerhorn, Goldschmid, and Shore, 1975). Fifth- and ninth-grade pupils as well as university students studied probability at their respective intellectual levels for two class periods using the learning cell. All age groups showed significant learning after reading and formulating questions and after discussion with their partner.*

While learning cells work in general, they work better for some students than others. Leith (1974) found that introverts did about as well studying alone as in learning cells; extroverts did better in learning cells, but only if their partners were also extroverts. A learning cell composed of an extrovert paired with an introvert was no more effective than individual learning.

Students Teaching Students

I shall discuss another method in which students teach students, the Keller Plan, in Chapter 11. In this chapter I have shown that well-planned use of students as teachers of one another is very effective educationally. There are at least two theoretical reasons why this may be so:

1. If students are to learn—to form new ways of organizing ideas in their minds—it is important that misunderstanding, emotional biases, and barriers to change be revealed and dealt with. Students are more likely to talk in small groups than large; students are more likely to ask other students questions about their difficulties or failure to understand than to reveal these problems with a faculty member present.

---

* Taken from Goldschmid (1975).

2. Remembering and using learning depends upon restructuring and relating it to other meaningful experience. Students teaching other students must actively organize and reorganize their own learning in order to explain it. Thus they themselves learn from teaching.

SUPPLEMENTARY READING

One interesting use of students as observers in panel discussions is reported by Meyer M. Cahn, Teaching through student models. In P. Runkel, R. Harrison, and M. Runkel, ed., *The changing college classroom* (San Francisco: Jossey-Bass, 1972), pp. 36–51.

10

Reading, Programmed Learning, and Computer-Assisted Instruction

While professors like to think that students learn from professors, it seems likely that students learn more from reading than from listening.

Reading and Textbooks

For the past three decades the demise of the textbook has been eagerly predicted by advocates of each of the new panaceas for the problems of education.* First television, then teaching machines, then the computer—each was expected to revolutionize education and free students and teachers from their longtime reliance upon textbooks. Even the major book publishers scurried to the arms of elec-

---

* Much of the following section was included in a letter I wrote to the editor of *Change Magazine* published in May–June 1971. It was stimulated by an article predicting the demise of textbooks.

tronic manufacturers and set up new nontextbook divisions to keep up with the coming age of educational media.

But each of the new media has settled into its niche in the educational arsenal without dislodging the textbook. In fact, the greatest revolution in education has come not from teaching machines or computers, but from the greater availability of a wide variety of printed materials.

The introduction of open-stack libraries, paperback books, inexpensive reprint series, and the Xerox machine has given the college teacher the opportunity to choose from sources varying in style, level, and point of view. Many teachers are substituting paperback books, reprints, and collections of journal articles for the textbook as the sources of the basic information needed by students. The students thus have an opportunity to organize the material in a way meaningful for them. But in most undergraduate courses there is little hope that bits and pieces will be integrated by students into a meaningful whole despite the valiant efforts of instructors to give assistance. They know that learning is facilitated by organization and that, lacking organization, facts and concepts become so many nonsense syllables subject to interference, quickly forgotten and inaccessible. With inputs from field experience, discussion, paperbacks, reprints, and other sources, the student needs more than ever some frame of reference within which to assimilate the boomin', buzzin' confusion of points of view present in a modern course.

Ideally, the textbook can provide such a structure. That structure need not be dogmatic, but it need not be gutless. It need not be presented as irrevocable truth. Inevitably, certain parts of textbook information become dated. If teachers fail to recognize what is obsolete and insist on its memorization, the students' education is harmed rather than aided. Probably the main drawback of textbooks as teaching tools is their tendency to encourage encyclopedic learning of factual material rather than achievement of the facility to deal with the ideas that have a longer half-life in their application to the transfer-of-learning world. But dogmatic, out-of-date teachers can misuse any source. A good textbook can counter instructor dogmatism by presenting a more open framework. Structures should be presented as tentative, temporary, and incomplete. Textbooks should be up to date and frequently revised. That textbooks in the past have often been little more than a collection of topics is no reason to reject their potential usefulness in meeting important needs for the student learner today.

Modern education is focusing less on imparting facts and theories and more on development of student capacities for judgment, fact-gathering, analysis, and synthesis. Thus the encyclopedic textbook is an anachronism promoting the wrong kind of education. But the modern textbook can and should be aimed at the very goals that are now evolving. None of these desired capacities for critical thinking and usefulness for action can be developed without some grounding in essential facts and concepts. Without the structure provided by a good textbook, students, required to gather, judge, evaluate, analyze, and synthesize a diversity of sources and experiences by themselves, simply end in confusion and frustration.

Certainly, modern teachers should provide a variety of learning experiences for students. If individual differences are to be attended to in teaching, students need an opportunity to learn in laboratory settings, field experiences, discussion, lectures, or reading from diverse sources. Textbooks are an important part of the teachers' compendium of tools, and the newer teaching methods and aids supplement rather than supplant the textbook.

Research on Learning from Reading

An early study (Greene, 1928) found that students learned as well from reading material as from listening to the same material read aloud. The better students, moreover, profited more from reading than from listening. A number of other studies have compared printed materials with lectures, and the results—at least with difficult materials—favor print (Hartman, 1961). However, the amount of research on books or articles as media for teaching is remarkably small considering their widespread use. There have been studies of size of print, readability, and effectiveness of illustrations (illustrations apparently do not contribute much to learning as measured by conventional tests), but much more needs to be done.

Fortunately the eruption of research in cognitive psychology has pushed the frontiers of research into studies of meaningful prose passages. Most of the research to date has been on brief passages, but there are now a number of studies using material like textbook passages. The theoretical changes resulting in these studies will be discussed in Chapter 23, but some studies with practical implications will be reviewed here. Hiler and McKeachie (1954) demonstrated that students read more efficiently when they are given questions to answer on the material. The classic study of Gates (1917) also illustrates the value of active questioning and recitation vs. passive reading. Kaplan (1964) describes the use of reading logs in courses where students spend a major part of their study time reading books and articles of their own choice. He reports (and my own experience confirms) that students not only read a great deal but that their logs show marked improvement in critical and integrative ability during a term. The key to this improvement probably lies in extensive teacher comments upon the logs, which are periodically turned in to the instructor. Kaplan reports favorable student reactions, but little research has been reported comparing different techniques of utilizing such printed materials.

The group of researchers at the Institute of Education, University of Goteborg has carried out a number of studies applying concepts of cognitive psychology to the learning of chapters of textbooks and other meaningful, relatively complex reading. Their results, like those of Gates and other pioneers, indicate that questions can influence student learning. Marton and Saljo (1976b) found that questions designed to produce more thoughtful, integrative study were more effective than questions of fact. Nevertheless, study questions are not automatically a guarantee of better learning. Students sometimes tended to look only for answers to the questions while disregarding the other content of the chapter (Marton and Saljo, 1976a). Research by Rothkopf (1972) and other students of prose learning lead me to believe that factual questions after reading may be more effective than factual questions before reading. What instructors need are questions that get students to *think* about the material and relate it to other things they know.

Programmed Instruction

In the 1960s "programmed textbooks" began to appear. These are instructional books developed by utilizing the learning-in-small-steps sequences advocated by B. F. Skinner. Such books and booklets have sometimes been designed as adjuncts to normal teaching materials, but often were intended to replace textbooks.

The teaching machine, like the programmed book, is a device for presenting questions in predetermined sequence and then providing immediate knowledge of results to active learners. Teaching machines do not ordinarily permit the learners to proceed at their own rates, since they ordinarily respond by writing an answer or pressing a button before additional information or the next question is presented. This means that progress is generally slower than with conventional books. Nevertheless, the learners have more control over the pace of learning than they do with television or most large lectures. In programmed methods the successive questions proceed in small steps from the simple to the complex. With some machines the students may, if they make a series of correct responses, adjust the machine to skip some steps; if they fail items, the items are repeated. The program of the lesson may include hints or other guidance.

There have been two general types of approaches to the use of teaching machines. Pressey (1926) used the teaching machine primarily as a device to provide prompt knowledge of results of conventional testing procedures. The testing machine was thus simply a supplement to the conventional teaching methods. The second approach, originated by Skinner and his followers, used the teaching machine as a substitute for other teaching methods; the teaching machine was either the sole instrument of instruction, or at least a major method that could be supplemented by the teacher. The phrase "programmed instruction" is now used to refer to any carefully sequenced presentation whether by teaching machine, book, lecture, film, or television.

Some research evidence supports the use of teaching-testing machines as supplements to conventional instruction. Angell (1949), Peterson and Peterson (1931), and Stephens (1953) found that immediate knowledge of results on a quiz or special answer sheet produced results superior to those obtained when such knowledge was delayed until the next class meeting.

The research with Skinnerian types of programs has been less encouraging. Students do learn from the programs, but learning is generally slower than with conventional printed materials (but faster than lectures) (Smith, 1962). In some cases, achievement is higher for the programmed learners (Williams, 1963), and you must judge whether the extra investment in time is justified by the gain in learning. In other cases, programs produce less learning than conventional sources.* However, reviews of research by Schramm (1964), Lange (1972), and Nash, Muczyk, and Vettori (1971) show programmed instruction superior to traditional instruction in about 40 percent of the over one hundred research studies reported, equally effective in about half the studies, and relatively seldom less effective.

The controversy over whether students need to make a response has largely abated. If the response itself must be learned, as in teaching typewriting or a new vocabulary, an overt response is required, but in most college courses the responses required are already in the students' repertoire and they learn more rapidly by not stopping to fill in blanks (Lumsdaine and May, 1965). An occasional overt response, however, may be useful in maintaining attention (Sime and Boyce, 1969).

One would expect strict control over the structure and pace of learning to be most helpful to students with poor study habits, those who read passively and tend to slide over important uncomprehended points, but little research has been done to determine what kinds of students gain from programs or what types of objectives can be most efficiently achieved. On the basis of the theoretical relationship between uncertainty and curiosity, it might be expected that most students would be bored by the practice of writing programs so that every question is answered correctly by almost every student. From Atkinson's theory it would be expected that students with a high need for achievement (those who work hardest in situ-

---

* J. J. Wulff and D. L. Emeson, The relationship between "what is learned" and "how it is taught." In A. A. Lumsdaine, ed., *Student response in programmed learning: a symposium*, Publication 943 (Washington: National Academy of Sciences-National Research Council, 1961), Chapter 30. Wulff and Emeson reported that in learning the names of electrical circuits, students did better studying by themselves than learning from a structured program. Also see: C. G. Zuckerman, G. R. Marshall, and S. Groesberg, Research in the automation of teaching, NAVTRADEVCEN 666–1 (Port Washington, N. Y.: U. S. Naval Training Device Center, February, 1961); J. F. Follettie, Effects of training response mode, test form, and measure on acquisition of semi-ordered factual materials, Research Memo. 24 (Fort Benning, Ga.: U. S. Army Infantry Human Research Unit, April, 1961) (mimeographed); M. E. Feldman, Learning by programmed and text format at 3 levels of difficulty, *Journal of Educational Psychology*, 1956, *56*, 133–139; W. H. Bartz and C. L. Darby, A study of supervised and nonsupervised programmed instruction in the university setting, *Journal of Educational Research*, 1965, *58*, 208–211. This study found that supervised programmed instruction was not inferior to formal instruction even though unsupervised programmed instruction was inferior.

ations with 50-50 probabilities of success) would find the usual small-step program more boring than other students would. And this is what Moore, Smith, and Teevan (1965) discovered.

But even for students in general, the University of Illinois project suggests that a logical sequence of items may be less efficient for learning than a random sequence.* This makes sense in terms of the motivational theory that lack of change or surprises makes for boredom and also helps to explain why short programs, requiring half an hour or less, seem to be more effective and less boring than longer programs covering large blocks of material or an entire course (Beard, 1972).

One reasonable finding about the types of students doing well or poorly with programmed instruction is that students scoring high on a sociability test did poorly with programmed instruction (Doty and Doty, 1964). Lublin (1965) reports that students low in need for autonomy achieved more in a programmed course than students high in this need. As more complex integrations of programs, computers, discussion groups, and teachers are developed, the dimension of students' autonomy and desire for control of their own learning is likely to be important.

The fervor of the 1960s proponents of teaching machines has now subsided, and research is beginning to clarify the uses of programmed materials (Lumsdaine, 1963). For a while it appeared that programmed materials might enable educators to shortcut the difficult problems of curriculum and course organization, but programs that teach unimportant concepts or untrue information are not of much help to education, and it is now recognized that the writing of a good program requires as much scholarship as the writing of a good textbook (Krumboltz, 1964). Unfortunately, programming is difficult work, and as yet scholars seem less willing to write programs than to write books. Thus, there are still only a very limited number of good programs for college use. College-level programs adapted to computer-assisted instruction are particularly rare.

---

* See E. F. Rosen, G. L. Frincke, and L. M. Stolurow, Principles of programming: II, Champaign community unit school district number 4 high schools, *Comparative studies of principles for programming mathematics in automated instruction,* Technical Report No. 15 (University of Illinois, September, 1964); L. M. Stolurow et al., Pilot studies of principles of programming, *Comparative studies of principles for programming mathematics in automated instruction,* Technical Report No. 9 (University of Illinois, July, 1964).

Programmed instruction has also suffered from a lack of evaluation skills. To many of its advocates, it has seemed self-evident that any student who completes a program successfully has learned—the student has achieved the goals of the program. Professors like to make the same assumption about their lectures. But most teachers have had the disheartening experience of discovering that points made crystal clear in a brilliant lecture seem not to have penetrated the awareness of students sufficiently enough to be recalled and used in responding to a relevant examination question. One of the problems for programmers of college materials is that in college teaching the level of conceptualization is such that the students' required response to a program question is only one of a class of related responses to a group of stimuli. The fact that the students make the appropriate program response is not prima facie evidence that they have learned the concept or class of responses. Sometimes the programmer provides irrelevant cues to which the students learn to make the desired response; at other times the response required in the program is irrelevant to the goal of teaching; for example, the response may simply indicate that the students have read the frame, as when they are asked to fill in a trivial word.

Some program writers have recognized the importance of tests of learning apart from the program, but such tests frequently contain items from the program or simple paraphrases of these items. Correct answers to such items are not very reassuring to the skeptic, since it is possible that a high score can be obtained by someone who has learned to respond to irrelevant cues or has learned only the specific responses taught in the program rather than the principle or concept desired. Ideally, the test should measure achievement of the goals of the program in a manner as different as possible from the program items. These problems are not unique to the evaluation of programmed instruction, but have marked much other research on teaching methods, especially that on PSI, Keller's Personalized System of Instruction.

The programmed-learning movement has had the healthy effect of forcing clarification of educational objectives. But after asking for a list of objectives precise enough to serve as guides for programming, the programmed-learning protagonists have tended sometimes to dismiss as illegitimate any objectives that could not readily be specified at a level appropriate for programming. The result has been that programs are often aimed at the most trivial objectives.

Disillusionment with the programmed-learning movement has sprung in part from the fact that once a program had been written, educators too often discovered that what it taught was not really what their students needed to learn.

Despite these problems, programmed learning is here to stay and can still make a contribution to higher education. Few teachers enjoy the role of drillmaster; yet drill is necessary if students are to master thoroughly certain necessary facts, schemata, or responses. This, at least, is a task programs can perform, freeing the instructor for other functions.

Computer Uses in Teaching and Learning

Computers can individualize instruction as printed programs do not. Early attempts to use computers in instruction simply put conventional linear and branching programs into the computer so that the capacity of the computer was not really used to increase the complexity of the teaching. Feurzeig, Swets and others (1964) at Bolt, Beranek, and Newman, Inc., however, used computerized techniques to develop analytical thinking, such as that used in medical diagnosis. A similar program for simulating a laboratory in qualitative analysis was described by Hirsch and Moncreiff (1965). In these systems, students could ask questions as well as answer those posed by the computer. Students could also volunteer assertions or solutions whenever they wished. The computer responded in a meaningful way both to student questions and assertions. It recognized inappropriate responses and remembered previous responses. The anthropomorphic terms "recognized" and "remembered" are not really inaccurate, for they describe the phenomenal experience of the student interacting with the computer. While it might be more objective to say that the program is written in terms of strings of conditional "if-then" probabilities, much of the motivational value of the computer lies in the student's attempt to test its humanlike qualities.

Bork (1975) and Pask (1976) have developed teaching "dialogues" or "conversations." Bork's dialogues are concerned with teaching content, concepts, and problem-solving skills in physics. Pask's "conversational domains" have been developed for physics and statistics. Both of these approaches involve extensive analysis of the conceptual structure of the material to be taught. Probably the major reason that computer assisted instruction has not spread more rapidly is the time-consuming, difficult work necessary to develop a system that uses the memory and adaptive capacity of the tutor.

Three experiments in computer-assisted college-level instruction (Grubb and Sefridge, 1963; Schurdak, 1965; King, 1977) showed savings in time and improved performance compared to conventional instruction and/or instruction with programmed text. Moreover, students enjoyed studies with the computer. With computer programs the motivational value of unexpectedness can be retained, and programs can be adapted for students of differing types. Jamison et al. (1974) and Edwards et al. (1975) have reviewed research on CAI (Computer-assisted instruction) and conclude that it is about as effective as traditional instruction, and sometimes saves time of students and teachers.

In addition to using computers as instructional devices, teachers have used computers in testing. TIPS, which I will discuss in the next chapter, is one such system. One of the advantages of computerized testing is the ability to collect data on items over time so that a test can be constructed with reasonably good estimation of its difficulty and of the level of outcomes being assessed, so that a test is not primarily measuring low level knowledge rather than application, analysis, or other more important goals.

On the whole it appears that CAI has no special magic that will solve instructional problems. It can relieve teachers of some time spent on drill (as can printed programmed instruction). Whether CAI is better in this respect than arranging for pupils to tutor one another is not known. Intuitively instructors feel that the computer should have great instructional potential, but it is apparently not going to be realized without a great deal of arduous work.

One promising direction for this research is the approach used by Pask and associates (Pask and Scott, 1973), who carry R. C. Atkinson's (1972) encouragement of response-sensitive paradigms to the point of a colloquy between the computer and the learner to determine the learner's preferred learning strategy. Pask demonstrates that matching the structure of the learning program to the learning strategy (holist or serialist) of the student results in more effective instruction than learner control or an incompatible program. In general, the research on learner control of CAI is inconclusive, leading Judd (1973) to conclude his review with the suggestion that students may need specific training to exercise effective control of their own instruction.

Effective computerized instruction will demand the development of more complex teaching strategies. CAI has not turned out to be the revolutionary panacea some expected, but the impact is gradually increasing. The computer has the potential not only to adapt to learners' learning strategies or styles but also to help students *learn* about their learning strategies so that they can become more efficient learners (Pask and Scott, 1973). For the moment the hardware has outstripped the educational uses. Minicomputers and microcomputers are proliferating. Before too long many or most homes will have computers with the ability to use the television set as a video display unit. At the moment the market is for games; in the future it could be for education.

Supplementary reading

For more detailed discussion of computer uses in education three good sources are:

B. Hunter et al., *Learning alternatives in U.S. education: where student and computer meet* (Englewood Cliffs, N.J.: Educational Technology Publications, 1975).

R. E. Levien, *The emerging technology: instructional uses of the computer in higher education* (New York: McGraw-Hill, 1972).

J. F. Rockart and M. S. S. Morton, *Computers and the learning process in higher education* (New York: McGraw-Hill, 1975).

11

PSI, TIPS, Contract Plans, and Modular Instruction

This chapter deals with a group of methods for segmenting and structuring a course. They probably have had more impact upon college teaching in the 1970s than has any other innovation.

The Keller Plan or Personalized System of Instruction

The most influential recent plan for individualizing college instruction is described by psychologist Fred Keller in his 1968 paper "Goodbye, Teacher..."* The method, first used in 1964 by Keller and his colleagues at the University of Brasilia, is most often referred to as the Keller Plan or the Personalized System of Instruction (PSI), a term that seems somewhat misleading since the method

---

* This section is adapted from W. J. McKeachie and J. Kulik, Effective college teaching. In F. Kerlinger, ed., *Review of research in education*, Vol. 3 (Itaska, IL: F. E. Peacock Publisher, 1975), pp. 166–174.

is less personalized than most other methods of teaching. The method has been used in at least 850 college courses in psychology alone, and that is probably less than half the total number of such courses. It has also been extensively studied. Hess's bibliography of November 1972 (Hess, 1972) lists 261 published and unpublished papers. This widely used and widely studied method will be the focus of my discussion of individualized approaches to college teaching.

Basic Features of the Keller Plan

Like other systems of individualized instruction, the Keller Plan involves a sequence of units of material, frequent readiness testing, and individual pacing. Its distinctive features are heavy emphasis on instructor-prepared written materials to supplement textbooks and extensive use of tutors for individual assistance and evaluation of students. In 1968, Keller described the five features that distinguish the Keller Plan from conventional teaching procedures: it is individually paced, mastery oriented, and student tutored; it uses printed study guides for communication of information; it includes a few lectures to stimulate and motivate students. Each of these elements contributes to the success of the plan. (Calhoun, 1976).

Students beginning a Keller course find that the course work is divided into topics or units. In a simple case, the content of the units may correspond to chapters of the course text. At the start of a course, the students receive a printed study guide to direct their work on the first unit. Although study guides vary, a typical one introduces the unit, states objectives, suggests study procedures, and lists study questions. Students may work anywhere to achieve the outlined objectives.

Before moving on to the second unit in the sequence, the students must demonstrate their mastery of the first unit by perfect or near-perfect performance on a short examination. They are examined on the unit only when they feel adequately prepared; they are not penalized for failure to pass a first, a second, or later examinations. When the students demonstrate mastery of the first unit, they are given the study guide for the next unit. They thus move through the course at their own paces. A student may meet all course requirements before the term is half done, or he may require more than a term to complete the course.

The staff for implementing the Keller Plan includes the instructor and undergraduate tutors. The instructor selects and organizes material used in the course, usually writes study guides, constructs examinations for the course, and gives fewer lectures and demonstrations than in a conventional course (perhaps six in the course of a semester). These lectures are not compulsory, and examinations are not based on them. The tutors evaluate readiness tests as satisfactory or unsatisfactory. Since they have been chosen for mastery of the course content, the tutors can prescribe remedial steps for students who encounter difficulties with the course material. The tutors also offer support and encouragement for beginning students. For further details see Keller and Sherman (1974).

Student Ratings

In his initial description of the plan, Keller (1968) reported that students rate personalized courses as more enjoyable than conventional ones. Research papers since Keller's confirm that most students are highly pleased with the method. The Keller Plan is sometimes, but not always, associated with a high rate of withdrawal. The generally favorable ratings are not merely a function of dropout by dissatisfied students; highly favorable ratings have been reported where dropout rates are high, medium, and low. Born's (1971) careful analysis of the dropout question suggests that Keller courses have high withdrawal rates when they are arranged so that students delay starting the course, put off taking tests, and generally procrastinate.

Content Learning in Keller Courses

In the first courses offered by the Keller Plan, it appeared to teachers that students seemed to learn course materials remarkably well. About 50 percent of the students received A's as final grades. Grades in Keller courses, it should be noted, are assigned on a different basis than grades in lecture courses. Anywhere from 50 percent to 100 percent of the student's grade in a Keller course comes from a number of repeatable examinations passed on short units of content. In lecture courses, grades are most often assigned on the basis of quality of performance on midterms, finals, and term papers. Differences in grade distributions for the two types of classes may therefore reflect either the differences in grading method or differences in amount of content learned. There is complete confounding.

Studies comparing examination scores of students in Keller and lecture courses offer more promise, but the ideal experimental design is easier to imagine than to achieve. A number of methodological precautions must be taken. Comparison groups must be equivalent, the performance of each subject in the two comparison groups must be taken into account, and students must not be "taught the test" to different degrees in the two groups. Of the studies listed in Table 4–1, fifteen compare examination results in Keller and conventional courses. Of these fifteen studies, eleven reported superior performance for the Keller section, and four reported no significant difference between the two kinds of classes. At least four of these studies seem relatively free of difficulties in design and analysis, and in each of these the performance of the Keller section was superior to that of the conventional section.

In McMichael and Corey's (1969) study a final examination in which items did not overlap with unit tests was administered to students in an experimental section and three control sections of a course in introductory psychology. Sections were very large (about 200 per section), and students registered for these sections without prior knowledge of the teaching method to be used in the section. Withdrawal rates for the four sections were nearly equal. The experimental group performance exceeded that of each of the control groups.

In the fifth semester of offering a personalized course in digital systems, Roth (1972) compared the final examination performance of his PSI section with the performance of a concurrently offered lecture section. Students were assigned to lecture and PSI sections according to time preference, and both sections were comparable in grade-point average. The two sections used the same text and study guides. On the final exam, prepared jointly by the PSI and lecture instructors, the performance of the PSI students was significantly and considerably higher than the performance of the students in the lecture section.

Other good studies are those of Witters and Kent (1972) and Morris and Kimbrell (1972). In these studies, the Keller sections clearly did better than lecture sections on hourly and final exams. Neither of these studies is plagued by problems of initial differences between experimental and control groups or overlap of items on unit tests and other examinations. There were apparently no withdrawals from courses described by Witters and Kent, and the withdrawal problem was handled by the appropriate statistics in the study reported by Morris and Kimbrell.

A number of investigators have compared long-term retention in individualized and lecture courses. In two studies (Corey, McMichael, and Tremont, 1970; Corey, Valente, and Shamow, 1971) Corey and his colleagues found striking differences between these groups in long-term retention. PSI students performed significantly better on retention measures than students in lecture courses. Moore, Hauck, and Gagne (1973) also found greater retention of material by students in an individualized section. While Breland and Smith (1974) found better retention of basic concepts by Keller students, these authors found no difference between Keller and lecture students on a test of retention of more obscure concepts. Kulik, Kulik, and Smith (1976) found nine studies of retention of PSI content, and in all nine PSI results were superior to lecture. Five studies compared PSI and conventional student performance in subsequent courses. In all five, PSI students were superior.

On the basis of present evidence, it can be concluded that content learning (as measured by final examinations) is adequate in Keller courses. In published studies, content learning of the material taught under the Keller Plan at least equals, and often exceeds, content learning under the lecture method. The only cloud dampening enthusiasm about these results is a methodological problem troubling almost all studies comparing teaching methods. Typically the evaluation of achievement is based on the only content common to two methods—in most cases, a textbook. Ideally what instructors would like is a sample of all learning achieved by either method. If one method covers a great range of material, of which only a small part overlaps with another method, and the other method teaches very little except the content overlapping with the first method, an achievement test on the overlapping content is not an adequate basis for a comparison of the relative educational effectiveness of the two methods. I suspect that in the experiments cited students in the lecture groups might have learned much not covered in the criterion tests; at the same time those in the Keller Plan may have had tutors who took them beyond the prescribed materials. The ideal evaluation would sample from this entire domain. Moreover, the ideal evaluation would also attempt to sample systematically from the higher levels of cognitive objectives of the Bloom (1956) taxonomy. (As an aside, it is worth noting that the high proportion of A's often assigned in Keller Plan courses is not justified by superior achievement. Even when Keller Plan courses are superior to conventional courses, the average level of achievement in the Keller Plan course is at the level of a B grade in the conventional course.)

Keller Plan Summary

A review of evaluative research on the Keller Plan establishes the following points:

1. The Keller plan is an attractive teaching method to most students. In published reports, students rate the Keller Plan more favorably than teaching by lecture.
2. Self-pacing and interaction with tutors seem to be the features of the Keller courses most favored by students. Frequent testing with immediate feedback is, however, the feature supported by research (Henderson and Wen, 1976; Kulik, Kulik, and Smith, 1976).
3. Several investigators report higher than average withdrawal rates for Keller sections.
4. Content learning as measured by final examinations is good in Keller courses. In the published studies, final examination performance in Keller sections equals, and sometimes exceeds, performance in lecture sections. Moreover, superior performance is found in courses following the PSI course.
5. Courses initiating the use of PSI often drop it, sometimes for noneducational reasons. For one account of the sociology and politics of PSI use, see Friedman et al. (1976).

TIPS

TIPS, an acronym for Teaching Information Processing System, was developed by Allan C. Kelley, an economist (Kelley, 1968, 1970). In TIPS students are given "surveys" eight to ten times a term. These surveys consist of nine to fifteen multiple choice questions intended to measure student achievement, but they are not used for grading. Rather, the students receive a "Student Report" shortly after completing the survey. The report provides a set of assignments for the ensuing period based on the students' mastery of previous material as assessed by the survey.

In addition to this feedback to students, students provide feedback to the teaching assistants and professor via regular reports. A computer is typically used to provide the prompt feedback, but computers are not essential for the system .

Contract Plans

Learning contracts, like PSI and programmed learning, provide students with a clear structure, but the contract method differs from PSI in being much more personalized. It gives students options about what they will do to achieve course objectives. Typically the student and teacher work out a set of *goals* to be achieved, methods of achieving the goals, and methods of evaluating achievement of the goals. When agreement has been reached, the teacher and student "contract" that if achievement is at the agreed-upon level, the teacher will give the grade contracted for.

The contract method reduces the student's uncertainty about what is expected and clearly places the responsibility for learning on the student. In practice, it has two difficulties:

1. The method often consumes inordinate amounts of teacher time in a tutorial mode. This can be avoided by careful attention to the teacher's side of the contract.
2. Grades are often higher than for comparable achievement in other classes. This derives in part from a tendency to phrase contracts in terms of quantity rather than quality of work. Reading five more books and writing an extra paper does not necessarily merit an A if the paper is of B or C quality. This problem can be reduced by specifying that the contracted grade depends upon the quality of the work done, but this implies that the teacher needs to make clear to the student what the standards of quality are. (Not a bad idea for any course!)

Research results do not reveal significantly higher achievement in contract groups as compared with conventional classes (Poppen and Thompson, 1971).

Modular Methods

Modular methods of teaching essentially involve analysis of course content and division into relatively independent units or modules.

Typically, modules are intended to be self-instructional and often include tasks involving field work or audiovisual media. The Keller Plan is one example of a modular approach, and modules are often used as well with computer-assisted instruction (CAI), contract plans, or other methods.

The Keller Plan typically presents material in a fixed sequence. Leith (1974) has suggested that the structure of a course may have either a linear, network, or spiral structure. A *linear* structure is one in which each unit of a course depends upon and builds upon the previous one. Mathematics courses, for example, are often linear. In *network* or *spiral* courses many starting points are possible, leading to relationships that become part of larger and more detailed structures. In a *spiral* structure there are, presumably, certain natural relatively complete structures or loops that can provide the base for the next loop of a spiral of greater breadth and comprehensiveness.

A fixed sequence, such as that of the Keller Plan, is thus appropriate for content structured in a linear (or skyscraper?) fashion. When dealing with content structured in a network or spiral, instructors may offer students a choice of starting points and sequences. It is here that modularization is helpful. You may offer each student a choice of modules, but Leith forms teams of five or six students. Each module consists of a problem, a group task with specific individual assignments, and a report to be made. In carrying out the instructions and organizing their efforts team members should engage the material much more actively and thoughtfully than if they were simply to read the material individually. Leith uses this approach with self- and group-evaluation to achieve the goal of developing skill in self-evaluation. I will discuss one of the better known modularized approaches, Audio-tutorial, in the next chapter.

SUPPLEMENTARY READING

J. G. Creager, and D. L. Murray, eds. *The use of modules in college biology teaching.* Commission on Undergraduate Education in the Biological Sciences (Washington, D.C.: 1971). This brief book includes general as well as biologically oriented articles.

R. B. Johnson, and S. R. Johnson, *Assuring learning with self-instructional packages or, up the up staircase, a how-to-do workbook* (Chapel Hill, NC: Self-instructional Packages, Inc., 1971).

12 _____

Audiovisual Techniques:
Television, Films, Radio,
Slides, Transparencies,
Audiotutorial, and
Media-activated Learning Groups

The impending shortage of college teachers has sparked several hotly contested skirmishes about the virtues or vices of various techniques of teaching with devices substituting for a portion of the usual face-to-face interaction between instructors and students. Since some college faculty members are anxious about technological unemployment and resist innovations, research has more often been used as a technique of infiltration than as a method of developing and testing educational theory. Despite many inconsequential studies, a few carefully executed programs of research have emerged. Representative studies are described in the following sections.

Television

The most glamorous of the newer technological aids to education is television. Before reviewing the research on teaching by television, consider two hypotheses that may help in analyzing the research results.

Television is not a method of instruction in the sense that discussion and lecture are methods of instruction. Rather, it is a means of giving students a clear view of an instructional situation. Therefore one would expect that the relative effectiveness of teaching via television will vary depending upon the importance of being able to see clearly. For example, I would expect television to be effective when it is important for students to see demonstrations, visiting lecturers, or films, but to have little advantage when the communication is primarily verbal.

Television reduces the opportunity for students to communicate with teachers and for teachers to interact with students. I would thus expect that the effectiveness of television will vary inversely with the importance of two-way communication, not only for feedback to the students but particularly for feedback to the teacher.

Research at Pennsylvania State University

In 1954 Pennsylvania State University (Carpenter and Greenhill, 1955, 1958) received a grant from the Fund for the Advancement of Education to study the effectiveness of conventional courses taught for a full semester over closed circuit television as compared with the same instruction given in the usual manner. Using these funds, Penn State set up a program of research on the courses General Chemistry, General Psychology, and Psychology of Marriage. In 1957 the research program was continued in additional courses with the goals of, 1) extending the project to additional courses, 2) studying instructional variables, and 3) working on methods of improving televised instruction.

The results of this research may be used either to extoll or damn television. Essentially they indicated that there is little loss in student learning in courses taught by television as compared with courses taught conventionally. For example, the first experiment dealt with the lecture portion of courses in general chemistry and general psychology. In the chemistry course the differences between methods in objective measures of information were not significant. In the psychology course the conventional class did prove to be slightly superior in knowledge gain over the televised class.

Students learned the information needed to pass examinations, and most did not object strongly to the televised classes although they preferred live instruction. Students in psychology were asked "How much they liked psychology" and "How much it contributed to their education as compared with other courses they were taking." On both counts ratings by the students in the television classes were lower than those of students who were in the same room as the instructor. The psychology students were also asked if they would like to take another semester course in psychology. About the same percentages signed up in all three types of classes, but when asked if they would prefer taking it in a large class or by television, a plurality preferred television. While students at other colleges also do not rebel at television, as at Penn State, research findings are unusually consistent in reporting less favorable attitudes toward courses taught by television as compared with conventional classes (see, for example, Lepore and Wilson, 1958; Macomber and Siegel, 1960).

Unimportant Factors in the Use of Educational Television

The heading of this section would normally be "Factors Conditioning the Effectiveness of Educational Television," but the results of the research are indicated by the title chosen. For example, recognizing that instructor-student interaction is sometimes important in learning, the Penn State staff installed two-way microphone communication in the receiving rooms so that students in the receiving rooms could ask questions. (This technique has been used even more extensively at Iowa [Stuit, 1956] and at Case Institute of Technology [Martin, 1957]. All found that this method of instruction was not superior to simple one-way communication [Martin, Adams, and Baron, 1958]. Similar results were found in the Army's research on television instruction [Fritz, 1952]).

Another attempt to combine the value of interaction with that of television was an experiment in presenting a thirty-five-minute television lesson followed by a discussion period of fifteen minutes in each of the receiving rooms. Other students in the same course observed by means of television the fifteen-minute discussion conducted by the instructor with the eight students in the origination room. Still other students were allowed to leave or to study their notes. As with the other attempt to provide interaction, results showed no significant difference in test performance among students taught by each of these three methods. A poll of students indicated that they preferred two hours of lecture followed by a full period of discussion to a short discussion each period.

Size of the viewing group was also not an important variable in television instruction. Neither do proctors in the viewing rooms contribute to student learning. Adapting a course for television by adding supplementary visual aids also proved to be no more effective than televised lecture-blackboard presentations. In fact both at Penn State and NYU (Adams et al., 1959) the "visual" productions tended to be less effective than "bare bones" television. This result should probably not be startling considering the Parsons, Ketcham, and Beach results with independent study. Just as discussion and lecture apparently interfered with learning the textbook, so here visual materials may have distracted the students from the verbal content upon which the tests were based.

The Pennsylvania State research does provide some support for the idea that television's effectiveness is related to how good the students' view is. In one experiment students were given their choice, after three weeks of instruction, of whether to finish the course in television classrooms or in the originating room. Depending upon the course, one-third to two-thirds of the students chose television. The most interesting aspect of this finding was that these students were predominantly those who had been assigned seats toward the back of the lecture hall.

Research at Miami University

A second major project in closed-circuit instruction was at Miami University (Macomber and Siegel, 1956, 1957, 1960). Miami's research compared closed-circuit television with both large lecture classes and small semi-discussion classes, and the Miami staff studied the possible differential effect of different types of instruction upon students of varying abilities and attitudes.

Miami attempted to use each method at its best. The television courses utilized professional directors, and audiovisual assistance was available for use in both television and in other classes. The result was that the television classes gained and held student attention as well as most good classroom lectures. (But remember the NYU and Penn State findings that visually enriched productions produce inferior achievement.)

In Miami's first experiment, the primary measure of achievement was the final examination in each course, and the television classes were not inferior on this criterion. In fact, in Human Biology the television students scored higher than the conventional classes, although there were other factors that might have contributed to this difference. However, in the second year of telecasting, live teaching produced superior achievement to TV in the second semester of the four courses and in economics proved to be superior in producing gains in critical thinking. Results of third-year experiments were less damning to television, although television classes in zoology proved inferior to conventional classes on a test of problem solving.

Since television is usually considered a substitute for large classes, it is worth noting that large "live" classes did not consistently produce the inferior results of television in the cognitive outcomes, but did tend to be inferior to conventional classes in effecting changes in attitudes.

Other Experiments in College Teaching by Closed-Circuit Television

Among the largest and best designed of other experiments on television teaching are those carried out at Purdue, Iowa, NYU, and San Francisco State. While these experiments have already been cited where relevant in my discussion of the Penn State and Miami experiments, a few points remain. One of these relates to the teaching of English composition by television. Even though the Purdue experiment (Seibert, 1958) used television for only two of the three instructional periods per week, and television students apparently had a good deal of practice in theme writing, television instruction proved to be significantly inferior to conventional instruction in several comparisons. The superiority of conventional teaching was most marked for the student of lower ability. NYU did not find similar ability-level differences, but did find evidence of superiority of conventional methods as measured by theme writing. Similar differences favoring conventional instruction using objective tests of achievement were found during the first semester, but reversed during the second.

Purdue also found television instruction to be inferior to conventional instruction in mechanical engineering (Seibert and Honig,

1959), military science (Kasten and Seibert, 1959), and, on some tests, in calculus (Seibert, 1957).

When a course demands the demonstration of small objects or parts, the use of television or film should be advantageous. In an experiment at Rensselaer Polytechnic (Throop, Assini, and Boguslavsky, 1958) in teaching strength of materials, television was not inferior to conventional methods in teaching instrumentation and specimen behavior, but was inferior in teaching theory and familiarity with machinery.

Student ability generally did not make a difference in the relative effectiveness of television. At Miami, low-ability students in "Foundations of Human Behavior" and "Government" achieved more in conventional classes than in television classes, but, in physiology and zoology, low-ability students did better in television classes than in conventional classes. However, better students disliked television and large classes more.

In both large lectures and in television sections, students complained of lack of contact with the instructor, but Miami students disliked television less than large lectures, while NYU students tended to prefer lectures. The attitudes toward television of both groups tended to become more negative during a second semester of television. (This was true in several studies.) If they could have had the same instructor, students generally preferred a small section to television or a large class. But they preferred television or a large class to a small class if they could be sure of an excellent instructor in the television or large class and had to take their chances in electing a small class. This is probably a realistic alternative, although the student's choice may not always be wise, for in three experimental comparisons Miami graduate assistants proved to be superior (as measured by student achievement) to regular staff members in one course even though inferior in another. Moreover, students taught by graduate assistants did more outside reading.

Uses of Television

From the hypothesis that television would be of most value in courses depending upon visual presentation of information, it might be expected to be more effective in science and engineering courses than in social sciences and humanities courses. From the hypothesis that television would be of less value in classes where interaction between students and instructor is important, it might be expected to be relatively less effective in psychology, speech, and languages than in courses usually taught by lecture. Such comparisons are difficult to make. However, as I have shown, in general psychology courses both at Purdue and Penn State, television students performed worse than students in conventional classes. In English, too, television proved to be inferior. This evidence is in line with the hypothesis.

Insofar as student-instructor interaction is important for teaching a course, television would appear to be of little help. Television does not permit more students to talk, even with two-way audio connections. It is apparent that the student's opportunity to participate is an inverse function of the number of students in the class. If actual participation is important, larger classes should be less effective whether they are taught in one classroom or by television.

Television can, however, have certain advantages in promoting interaction. On any large college campus one of the difficulties in education outside the classroom is that students have few common educational experiences. Since their common experiences tend to be social or athletic, these are likely to be the usual topics of conversation. Stephens College (1955) met this problem in a creative way by developing a required course—"Ideas and Living Today"—which consisted of brief lectures viewed by students in small faculty-led discussion groups. The course was craftily scheduled just before lunch so that discussions spilled over into the dining halls.

With reference to the hypothesis that television will be effective when a good view of the instructional situation is important, television was effective in teaching dentistry (Grossman, Ship, and Romano, 1961). Students learned as much by television as in conventional classes in chemistry both at Penn State and Purdue. If we simply look at the direction of the differences, about half the experiments in science classes favor television and half favor conventional instruction. In nonscience courses well over two-thirds of the differences favor conventional teaching.*

---

* Note that the tests used in most studies are verbal. In any course where visual identification or discrimination is an important goal, a visual test item might be expected to be more valid. While many instructor goals primarily involve abstractions and verbal or symbolic concepts, tests may underrepresent goals involving learning to deal with the real world of objects and events.

It seems safe to conclude that when used over an entire course, television instruction is generally inferior to classroom lectures in communicating information, developing critical thinking, changing attitudes, and arousing interest in a subject, but that this inferiority is not great. Although differences favoring conventional teaching appeared in about two-thirds of the studies reviewed, only a fifth of the differences were statistically significant. Schramm's review (1962) similarly reports three college-level studies in which television was significantly superior and thirteen in which it was significantly inferior. Dubin and Hedley's recent review (1969) reached similar conclusions. A person's view of these results depends a good deal upon individual bias for or against television. When contrasted with research comparing other instructional methods, the consistency of results favoring conventional instruction over television is unusual. However, when one weighs heavily the necessity for accommodation of higher education to large numbers of students, the differences between television and conventional instruction seem relatively small.

The preceding comments have been primarily concerned with closed-circuit television instruction on campus. Although it is difficult to do adequately controlled studies .of the educational effectiveness of broadcast television, it seems quite clear that students motivated enough to take a television course for credit at home may learn well and have favorable attitudes toward television (LePore and Wilson, 1958; Dreher and Beatty, 1958; Evans, Roney, and McAdams, 1954). The Open University in England and the University of the Midwest, covering states in the area around Nebraska, both use television as part of a system of bringing education to people who would not otherwise have access to higher education. While there has not yet been much evaluative research published, the television component seems to be appreciated by many learners who might not have responded to correspondence courses or other alternatives less expensive than television. Nevertheless, the number of students enrolling in broadcast television courses has generally been disappointing. Hoban (1968) suggests that this is a result of the serious limitations of television in giving students and teachers the sense of interpersonal interaction so central to higher level education. He suggests, and the Open University type of programs have often adopted, small group discussions following televised lessons.

Even if closed-circuit television were a potential answer to all educational problems, its success would probably depend to some extent on faculty acceptance. Apparently all of the colleges using closed-circuit televisions have found that many faculty members are skeptical (to say the least) of its value. Polls generally indicate faculty willingness to teach by television if necessary, but faculty preference is for traditional teaching methods.

Faculty acceptance of television seems to be greatest when the faculty has participated in planning for it. For example, the faculty of Stephens College seems to have accepted television more fully than the faculties of any of the other institutions, probably due in no small part to their involvement in the planning for their television course.

A second factor in the acceptance of television at Stephens was that the course offered did not set a particular department or instructor apart from the rest of the faculty. The course offered at Stephens was interdivisional and involved almost all of the faculty. Since the course was a new one, no local professor was pushed aside to make room for a "Master Teacher."

When television enables a department to provide instruction that would otherwise be difficult or impossible to provide, acceptance also seems to be good. Thus, Pennsylvania State found no faculty objections to teaching electrical engineering by television, when a large enrollment plus a staff shortage resulted in several unstaffed sections.

Finally, the support of administrative officials is of obvious importance. Since television teaching is difficult and time consuming, faculty members are much more likely to participate if they feel that this activity is valued not only by their colleagues but also by their administrative officials. (One evidence of such support is a reduction in teaching load for television instructors.)

Taking into account the results of all research on instruction by television, it seems safe to conclude that 1) television instruction for an entire course is inferior to classroom lectures in communicating information, developing critical thinking, changing attitudes, and arousing interest in a subject, but that, 2) this inferiority is probably not great. This conclusion may be surprising after reading the publicity releases reporting that no significant difference was found in this or that study. I have pointed earlier to the logical fallacy in concluding that no difference exists because the difference found is not great enough to disprove the null hypothesis. Aside from this, however, a different impression results from reviewing the mass of studies than from one alone. For example, in twenty of the twenty-six well-controlled experiments reviewed here, conventional classes were superior to television classes in achievement. Although few of the differences were statistically significant by themselves, simple application of the sign test indicates that the differences are not random.

Almost all research has dealt with television used as a major medium of instruction for a total course. While there is little research evidence, anecdotal accounts of the use of television as a teaching aid in conventional courses indicate that there are apparent advantages to its ability to magnify and to provide an unobtrusive means of observation. The development of hand held videotape cameras gives television much greater flexibility. Carrels with videotape increase flexibility for the learner. Frank Costin of the University of Illinois reports that twenty-five minute videotapes played in the discussion sections are much better liked by his teaching assistants and students than the live television presentations previously used in his course. The continuing technological advances in television give television more and more potential usefulness for higher education.

Films

Motion picture films have been available for teaching for a good many years, but their impact upon college teaching has not been great. Nevertheless, well-made educationally useful films in most areas of the curriculum are now available, and it behooves college teachers to become familiar with the audiovisual resources available for their use.

The effectiveness of visual aids depends to a large extent upon the way they are used. Many films are not of great value if they are shown without comment or discussion. Before showing films to classes, instructors should have seen them, noting what points it illustrates, and in the case of many Hollywood films, what misconceptions may be inferred from it. Occasionally it may be a dramatic procedure to dim the lights as soon as the students have arrived and begin the picture immediately. Usually, however, the film is of more value if the students know what to look for and if it has been related to the subject matter of the course.* A study guide may be distributed in the class meeting before the class meeting of the film, or the instructor may give a verbal introduction to the film. If the film is silent, comments may be made while the film is being shown; sometimes verbal comments may be used to occupy periods when the film is of little interest. However, unless you are familiar with the film, your comments may run over into the next scene and be lost in a chorus of laughter.

Instructors should not usually expect a film to offer proof of a given principle. Ordinarily the film offers visual demonstrations or illustrations of a principle or the way in which proof was obtained. Before showing a film, instructors should consider their objectives in showing the film, and then plan how they can best utilize the film to attain these objectives. According to the results of experiments on the use of films, repeating the film adds much to its educational value.

Many of the newer educational films attempt to accomplish certain objectives in the films themselves without regard to the instructors' introductions of the films or the classroom activities following the film. Adding to the versatility of films are single-concept films designed specifically to teach a particular concept. Often, newer colleges are providing facilities for student viewing of such films outside the classroom so that films may be used for student learning almost as conveniently as books. And just as with readings, instructors may use films to provide background and stimulation for discussion. Thus, instructors may break a class into small buzz groups or lead a class discussion in which the students use the film materials in analyzing and understanding the phenomena depicted.

One of the biggest difficulties in using films is knowing which films to use. Previewing as many films as possible seems to be the usual solution, but there are increasingly available critical reviews of most films for college teaching.

The great mass of research on instructional films is relevant to our topic, even though most of it has not been concerned with college teaching. While it would be impossible for us to summarize all of the relevant studies, certain principles have emerged (for a more complete analysis, see Miller, 1957):

---

* Experiments in the Armed Forces support this. See C. A. Lumsdaine, C. Hovland, and F. Sheffield, *Experiments on mass communication* (Princeton: Princeton University Press, 1949).

1. Students can learn from films, and usually do learn at least as much as from a poor teacher (Vandermeer, 1950).
2. Such learning is not confined to details, but may include concepts and attitudes (Kishler, 1950; Mertens, 1951; Hoban and Van Ormer, 1950).
3. Outline material, such as titles and commentary, increases learning if a film is not well organized (Northrop, 1952).
4. For less intelligent students, repeating the film increases learning (McTavish, 1949).
5. Students learn how to learn from films; for example, students with previous experience with instructional films learn more than students without previous experience (Vandermeer, 1951).
6. Presenting pictures is more effective than presenting words as stimuli in rote association tasks such as learning a foreign language (May and Lumsdaine, 1958; Kapstein and Roshal, 1954).
7. Participation increases learning (Hovland, Lumsdaine, and Sheffield, 1949). In this study, active response with prompting and feedback was most effective on the most difficult material with the least motivated, least able students—a finding that probably has wide generality in teaching (also see Michael and Maccoby, 1953). However, Ash and Carlton (1951) found that notetaking during a film was not effective when a test was administered immediately after the film. This suggests that active participation needs to be planned in the production of a film or television presentation rather than being interjected as an additional task for the student.

Telephone and Radio

Cutler, McKeachie, and McNeil (1958) compared the effectiveness of teaching equal-size groups in face-to-face groups or by telephone. Both groups showed significant learning and attitude change, and there was no significant difference in the two methods' effectiveness. Thus, if economy in instruction is desired, perhaps the expense of television cameras and receiving tubes is unnecessary. One of the few experiments comparing the effectiveness of radio and television, however, showed better learning and retention for television (Paul and Ogilvie, 1955), and experiments conducted a generation ago tended to find differences in change of attitude favoring face-to-face instruction over radio or printing (for example, Wilke, 1934). Recently there have been a number of accounts of the use of telephone to bring students into contact with well-known public figures, but no systematic evaluation has yet appeared.

A unique study by Newman and Highland (1956) suggested that mass media may be more effective in information-giving early, rather than late, in a course. In the course "Principles of Radio," they compared:

—Presentation by tape recordings and workbook.

—Presentation by supervised readings.

—Presentation by tape recordings and slides.

—Instructor presentation.

The three mass media methods were as effective as the instructor for the first two-thirds of the course, but less effective for the last third.

A new alternative extending the scope of teaching by telephone is "blackboard-by-wire" and "picture-phone," devices for presenting relatively static pictures over ordinary telephone circuits (Ristenbatt, 1968).

Language Laboratories and Cassette Recorders

Cassette recorders are now convenient and relatively inexpensive tools available for teaching. The original and most common use of tape recorders was in language laboratories. Developed in the Army's intensive language training programs during World War II, language laboratories multiplied rapidly in the postwar years and boomed under the financial impetus of the National Defense Education Act of 1958. The core of the language laboratory is the tape recorder, which can present foreign language sounds and utterances with accuracy, fidelity, and endless patience.

With its emphasis upon the prepared recorded sequence of stimuli with frequent opportunities for student responses, the language laboratory has close kinship to the programmed-learning movement. Language laboratories are now an accepted part of the college scene, but experimental tests of their value are nonexistent, so far as I can ascertain. At other educational levels there is scanty evidence, some of which is favorable. For example, Allen (1960) reports higher achievement for high school students with language laboratory experience, and Banathy and Jordan report favorable experience at the Army Language School (1969). Bauer (1964) found that the success of the language laboratory depended upon the amount of supervision —a finding reminiscent of some of those in programmed learning and in independent study.

Other imaginative uses of tape recorders are in presentation of oral questions in programmed teaching, in dictation of comments about student papers, in lecture-poster or slide presentation (Johnston, 1969), in an automated taped lecture, programmed-question, film-strip presentation (Postlethwait et al., 1969), and in recording lectures prepared by students as a technique for developing student motivation and active integration of material (Webb, 1965). So far as I can find, the only empirical study of the effectiveness of tape recording was a study of a thirty-minute lecture by Bligh (1970). In this study the lecture was given live, audio-taped, and transcribed by a secretary. A multiple-choice test given immediately after students had heard or read the lecture revealed no difference in overall learning, but a possibility that the tape was superior for the higher level questions requiring synthesis and evaluation.

Photographs, Transparencies, and Other Visual Aids

In contrast to the dearth of evidence about the use of language laboratories, research on other types of audiovisual aids has been encouraging. Carroll (1963) reports successful use of an audiovisual teaching machine to teach the Arabic writing system. Antioch College (1960) used acetate visuals projected with an overhead projector coupled with a language laboratory to achieve substantial savings of instructional time and improve instruction as measured by a test of reading ability. Similarly, Chance (1961) found that the use of overhead projected transparencies and overlays was significantly superior to conventional instruction (using the blackboard) in teaching descriptive geometry to freshman engineers.

Slide projectors that permit showing slides in a lighted room have added much to the value of this type of visual aids. While many excellent slides may be secured from commercial sources, slides made to meet individual instructor objectives may be especially helpful. I have found that cartoons from popular magazines may be used not only to illustrate academic principles, but also to add humor and variety to the lecture.

One of the problems faced by the instructor with a large section is that of getting the students settled and quiet in order to begin the lecture. Louis Berman, while in charge of visual aids for a lecture section of 500 students at the University of Michigan, conceived of showing slides of review material, cartoons, and questions for the ten-minute period between classes. This directed the attention of arriving students to the front of the auditorium and eased the instructor's task of gaining attention.

Photographs can hardly be included among new media. Yet recent years have seen some innovations in their use in teaching. Novak (1958), for example, successfully used labeled photomicrographs in teaching botany.

One experiment in the use of tape recording and visual displays in place of face-to-face lectures in teaching introductory psychology indicated superiority of the conventional method (Johnston, 1969). In another study no significant difference was found.

Audiotutorial

The Audiotutorial method was developed by Postlethwait for use in a Purdue University biology course (Postlethwait, Novak, and Murray, 1969). It involves a combination of individual study of modules, including audiotapes, slides, and other media with a general assembly used for guest lecturers, films, and examinations. In addition, weekly small-group quiz sessions are held. Mintz (1975) reviewed research comparing audiotutorial and conventional approaches and found six studies, of which three favored audiotutorial and one conventional instruction. Fisher (1976) reported that six of ten studies favored audiotutorial over lecture. Kulik and Jaksa (1977) found twenty-four studies, nine of which favored audiotutorial and two the conventional class. Thus the audiotutorial approach seems well worth instituting as a method in courses such as the sciences, where visual, auditory, or laboratory experience is needed in order to achieve course goals.

Media-Activated Learning Groups

The Technical University of Denmark has made effective use of a method described by Berman (1973, 1974). In media-activated learning groups a structural audiovisual program of transparencies and audiocassettes orients and directs activities of students who meet without the instructor. Such groups proved to be equal in achievement to lecture groups.

Automation: A Summary

The research to date indicates that television, films, and other media can be used to achieve educational objectives. The usefulness varies depending upon the objective, characteristics of the students, and the excellence of the materials. Research at present reveals no likelihood that they will eliminate the need for face-to-face contacts between professors and students; one of the most useful audiovisual devices continues to be the blackboard.

SUPPLEMENTARY READING

A good general reference on audiovisual methods is W. A. Wittich and C. F. Shulder, *Instructional technology: its nature and use,* 5th ed. (Harper & Row, 1973).

13

Role Playing and Microteaching

This chapter focuses on role playing and microteaching, a form of role playing.

Role Playing

Role playing as a teaching device developed from the psychodramatists centered around Moreno and the group dynamicists. Briefly, role playing is the setting up of more or less unstructured situations in which students' behaviors are improvised to fit in with their conceptions of roles to which they have been assigned. Role playing is like a drama in which each participant is assigned a character to portray, but where no lines are learned. The individuals portraying specific roles improvise their responses to the situation.

The purposes of role playing as used in my classes are:

1. To give students practice in using what they've learned.
2. To illustrate principles from the course content.

3. To develop insight into human relations problems.
4. To provide a concrete basis for discussion.
5. To maintain or arouse interest.
6. To provide a channel in which feelings can be expressed under the guise of make-believe.
7. To develop increased awareness of one's own and others' feelings.

Role playing can be utilized in a variety of classes, ranging from complex simulations of political or international situations to language classes in which role playing is used for practice of the language. In language classes, for example, role playing can provide useful linguistic information on appropriate speech levels (how to respond to rude questions, how to be politely evasive, persuasive, firm, and so on), use of gestures, and cultural points such as distance between speakers. Students may write and/or act out more than one way of handling a situation; they generally prefer role playing that allows them to express dissatisfaction, anger, or rudeness. Sometimes teachers take part in the role playing as participants; sometimes they act as "coaches."

In using role playing instructors may begin by bringing to class a problem situation that does not have too direct a relationship to the students' own personal problems. The situation should be one that is familiar enough so that members can understand the roles and their potential responses to the problem. Ordinarily, role playing seems to work best when it arises rather spontaneously from a problem being discussed in class. This does not mean, however, that instructors cannot foresee problems likely to arise and need role playing. In fact, until they have had some experience with role playing, they will probably role play only those situations they have worked out rather explicitly before class. Nevertheless, instructors should be willing to change plans in accordance with the needs of the group.

Instructors should have in mind some objective for the role playing other than that of showing off a new trick. In introducing the first role-playing situation to the class the instructor should describe the situation quite completely, picturing the roles required and the objective of the role playing before asking for volunteers for the roles.

For example, the instructor in a psychology class might say,

> We've been learning about the differences between Skinnerian and Freudian approaches to treatment. Let's imagine that Freud has come back to life and that he and Skinner have just read an account in the

morning paper of a baseball player who punched his manager. Skinner and Freud are having coffee with a student who asks them, "What should be done about this player who punched his manager? This is the third time he has been in trouble for fighting." Who wants to play the role of the student? Who will volunteer to be Skinner? Who will volunteer to be Freud? ... O.K. Here are three chairs; we'll imagine that you're sitting around a table. Let's begin by the student asking her question.

The goal of this role-playing situation would be to get the class actively involved in comparing Skinner's and Freud's viewpoints. The situation can be far-fetched or realistic, so long as it is interesting and involving. You might, in fact, even get the class to help you develop the description of the situation to increase their involvement.

Here is another role-playing situation used in language courses:

Students are shown a picture of an apartment building. Students work in pairs, writing their dialogues first.
Grammar points: Modal verbs; *too, very*.
Instructions: You are the man who lives in the apartment that is too noisy. Call up the mother of the children who are playing football in their apartment. Be polite. *or* You are the man who lives in the apartment that is too noisy. Call up the mother of the children who are playing football in their apartment. Be rude. Be angry.

General considerations in handling role playing are:

—If you wish to point out different responses or solutions to a given problem, use two or more presentations of the same situation with different participants or have participants switch roles. In such cases more natural behavior and more convincing differences are obtained by not permitting participants in the replay of the situation to see the first presentation. This also prevents the feeling of the first group that the second group is trying to show them up.

—Even if you know the class fairly well, it is usually preferable to get volunteers for the roles rather than to choose participants, for volunteers are less likely to feel on the spot.

—For the usual class situation, it is better to direct discussion away from the reactions of specific participants to the reactions of people in general in such a situation. As the group gains a sense of security, more attention can be paid to feelings of the actual participants, provided you are aware of the possibility of mobilizing anxiety with which you may not wish to deal. Situations involving morals or subjects of high emotional significance, such as sex taboos, are apt to be traumatic to some students. The situations that are most interesting and reveal the greatest differences in responses are those involving some choice or conflict of motives. Often the students themselves will suggest good situations for illustrating certain principles. In any case, situations that are unrelated to student experience are apt to fall flat. The teacher can to some extent control the depth of emotions and attitudes aroused by the context of the situation. For example, the same situation might be set up as father and son, dean and student, or boss and employee.

To help the nonparticipating members of the class observe skillfully, assign individuals to watch for specific things. For example, one observer may be asked to particularly observe expressive movements of the participants; another may observe the pattern of interaction between the participants. The class itself may suggest points to look for and to discuss.

—Some role-playing situations may end themselves. Usually, however, the instructor will have to "cut" the action. Generally the beginner lets the role playing run too long. Ordinarily three to six minutes is sufficient to spark discussion.

—Players feel less defensive if they are asked to discuss the situation before the rest of the class begins discussion.

—After discussing the situation, you may wish to replay the situation reversing the roles, changing one role, altering the situation, or playing a probable following scene.

—In general, role playing seems to stimulate much interest and give students the feeling that they are actually making use of what they've learned.

—As in most other novel teaching techniques, the effectiveness of role playing depends to a large extent upon the confidence of the instructor in the procedure and the students' feeling (gained from the instructor's attitude) that it is going to be a successful and valuable aspect of the course. Like any other technique, it can be used to such an extent that it becomes repetitious, but if used to accomplish definite goals, and if students perceive their progress toward those goals, it can be an extremely rewarding technique.

Microteaching

Microteaching is a technique primarily used in teacher training, but is also potentially useful for training in public speaking, interviewing, leading groups, or other communication or interpersonal skills. Microteaching involves presenting a lesson, speech, and so on in a brief period; for example, five minutes. The microlesson focuses on the use of a particular skill, such as asking questions, establishing rapport, or eliciting student comments. Often the microlesson is videotaped to facilitate review and further practice of the skill desired. Microteaching is a form of role playing, and research results indicate that it is effective in teacher training. But even though you are not in teacher education, you may wish to consider microteaching as a means of enhancing your own skill as a college teacher or you may find the emphasis upon specific skill and videotape feedback a useful adjunct to your use of role playing.

SUPPLEMENTARY READING

For further discussion of the use of role playing in teaching, I recommend:

Adult Education Association, *How to use role playing*, Leadership Pamphlet #6 (743 N. Wabash, Chicago, Ill.: Adult Education Association, 1959).

R. G. Baker, Psychodrama in teaching scientific method in the social sciences, *Sociatry*, *1*, 179–182.

C. C. Bowman, The psychodramatic method in collegiate instruction: a case study, *Sociatry*, *1*, 421–430.

W. Coleman, Role-playing as an instructional aid, *Journal of Educational Psychology*, 1948, *39*, 427–435.

L. W. Kay, Role-playing as a teaching aid, *Sociometry*, 1946, *9*, 263–274.

L. W. Kay, Role-playing as a teaching aid—some theoretical considerations, *Sociometry*, 1947, *10*, 165–167.

N. R. F. Maier and L. F. Zerfoss, MRP: A technique for training large groups of supervisors and its potential use in social research, *Human Relations*, 1952, *5*, 177–186.

F. Moreno, The learning process in nurse's training, *Sociatry*, *2*, 207–214.

G. Stanford and A. E. Roark, *Human interaction in education* (Boston: Allyn and Bacon, 1974).

A. Zander and R. Lippitt, Reality practice as educational method, *Sociometry*, 1944, 129–151.

For Microteaching, see:
D. N. Allen and K. Ryan, *Microteaching* (Reading, Ma.: Addison-Wesley, 1969).

14

Term Papers, Student Reports, Visiting Experts, and Field Trips

This chapter contains miscellaneous observations about practical teaching problems that don't fit into other chapters, but which are nonetheless real and confront teachers almost daily.

Term Papers

My experiences with term papers have not always been happy ones. Yet the potential values for students who do a good job are so great that I almost invariably use them in my courses.

When undergraduates are required to turn in a term paper, they seem to face three alternatives:

1. Buy one or to borrow one from a friend or fraternity or sorority file. The student may have this retyped or, if there are no marks on it, simply retype the title page inserting his own name for that of the author.

2. Find a book in the library that covers the needed material. They may then simply copy it with varying degrees of paraphrasing and turn it in. Whether or not to list this book in the bibliography is a problem not yet adequately covered by student mores, although it is agreed that if it is listed in the bibliography it should be well hidden between two references with Russian (first choice) or German (second choice) authors.

3. Review relevant resources and, using their powers of analysis and integration, develop papers that reveal understanding and original thinking.

Most teachers prefer that their students adopt the third alternative. Few of us, however, have evolved techniques for eliminating the first two. Here are a few things I've tried:

1. Don't give students complete freedom in choice of topics. Most students have difficulty in selecting a topic and are happy to have suggestions. If you can vary these topics each time you teach the course (and change jobs when you run out of ideas), you can reduce the use of alternatives 1 and 2 in the preceding list.

2. Include on a test some question that will require the student to use knowledge gained in preparing the term paper.

3. Require students to make oral reports on their papers and answer questions from the class.

Student Reports

Typical student reports to the class are mumbled readings of uninspired papers, not unlike the papers of their professors at the annual meetings of their scientific societies. Like the professors' colleagues, the students' audience is likely to be bored and inattentive. If you wish to use student reports, I would advise that they be given in a manner in which the presentation is broken up by discussion, questions, or demonstration. One method is to have the students who are to give the reports form a group for a forum or panel discussion.

Sometimes teachers will schedule student reports as a method of saving themselves preparation time. This usually doesn't work. If student reports are to be effective, instructors usually need to schedule conferences with the students reporting and spend time going over both the content and presentation of the report.

If term papers and student reports are frequently so inadequate, why would instructors bother to use them? As I see it, term papers and student reports attempt to gain two objectives:

1. To provide an opportunity for students to go beyond conventional course coverage and gain a feeling of expertness in a limited area. I feel that this is an important way in which students learn to value knowledge and the rational process by which knowledge accumulates.
2. To give students an opportunity to explore problems of special significance to them. In this way instructors hope to capture increased motivation.

Even though term papers fail to achieve these objectives for many students, they provide one of the few means by which instructors can handle individual differences in ability and motivation. Even if they stimulate only a few very bright students who are bored by class discussions and lecture, term papers are well worthwhile.

Individual Instruction

In laboratory courses and fields such as dentistry, nursing, and medicine much of the instruction is individual. My guiding principle, here, is to permit students the maximum freedom to experience successful completion of a task or a part of a task, but to give enough guidance so that they will not get bogged down in a rut of errors. This implies that the learning experiences of students go from the simple to the complex, with the steps so ordered that each new problem can be successfully solved.

This principle does not mean that instructors should be mere observers of the learning process. Sometimes they may act as examples to the students. However, it doesn't usually do the students much good simply to observe skill in another which they must develop themselves. When instructors perform, they should utilize the same techniques they use in presenting other visual aids, particularly in directing the students' attention to crucial aspects of the problem.

One of the goals of individualized instruction, and of all instruction, is that students should learn to evaluate their own work. This means that students should be given opportunities for self-evaluation, and that you should point out carefully the basis for your evaluations. Many of the problems students bring to their instructors are directly or indirectly the result of inaccurate self-evaluations.

Visiting Experts

The visiting expert is frequently only an easy way for instructors to save themselves the trouble of preparing a lesson. However, if used sparingly, a visiting expert can provide a welcome change of pace in the course routine. If this device is used many times during a single term, students may complain of lack of continuity in the course, for it is difficult to get experts who use the same concepts and build upon the students' previous learning.

For maximum success I suggest that the students be prepared for the visitor and some effort be made to get the class to formulate the questions the expert will attempt to answer. The visitor should be warned to allow some of the class period for questions so that students can follow up with the questions formulated before the visit. Then part of the following class period should be allotted to discussion of the visitor's contributions.

Field Trips

The sequence of preparation, learning experience, and follow-up applies to field trips as well as to visiting experts, demonstrations, and movies. The field trip not only gets the students away from the classroom, but gives them actual first-hand contact with data in the course area. I would suspect that such concrete experiences would be more effective in promoting learning than the more abstract, but less time-consuming, presentation of a lecture or textbook, but experience alone may be less helpful than experience accompanied by verbal analysis and conceptualization that enables the experience to be generalized to other situations. Moreover, just as extraneous details may decrease learning from films or case histories, incidental elements of the natural situation may be distracting. Thus, preparation is especially important for field experience learning.

SUPPLEMENTARY READING

In *The craft of teaching* (Chapter 10), Kenneth Eble argues against assigning term papers.

Bligh et al. (1975) describes the "syndicate method," in which groups of five or six students carry out field and/or library work in order to write a joint report.

15

Instructional Games, Simulations, and the Case Method

For some students and some teachers education and games are simply at opposite ends of a continuum—they find it hard to conceive of games as educational. Yet in the past decade an increasing number of teachers have been finding games to be an important part of their educational resources. It may well be that within the next decade educational games will replace many of the noneducational game shows now on television.

Games and Simulations

An educational game involves students in some sort of competition or achievement in relationship to a goal, a game that both teaches and is fun. Many games are simulations; for example, they attempt to model some real-life problem situation. Thus there are business games, international relations games, and many others. Whatever the topic, the planner of the game needs to specify the teaching objectives to be served by the game and then plan the game to highlight features that contribute to those objectives.

The chief advantage of games and simulations is that students are active participants rather than passive observers. Students must make decisions, solve problems, and react to the results of their decisions. The research literature on gaming in higher education is surprisingly sparse and surprisingly lacking in support for educational superiority over other methods. Hsiao (1975), for example, found a nonsignificant superiority of a simulation group over a traditional class in economic knowledge. Student evaluations of the simulation were very favorable. Games typically create a high level of student involvement and can be a worthwhile adjunct to many courses. Following is a description of a game used in Russian History.*

Simulation in a Survey Course in Russian History

Game: Parties and Constituencies in Russian Revolution.

Instructor: Bill Rosenberg, Associate Professor of History.

Course: History 503, Survey of Twentieth Century Russian History.

Enrollment: About 100 students.

Game Time: 1½ hours (up to 2 hours).

Preparation: Four or five students volunteered to work out this game as their course project; two or three took a leadership role. The instructor consulted with them in planning; he suggested readings and consultation with an instructor who had worked on gaming and simulation.

The students prepared a twelve-page document on four parties and four constituencies that took part in the Russian Revolution. This program told each group what its orientation was (for example, peasants wanted land), what its members were striving for, and what their methods tended to be. The program was given to students to read in advance of the day of the simulation.

Purpose of the Game: To look at the electoral processes, in terms of, 1) where groups of people stood, and 2) how they related to each other politically.

---

* Many of the games used at the University of Michigan have been developed in workshops directed by Barbara Steinwachs and the staff of the Gaming Service of the University Extension Service.

Structure of the Game: There were, historically, two elections: in the middle of 1917 and at the end of 1917. One of these elections took place in the game situation after parties and constituencies had been playing their parts for an hour. The game then went on for another half hour or more.

Students volunteered for four "party groups" and four "constituency groups." A few were assigned to groups or chose not to participate. Each group consulted the program and met in caucus to decide on its actions. They could do about anything they wished: attempt to form alliances, appeal to another group for support, influence others, and even lie. Delegates were sent from caucuses to different groups and returned for further strategy discussions.

After an hour, an election was held and tallied on the blackboard. The game continued for about half an hour after the election.

Physical Setting: The game took place in the usual large lecture hall, but smaller groups spilled out into the hallway and beyond the room. The usual lecture time of one hour was extended to two hours that day.

Evaluation: The instructor felt that the simulation was remarkably effective as a recreation of what actually took place in 1917. For example, the Bolsheviks were clear about what they wanted and went directly to the point of gaining power, while the Liberals were meeting in the hall and came in to ask at an advanced stage of the play whether the game had actually begun.

Evaluations of this session were elicited from students, who were uniformly positive. There were some suggestions that the instructions could have been clearer and more time might have been taken to explain in advance.

The educational use of the game might have been strengthened by planning for more student discussion afterwards. About twenty minutes or so were spent in discussion after the game in the lecture room, and there was some discussion in section meetings. However, more planning for postgame discussion might have strengthened this game as a teaching technique.

There are now a number of well-designed games that have been used in enough situations to have the kinks worked out. Some use computers to implement the complex interaction of various decisions. Two examples are SIMSOC (Gamson, 1966), a sociological game in which students are citizens of a society in which they have economic and social roles; for example, some are members of political parties, some have police powers; and METRO, an urban planning game involving conflicts between politicians, landowners, planners, school personnel, and so on.

The Case Method

Case methods, like games and simulations, are intended to develop student ability to solve problems using knowledge, concepts, and skills that may have been learned in previous courses, or which the students are expected to be motivated by the case to learn from readings, lectures, or other resources. Typically the case method involves a series of cases, but in some case method courses the cases are not well chosen to represent properly sequenced levels of difficulty. Often, in order to make cases realistic, so many details are included that beginning students lose the principles or points the case was intended to demonstrate. As in classic studies in discrimination learning in the laboratory, teachers attempting to help students learn complex discriminations and principles in problem solving need to choose initial cases in which the differences are clear and extreme before moving to more subtle, complex cases. Typically, one of the goals of the case method is to teach students to select important factors from a tangle of less important ones that may, nevertheless, form a context to be considered. One does not learn such skills by being in perpetual confusion, but rather by success in solving more and more difficult problems. For a more detailed exposition see Hunt (1951) and Maier (1971).

Cases, simulations, and games involve getting, recalling, and using information in order to solve problems. As I shall show in Chapter 23, this involves the kind of restructuring that is likely to result in better retention, recall, and use of the information outside the classroom.

SUPPLEMENTARY READING

A good source for business simulations is P. S. Greenlaw, L. W. Herron and R. H. Rawdon, *Business simulation* (Englewood Cliffs, N.J.: Prentice-Hall, 1962).
More general references are
H. S. Guetzkow, *Simulation in social sciences: readings* (Englewood Cliffs, N.J.: Prentice-Hall, 1962).

D. W. Zuckerman and R. E. Horn, *The guide to simulations/games for education and training* (Lexington, Mass.: Information Resources Inc., 1973). This not only includes descriptions of over 600 games, but also tells how students can make their own simulations.

Clark Abt, *Serious games* (New York: Viking Press, 1970).

M. Inbar and C. Stoll, *Simulation and gaming in social science* (New York: Free Press, 1972).

R. L. Dukes and S. J. Waller, "Towards a general evaluation model for simulation games: GEM, *Simulation and Games,* 1976, 7, 75–96.

16

Examinations

Most instructors in colleges with traditional grading systems deplore the emphasis students place upon getting a good grade from the course. Usually instructors attempt to minimize this aspect of the course by stating that the important thing in the course is what the students gain, not what grade they make. Sometimes a few students nod their heads in agreement. While such words are intellectually accepted, motivationally the grade remains the most important aspect of the course for most students. Since grades in large courses are determined to a great degree by scores on tests, the tests are among the most frustrating aspects of the course to many students, and usually arouse a great deal of overt and covert aggression. If teachers, using objective-type tests, attempt to go beyond the usual practice of asking simply for memory of information from the textbook or lectures, they are immediately deluged with the complaint, "These are the most ambiguous tests I have ever taken!"

Reducing Student Aggression

To most beginning teachers the aggression that students direct against them after a test is very disturbing. It is likely to impair the rapport of the instructor with the class and may in some cases actually be a block to learning. Hence, devices for reducing the aggression seem to be worthwhile.

The most obvious solution to the problem is to reduce the frustration involved in taking tests. The most important aid in this area is to emphasize the contribution the course can make to the long-range goals of the students, so that the need of a good grade is not the only one involved in the situation. Emphasizing the educational and diagnostic value of tests is one application of this principle. Yet, no matter how much the instructor emphasizes long-range goals, the tests are going, in a large measure, to determine the students' goals. Do you want the students to memorize details? Then give the usual memory-of-details sort of test.

Thus, the first step in constructing a test is to list your goals for the course. Not all goals can be measured by a test. New attitudes and interests, for example, are not measured by classroom achievement tests, but this should not be used as an excuse for avoiding the effort necessary to specify outcomes in measurable terms. Once you have specified objectives you can determine how many test items embody each category of objective. You'll probably be surprised to find out how many of your test items pile up in certain categories.

One way of helping to maintain a balance is to construct a grid, listing objectives along the side of the page and content areas along the top. If you then tally items as you write them, you can monitor the degree to which your test adequately samples the objectives and content desired.

Because some course examinations emphasize recall of facts, many students demand teaching that emphasizes memorization of facts. One student wrote on a slip evaluating me, "This instructor is very interesting and worthwhile, but I have rated him low because he doesn't give us enough facts. The sort of job I get will depend on my grades, and I have little chance of beating other students out for an A unless I can get a couple of pages of notes each period."

Because our objective was not simply memory of facts, but ability to apply principles, the general psychology teaching staff at the University of Michigan attempted to construct items that would measure the students' abilities to apply principles and give them the feeling that application of learning was an important objective of the course. As might be expected, scores on our application items correlated more highly with intelligence as measured by the Otis Test of Mental Ability than did scores on items primarily testing memory (0.41 vs. 0.17). Nevertheless, this correlation was not high enough to indicate that intelligence was the only factor tested, and a semester of psychology does result in gains on these items.

Students may object at first to items requiring them to think, but if you emphasize that the tests will measure the students' abilities to use their psychological knowledge, you can greatly influence their goals in the course. This is indicated by a student comment we received, "More of the course should be like the tests. They make us apply what we've learned." Marton and Saljo (1976b) showed that questions demanding understanding rather than memory of detailed facts resulted in differing styles of studying for later tests and better retention.

Student participation in test construction also seems to reduce the aggression occasioned by tests. Explaining the type of test you give, discussing your reasons for using this type, and asking students who would like to contribute items for the next test to submit items helps you tear off some of the cloak of mystery surrounding the test. Actually using some items submitted by students rewards those students who submitted them. Devising questions helps make the students aware of the problems involved in item construction, as well as giving them a good review of subject matter.

Nevertheless, I cannot overemphasize the importance of relating test items to objectives. Admittedly it is more difficult to devise measures of the more complex, higher level objectives. Yet the very effort to do so will, I believe, have an influence on student motivation and learning. Moreover, consideration of these objectives may help you break out of the conventional forms of testing. For example, in my classes in introductory psychology, the desired goals include developing greater curiosity about behavior, awareness of dimensions of behavior that might ordinarily be ignored, and increased ability to describe and analyze behavior objectively. To get at this I have sometimes used a film as a stimulus, with the test questions having to do with the students' reactions to the film; or I have asked students to leave the classroom for fifteen minutes and then return and report on some interesting behavior they have observed. I have brought in collections of journals and asked them to find an article of interest and to write their reactions to it. I have asked for analyses of newspaper items to get at the degree to which students can read critically. Using materials with somewhat greater apparent relevance to course objectives than typical test items is more fun for the students taking the test—and more fun to grade.

When to Test

Because tests are so important in operationalizing goals and influencing student methods of learning, I like to give a test early in the term —after the third or fourth week of a fourteen-week semester. To reduce the stress, I weight the test very little in determining the final grade, perhaps a third of a comparable hour test given later in the term. Such an early test gets students started, rather than delaying their studying until the conventional midterm examination, and it helps you, or your teaching assistants, to identify problems early while they are still remediable. Thus, this test should demand the style of learning you expect and needs to be constructed carefully, even though its purpose is more motivational and diagnostic than evaluative.

I usually also give midterm and final examinations, but the amount and frequency of tests should depend upon the background of your students. In a freshman course in an area new to students, frequent short tests early in the term facilitate learning, as demonstrated in the Keller Plan. Generally, however, I want to wean students from studying for tests to become lifelong learners who will be able to evaluate their own learning. This implies less frequent testing as learners become more experienced. It probably also implies questions requiring broader integration and more detailed analysis as the learners advance. For this reason my tests are all cumulative; that is, they cover material previously tested as well as material learned since the last test.

Test Construction

This is not the place to engage in an extended discussion of test-construction theory. Let me, however, confess that from the students' point of view, tests and marks are frequently the most important part of the instructor's job. Because of this, these topics deserve some consideration.

Choosing the Type of Question

I shall begin by pointing out that the instructor who is about to give an examination is in a conflict situation. There are two time-consuming procedures involved in the administration of an examination: the first is the construction of the examination; the second is the grading. Unfortunately, it appears to be generally true that the examinations that are easiest to construct are the most difficult to grade and vice versa. Essay examinations that can be made up in a few minutes require hours to grade. Multiple-choice examinations, which can be constructed by an experienced item builder at the rate of 3–5 items an hour, can be corrected at the rate of about 20–30 seconds for a 60-item test. Short-answer examinations fall somewhere between these two extremes.

Teachers often choose questions solely in terms of class size, using multiple-choice tests for large classes, short-answer questions for medium-sized classes, and essay questions for small classes. Class size is obviously an important factor, but I urge that your educational goals take precedence. This almost always implies use of some essay or other questions requiring analysis, integration, or application.

● *Short-answer tests.* An example of a short-answer item might be this: "What was the important finding of Coghill's study of amblystoma?" The answer that I, at least, would expect would be to the effect that stages in behavioral development were found to be correlated with stages in neural development. Such a question is restricted enough that it is not often difficult to judge whether the expected answer is there. Furthermore, such questions can be presented in a format that allows only a small amount of space for the answer. The student's tendency to employ the "shotgun" approach to the examination is thus inhibited. Finally, it has been my experience that the short-answer type of examination is respected by the students as, 1) being fair, and 2) permitting an adequate coverage of assigned materials without asking for petty details. Such a quiz can be made about as challenging as you choose to make it. Unfortunately, many short-answer questions test only recall of a specific fact.

Short-answer questions can get at other than informational outcomes. If you are trying to develop skill in analysis or diagnosis, for example, you may present case material or description of an experiment and ask the students what questions they would ask. You can then provide additional information that the students can then use in an analysis. Or a short-answer question can ask students to solve a problem or propose a hypothesis relevant to information learned earlier. An example is the following question from a course on the psychology of aging:

1. Given the *differences* in ways in which men and women experience middle age, and the fact that depression rapidly rises as a psychiatric symptom in middle age, how might the *causes* of the depression differ for men and women at this time in life?

● *Essay tests.* Although the short-answer examination is very useful in certain situations, I would recommend that, if possible, you include at least one essay question on examinations in most college courses. Whether or not essay tests are valid measures, experiments indicate that students study more efficiently for essay-type examinations than for objective tests (Monaco, 1977; McClusky, 1934).

Whatever the values of essay tests as evaluation devices, you should also take into consideration their potential educational value. Particularly where the tests can be returned with comments, essay examinations may give students practice in organized, creative thinking about a subject and an opportunity to check their thinking against the standards of someone with more experience and ability in the field. Moreover, they may, as we suggested earlier, orient students to work toward objectives beyond memorization of details. Johnson (1975) demonstrated that when marginal comments on earlier tests emphasized creativity, creativity on the final exam was improved. He also found that a training program incorporated into the course increased creativity.

Finally, if you read the examinations yourself (or at least some of them), you get some excellent information on what students are learning. While the teacher can also learn from students' responses to objective tests, the impact on the teacher of what students are learning seems to be greater and more vivid in reading essay tests.

● *True-false tests.* Although true-false examinations are rather easy to make up, I'm not sure what they measure, and don't advocate their use. This is partly a concession to student opinion. Students can usually figure out reasons why any particular item can be either true or false. Because of this, the true-false test tends to enhance the frustration which is inherent in the test-making situation anyway.

● *Multiple-choice tests.* For some purposes, objective items of the multiple-choice type are useful. Items need not be entirely verbal. Louis Berman of the University of Illinois has worked out a number of items using cartoons, sketches, graphs, and diagrams, which students feel are more interesting than all-verbal questions. Some students with little verbal ability do better on these questions than on the usual ones.

Good multiple-choice questions are difficult to construct. (As a matter of fact, the greater your experience in their construction, the longer it takes per item to construct a reasonably fair, accurate, and inclusive question.) Because of this difficulty, the construction of such items is probably not worthwhile unless they will be administered to several hundred students, either in a single year or in successive years. Here are some useful hints for their construction.

1. Teacher's manuals that are provided for many textbooks contain multiple-choice items. You will not be able to rely on a manual as the source of all your questions, because it will not often contain enough good questions of this sort.

2. A second source of such items is the students themselves. This is not a particularly satisfactory source of test questions because only about 10 percent of the items thus received will be usable. They are typically from obscure passages in reading materials; where they are not, they are apt to be duplicated by many students. As I have said before, however, this technique is a rather successful pedagogical device because it gets the students to read their assignment more analytically. It also gives the instructor a good index of what the students are getting out of the various sections of their reading.

3. Item analysis may be useful in improving the questions, but I have found that the best suggestions for improvement came from students themselves in their discussion of the test. It seems almost criminal to waste this experience with items; therefore I recommend a permanent file. I have found it to be a good procedure to keep multiple-choice items on 5″ x 8″ file cards, one item per card, rather than on sheets of paper. This system permits easy filing and the discard of individual items that have been unsatisfactory without the use of scissors and paste. New items can be filed in the

proper subject area. This card size permits revision of the item if some of the choices have turned out to be confusing ones. Our secretaries say that such copy is as easy to type stencils from as the copy on a few pieces of paper.

4. If you have a problem, but no good distracter (incorrect alternative), give the item in short-answer or essay form and use the students' own responses for alternatives for a later use of the item in multiple-choice form.

5. Multiple-choice questions typically have four or five alternatives. Rather than wasting your and your students' time with extra alternatives that don't test a discrimination that is important, use only as many alternatives as you can construct making meaningful discriminations. Costin (1972) has shown that three-choice items are as effective as four-choice.

6. For measuring understanding, I like questions that require the student to predict the outcome of the situation rather than those that simply ask the student to label the phenomenon.

7. General rules.

   a. The item as a whole should present a problem of significance in the subject-matter field.

   b. The item as a whole should deal with an important aspect of the subject-matter field, not with a minor element that is of significance only to the expert.

   c. The item as a whole should be phrased in language appropriate to the subject-matter field.

   d. Items that attempt to measure understanding should include an element of novelty, but too much novelty is likely to make the problem too hard. Trick questions should be avoided since they are always too difficult and represent abuse of the element of novelty.

   e. The items in the test should be independent of one another, and the information supplied in one item should not indicate the answer to another.

8. Rules for stating the problem.

   a. There must be a single central problem.

   b. The problem must be accurately stated.

   c. The problem should be stated briefly, but completely; hence, the problem should not test the student's ability to understand complex sentence structure except when the teacher is deliberately measuring that ability.

   d. The problem should contain only material relevant to its solution. However, the problem should be an interesting one even though padding is avoided.
   e. The problem should be stated in a positive, not a negative form. Somehow, even intelligent adults often fail to see a "not" in reading a sentence.
   f. It should be possible to understand the problem without reading the alternatives.
   g. Generally speaking, the test is more interesting if the questions are worded in concrete rather than abstract terms. Such items are particularly worthwhile if you wish to measure ability of the student to apply concepts to concrete situations.
9. Rules for developing the suggested solutions.
   a. The suggested wrong answers should represent errors commonly made by the students being tested, not popular misconceptions among the public at large.
   b. The right answer should be unquestionably right, checked by two or three independent experts.
   c. The suggested answers should be as brief as possible.
   d. The position of the right answers should be scattered.
   e. Numerical answers should be placed in numerical order.
   f. Even wrong alternatives should not contain words unfamiliar to students.
   g. The right answer should not be given away by irrelevant clues. A few examples of commonly occurring irrelevant clues are:
      1) alternatives that include absolute terms such as "always" and "never" are rarely right answers, 2) alternatives that are longer and more elaborate than the others are frequently right answers, and 3) if the lead of the item is an incomplete statement, then alternatives that do not complete it grammatically are obviously wrong.*

My colleagues and I have sometimes found it helpful to have students pre-test newly constructed tests. In this procedure, each section of the course selects a delegate to take the test a week before the rest of the class. After the pre-test, an instructor corrects each delegate's

---

* Many of the foregoing rules are derived directly or indirectly from notes taken in the "Test Construction" class of Dr. R. M. W. Travers. For a more detailed exposition, see his book, *How to make achievement tests* (New York: Odyssey Press, 1950).

paper with the delegate while the delegate points out ambiguous or unfair items and suggests changes. The test score of the delegate is not directly comparable to that of the students taking the revised test, but since different delegates are selected for each test, the instructor can easily devise a system for determining the pre-tester's grade. The students appreciate this expression of trust in them and to our knowledge have not violated that trust.

Usually the pre-testers will be most apt to criticize the more difficult items, but the instructor can also observe which items none of the pre-testers fail, and thus exercise control over the difficulty and discrimination ability of his test. By getting the pre-testers to think out loud about items, you can see if an item evokes the type of response you want.

Even if you don't pre-test the item on students, it is worthwhile to have someone take the test before it is in its final form. If you can persuade a skilled test-taker who doesn't know the subject-matter to take the test, you will probably be surprised at how many she gets right simply from cues you've provided in the questions.

How Many Questions Should I Use?

Obviously the number of questions depends upon the type and difficulty of question. I prefer to give tests without a time limit, but the constraints of class scheduling usually require that you clear the classroom so that the next class can begin. Thus, you must plan the length of the exam so that even the slowest students have time to finish before the end of the period. As a rule of thumb I allow about a minute per item for multiple-choice or fill-in-the-blank items, two minutes per short-answer question requiring more than a sentence answer, ten or fifteen minutes for a limited essay question and a half-hour for a broader question requiring more than a page or two to answer.

Instructions to the Students

The test instructions should indicate whether or not students are to guess, what the time limit is, and any other directions that define the nature of the expected responses. Emphasizing in the multiple-choice test introduction that the students should choose the *best* answer may help prevent lengthy discussion with the student who can dream up a remote instance in which the correct alternative might be wrong. Particularly in the case of multiple-choice examinations, I have found that a good morale builder is spending fifteen minutes or so before the first examination in telling the student how to take a quiz of this sort.

Some of the points which I make in such a lecture follow. The student taking a multiple-choice examination is essentially in the same position as a poker player. The object is to get into a position where you are betting on a sure thing. If this is impossible, at least make your bet on the choice where the odds are in your favor. In poker, you are obviously in the strongest position if you know exactly what the opponent has; and in the examination situation, you are also in the strongest position if you know the material. There is no substitute for study. At the same time, it is unlikely you will be absolutely certain of all the right answers. It is in these cases that certain techniques may help.

What I recommend to the student is this: Go through the examination a first time and answer all of the items of which you are fairly certain. In addition to getting a certain amount of the examination done without wasting too much time on single, difficult items, it is frequently true that having gone through the complete test once in this way will suggest the answers to questions that might have been difficult had they been answered in serial order. When you have gone through the test once in this fashion, go through it again and answer any questions that are now obvious. There will still usually remain a few questions that have been left unanswered. It is in connection with these that certain tricks may be useful. First of all, if the item is multiple choice, do not simply guess at this stage of the game. See whether it is not possible to eliminate some of the choices as incorrect. In a four-choice, multiple-choice item, the probabilities of getting the answer right by pure guesswork are one in four; if you can eliminate two of them, your chances are fifty-fifty. So take advantage of the mathematics of the situation.

Having eliminated some of the answers, there are still better ways of answering the questions than pure guesswork. One of these is to choose the answer that you first thought was right. A second is to choose one of the middle alternatives. If you have no notion at all as to the right answer, and if the "b" or "2" choice is one of the possibilities, use it. There are two reasons for this advice: 1) it gives you a rule of thumb by which you can answer all highly doubtful items, thus eliminating anxiety-building, trial-and-error behavior, and 2) it takes into account frequent instructor behavior in constructing items. When instructors set out to make up a multiple-choice item, they usually have, 1) a bit of information for which they want to test, 2) a notion as to what is the right answer, and 3) one or more "seductive" alternatives. The tendency is, in listing choices, to make the first choice one of the seductive alternatives, the second choice the right answer, and the remaining choices anything that they can think of. Most instructors have a feeling that the right answer sticks out if it is first or last. Hence the correct answer on instructor-made tests tends to be in the middle.

Once the examination has been answered completely, it is a good idea to go through the whole thing again to check your choices on the various items to make sure that they are. the ones you still regard as correct and to make sure that you have made no clerical errors in recording them on the separate answer sheets. In this connection, it is worthwhile pointing out the common misconception that, when you change your answers, you usually change from right answers to wrong ones. As a matter of fact, Kimble has made a check of this. In a group of about one hundred papers, he discovered that two-thirds of the changes made resulted in the selection of a correct choice rather than a wrong one. Similarly, Johnston (1975) found that over several quizzes 71 of 102 students made more changes from wrong to right as compared to 31 from right to wrong.

In taking a multiple-choice examination, the student has a right to know whether there is a penalty for guessing. For the typical classroom examination, there is no point in a correction for guessing.

Some will perhaps want to question whether it is wise to give away the secret of examination construction in the way in which this discussion obviously does. The answer to this question depends upon your purposes in giving the examination. If you want to test for "test taking" ability, you will not want to give the students these hints. If you are interested in eliminating this as a source of variaion, an orientation lecture of the kind that we have described is not ill advised. At any rate, it seems to have the effect of giving the students the notion that you are not out to "out-smart" them, but that you are interested in helping them get as high a mark as their information warrants. In this connection, it is a good idea to point out to the class that the instructor is not out to trick the student through the use of various kinds of sophistry in the examination, that ordinarily the answer that they think is the right one will be the right one, and that any attempt to read more into a particular answer than initially appeared to be there is a mistake.

Research by McKeachie, Pollie, and Speisman (1955) and by Smith and Rockett (1958) has demonstrated that the instruction "Feel free to write comments" and blank space by each question for comments results in higher scores, especially for anxious students.

Administering the Test

Handing out a test should be a simple matter. Usually it is, but in large classes, simple administrative matters can become disasters. It is hard to imagine how angry and upset students can become while waiting only ten minutes for the proctors to finish distributing the test forms. And if this doesn't move you, imagine your feelings when you find that you don't have enough tests for all of the students. (It has happened to me twice—deserving a place among my worst moments in teaching!)

How can you avoid such problems?

1. If you are having tests mimeographed, ask for at least 10 percent extra—more if the test is administered in several rooms. (Someone always walks off with too many.) This gives you insurance against miscounting and against omitted or blank pages on some copies.
2. Unless there is some compelling reason to distribute the tests later, have your proctors pass out the tests as students come in the room. This protects students from the mounting waves of panic while they wait for the test to be distributed.
3. Minimize interruptions. Tell students before the exam that you will write announcements, instructions, or corrections on the blackboard. Some exam periods are less a measure of achievement than a test of the students' ability to work despite the instructor's interruptions.

Cheating

In this section, I discuss how to handle cheating. It is never pleasant nor easy. To coin a phrase, "An ounce of prevention is worth a pound of cure."

It may be hard for you to believe that your students would ever cheat—"Maybe other students cheat, but not mine!" Unfortunately studies of cheating behavior invariably find that a significant percentage of students report that they have cheated. I believe that most students would rather not cheat, but the pressures for good grades are intense enough that many students feel that they, too, must cheat if they believe that other students are cheating. In my experience the most common excuse given by a student caught cheating is that other students were cheating and that the teacher didn't seem to care, or at least not enough to do anything to prevent or stop cheating. Many students thus feel less stress when an examination is well managed and well proctored.

Preventing Cheating

"O.K., so we want to prevent cheating. What can we do?"

An obvious first answer is to reduce the pressure. While you can't affect the general academic atmosphere putting heavy emphasis on grades, you can influence the pressure in your own course, for example, by providing a number of opportunities for students to demonstrate achievement of course goals rather than relying upon a single examination.

A second answer is to develop group norms supporting honesty. I frequently give my classes a chance to vote on whether or not we will conduct the tests on the honor system. I announce that we will not use the honor system unless the vote is unanimous, since it will not work unless everyone feels committed to it. If the vote is unanimous, I remind the students of it on the day of the exam and ask whether they still wish to have the test under the honor system. While I haven't collected data on the success of this approach, I've never had a complaint about it. Nevertheless, only a minority of classes vote for the honor system.

If the honor system does not work, what else can be done?

One principle is to preserve each student's sense that he or she is an individual with a personal relationship both with the instructor and with other students. Students are not as likely to cheat in situations in which they are known as in situations in which they are anonymous members of a crowd. Thus, if a large course has regular meetings in small discussion or laboratory sections, there is likely to be less cheating if the test is administered in these groups than if the test is administered *en masse*.

But even in small groups cheating will occur if the instructor seems disinterested and unconcerned. Typical graduate student teaching assistants are likely to feel that any show of active proctoring will indicate that they do not trust the students. There is certainly a danger that the teacher will appear to be so poised to spring at a miscreant that the atmosphere becomes tense, but it is possible to convey a sense of alert helpfulness while strolling down the aisles or watching for questions.

The most common form of cheating is copying from another student's paper. To reduce this I usually ask to have a large enough exam room to enable students to sit in alternate seats. I write on the board before students arrive, "Take alternate seats." Some students fail to see the sign, so in large exams you not only need two proctors at each door passing out exams, but at least one more to supervise seating.

In the event that you can't get rooms large enough to permit alternate seating, you may want to use an alternate form of the test. Since I prefer to have items on a test follow the same order as the order in which the material has been discussed in the course, I don't usually scramble the order of items as much as scrambling the order of alternatives of multiple-choice questions, and I typically write separate sets of essay questions for the two tests. Since it is difficult to make two tests equally difficult, you probably will want to tabulate separate distributions of scores on each form of the test.

All this advice will not eliminate cheating. It is a sad commentary on our educational system that it occurs, but recognizing and preventing problems is likely to be less unpleasant than ignoring it.

Handling Cheating

Despite preventative measures, almost every instructor must at some time or other face the problem of what to do about a student who is cheating. For example, as you are administering an examination you note that a student's eyes are on his neighbor's rather than on his own paper. Typically you do nothing at this time, for you don't want to embarrass an innocent student. But when the eyes again stray, you are faced with a decision about what to do.

Most colleges have rules about the procedures to be followed in case of cheating. Yet instructors are often reluctant to begin the procedures. The reasons for instructor reluctance vary. Sometimes it is simply uncertainty about whether or not cheating really occurred. Students' eyes do wander without cheating. Answers may be similar simply because two students have studied together. "If the student denies the charge, what evidence do I have to support my accusation?"

Again, unwillingness to invoke the regulations concerning cheating may be based upon distrust of the justice of the eventual disposition of the case. Cheating is common in colleges; few teachers have not been guilty themselves at some stage in their academic careers. Thus, most of us are understandably reluctant to subject the unfortunate one who gets caught to the drastic possible punishments that more skillful cheaters avoid. Such conflicts as these make the problem of handling a cheater one of the most disturbing of those a new teacher faces.

Unfortunately I've never been completely satisfied that I handle the problem adequately; so my "advice" should, like the rest of the advice in this book, be regarded simply as some ideas for your consideration rather than as dicta to be accepted verbatim.

First, let me support the value of following college procedures. Even though it may not be long since you were taking examinations yourself, your role as a teacher requires that you represent established authority rather than the schoolboy code that punishes "tattlers." Moreover, your memories of student days may help you recall your own feelings when you saw someone cheating and the instructor took no action.

Further, student or faculty committees dealing with cheating are not as arbitrary and impersonal as you might expect. Typically, they attempt to get at the cause of the cheating and to help students solve their underlying problems. Being apprehended for cheating may, therefore, actually be of real long-term value to the students.

There still remain cases where the evidence is weak and you're not even quite sure whether or not cheating actually occurred. Even here I advise against such individual action as reducing a grade. If you're wrong, the solution is unjust. If you're right, you've failed to give the student feedback which is likely to change his behavior. In such cases I advise calling the chairman of the committee handling cheating cases, the student's counselor, or some other experienced faculty member. It's surprising to find how often your suspicions fit in with other evidence about the student's behavior. Even when they don't, advice from someone who has additional information about the student will frequently be helpful.

Finally, let's return to the case of the straying eyes. Here you haven't time for a phone call to get advice; your decision has to be made now. Rather than arousing the whole class by snatching away the student's paper with a loud denunciation, I simply ask him unobtrusively if he would mind moving to a seat where he'll be less crowded. If he says he's not crowded, I simply whisper that I'd prefer that he move. So far no one's refused.

Scoring the Test

Once the test has been constructed and administered, the next problem is scoring it. One of the main advantages of the multiple-choice examination is that scoring can be extremely rapid even without the benefit of electric scoring equipment. Although fairly efficient scoring can be achieved without the use of separate answer sheets, such answer sheets are very useful. They can be obtained through the IBM company at about one cent each, or they can be mimeographed or lithoprinted. Unless you plan to use several thousand answer sheets a year, the IBM sheets are quite satisfactory and not too expensive. The advantage of the separate answer sheet is that it can be scored simply by placing a stencil, cut from one of the answer sheets, over the student's paper. In the stencil, you will punch holes in the space where the correct answers would be. All empty spaces on the student sheet are counted as wrong answers. The stencil, marked with the correct answers, can be punched out easily. Several potential stencils (five or six) can be stapled together and punched out simultaneously. Such a stencil can also be used for the correction of true-false examinations if, on the separate answer sheets, you instruct the student to use the "a" choice for true and the "b" choice for false.

If you mimeograph your own answer sheet, my experience indicates that an answer sheet set up in the form

1. a   b   c   d   e
2. a   b   c   d   e

is easier for students to follow and instructors to correct than answer sheets of the forms

    1. (b)
    2. (d)

or

<pre>
      a   b   c   d   e
   1. ( ) ( ) ( ) ( ) ( )
   2. ( ) ( ) ( ) ( ) ( ).
</pre>

In addition, allowing space on the answer sheet for student comments seems to reduce anxiety and help student performance (McKeachie, Pollie, and Speisman, 1955).

A method of using multiple-choice items has been developed by Coombs, Milholland, and Womer (1955). In this method the students are asked to cross out the wrong alternative rather than the right one, but are allowed to cross out as few or as many alternatives as they wish. Thus, if they know that two alternatives are incorrect and cannot decide between the other two alternatives (in a four-alternative item), they can indicate that they have some knowledge by crossing out the two alternatives they know to be wrong.

The test is scored by crediting the students with one point for each wrong alternative they have crossed out and subtracting three points for each correct alternative crossed out. This means that guessing is heavily penalized. The result is that personality variables related to risk-taking may influence scores. Since the score on each item can vary from +3 to −3, the range of scores is increased when this method is used, and students can be more reliably differentiated from one another.

Grading Essay Questions

I recommend that you use essay questions because of their powerful effect upon the way students study, but there is a drawback. Instructors don't grade essay tests very reliably.

One of the problems is that standards vary. First papers are graded differently than later papers; a paper graded immediately after several poor papers is graded differently from one graded after several good papers.

There are four procedures you can initiate to improve your evaluation of essay examinations—but they entail work. The first is to read all or several of the examinations in a preliminary fashion to establish some notion of the general level of performance. The second is to write out and refer to a list of points that should be covered in the answer to each question, remembering that this will probably check only the objective recall of information and that you will probably wish to include evaluation of other objectives. The third is to write or choose from your first reading models of A, B, C, and D papers to which you can refer to refresh your memory of the standards by which you are grading. This technique is particularly useful if an assistant is helping to grade or if grading is carried out over a period of time. The fourth procedure is to read essay exams without knowledge of the name of the writer.

Assigning a Test Grade

Whatever scoring method is used, there is often a question as to whether some more refined score should not be calculated. In addition to scores that are corrected for guessing, the choices include percentile ranks, standard scores, or some combination of these, such as scores corrected for guessing and then put into standard scores. In general, it seems to me that, except for the statistical information that is perhaps imparted by these arithmetic maneuvers, the use of special scores is of little value, except in the case of percentiles. There are two reasons for this: 1) nothing in the way of validity is gained, and 2) students have difficulty interpreting refined scores. In the case of corrections for guessing, to take one case, the correlation between corrected and uncorrected scores is usually in the very high nineties, so high that the time required to compute the corrected scores is exorbitant. The correction for guessing is only useful in the case where the university requires the assignment of grades on a percentage basis, that is, "A" for 90 percent correct, and so on. In this instance, if your examinations have a tendency to be too easy, the use of a correction for guessing may result in the assignment of a reasonable number of high marks.

Again, the chief argument against the use of standard scores is that you gain very little by going through a rather tedious arithmetic manipulation (even if you force an assistant to do it). If the standard deviations of the scores obtained on all of the tests that you give during a course are the same, the simple addition of all of the test scores for each student is the exact arithmetic equivalent of adding or averaging z-scores. I know of at least one case in which average z-scores were obtained for a series of four examinations in elementary psychology. When these z-scores were correlated with total raw scores, the correlation was .998 and all that was gained was a certain amount of calculating machine facility on the part of an assistant.

If the standard deviations are radically different from test to test, this arithmetic equivalence I have been discussing does not hold. This leads to the question of what is the main source of such variations in examination scores. By far the largest source of such variation is in different length examinations, long examinations tending to produce larger standard deviations than short ones. When you give a long examination, it is almost always true that you consider the materials covered by the long examination more important than those covered by the short one. In this event, you would probably want to weigh the long examination more heavily in the computation of a final mark than the short one. Simply adding test scores will do exactly this. The proportional weight will vary as the ratio of the standard deviations. The use of standard scores will weigh each examination equally unless you introduce some further arithmetic manipulation, which (if you do it) will involve a number of statistical assumptions, and, in the end, give you a result that is probably no more satisfactory than a cumulative total score. Add to all of this the fact that each additional arithmetic step presents one more opportunity for arithmetic and clerical error, and it becomes fairly obvious that the use of the various corrections and scalings has little to recommend it.

Grading based upon relative achievement in a given group may encourage an undesirably high degree of competition. Despite the absence of absolute standards in any very objective sense, I believe that attempts to approach grading on an absolute basis are worthwhile in terms of reduction of competitiveness and grade-centered study. When students perceive the situation as one in which a limited number of good grades are possible, the cards are stacked against cooperation, because helping classmates may lower one's own grade.

The problem of grading "on the curve" seems to arouse the most heated discussion around standards for assigning failing grades. Logically, it would seem that an instructor should be able to designate some minimum essentials, mastery of which would be necessary for a passing grade. At the University of Michigan an attempt was made to divide the psychology course examination into "mastery" and "proficiency" sections. The "mastery" section included items testing attainment of minimum essentials of the course and was designed to differentiate between passing and failing students. The "proficiency" section was designed to demonstrate higher degrees of achievement for discriminating between A, B, C, and D students. Unfortunately it is difficult to select items to test only minimum essentials, and some students who failed the "mastery" section excelled on the "proficiency" items. However, with a precise statement of course objectives and better pre-tested measures of their attainment, some more nearly absolute standards for grading may be devised. Keller Plan courses, programmed courses, and contract courses typically specify mastery of certain materials. As I shall show in the next chapter, so-called mastery grading has some serious pitfalls, but at least some attempt to get away from strict "grading on the curve" is likely to be helpful for class morale.

Returning Test Papers

Returning test papers to students promptly is much appreciated by the students and conforms to traditional learning principles. However, if you don't plan to discuss the papers, don't hand them back at the beginning of the hour, or you risk loss of attention the rest of the hour.

Students do like to have their examinations back. In the case of multiple-choice examinations, developed through a considerable amount of hard work, you will not want to let them have them, because you want to use the items another year. But you can do this: Return separate answer sheets so that your marking and arithmetic can be checked. Allow the students to have copies of the examination while you go through the test. If you do these things, certain questions arise. Does such a procedure destroy the validity of the item in future tests? Does the student profit from such experience? These are experimental questions to which we have only partial answers, but evidence suggests that validity is not lost and that students do learn from their corrected papers (McClusky, 1934). Although you may not wish to spend class time quibbling over some individual items, you should make known your willingness to discuss the test individually with students who have further questions.

If some ambiguities have gotten through the screening process, and an item is really capable of two equally correct interpretations, admit it and change scores. But remember that you can't escape aggression simply by changing scores, because every time you admit a new right answer the students who originally had the question right are likely to feel injured.

On questions that many students missed, I recommend this sort of procedure: When you read a particular question, do not merely read the stem of the question or answer the question with the correct choice. Instead, read the stem and each of the choices. For each of the incorrect choices give your reasons for regarding it as incorrect. This procedure gives you the "jump" on the chronic criticizer. It is more difficult to maintain that a given choice is right under these circumstances than it would be if you had said nothing about the various alternatives and students could argue that the correct alternative was not completely correct. But there will be cases in which a legitimate argument arises. In such cases, give the student the benefit of the doubt. Such items should either be eliminated or revised in future revisions of the examination.

Quibbling can also be reduced by a discussion of the methods used in test construction. This is helpful in convincing students of your desire to make the tests fair. Accepting students' suggestions for better wording of items also reduces their aggressiveness. You can prevent some aggression from being directed against yourself if you have items that are discussed and explained by the students who got them right. However, you should not call upon the same student to explain every such question or you may simply be substituting another scapegoat for yourself.

One of the techniques for returning tests that seems to reduce much aggression was, I believe, first used in the classes of Dr. N. R. F. Maier. Instructors using this technique break the class into small groups of five to eight students for discussion of the test. Each group discusses the test for part of the class period. When they have finished, unresolved questions are referred to the instructor as the expert. This method seems to permit dissipation of the aggressions aroused and limit arguments to points where there are several aggrieved students.

Make-up tests can involve a good deal of extra work for the instructor. If you devise a new test, you have no norms with which to compare grades on the make-up. If you use the same exam that the students have missed, you cannot tell how much the student has learned of the test from students who took it at the scheduled time. Hence, I don't usually give make-ups except for the final exam, and I simply use only marks from the tests the student did take to determine the grade, counting the missed test neither for or against the student. Most students are happy not to have to make up a test, and those who desire to may take the test for practice.

While these suggestions may save the instructor some bitter moments, they cannot substitute for the time (and it takes lots) devoted to the construction of good tests.

SUPPLEMENTARY READING

So far as I know there is still nothing better on constructing classroom achievement tests than R. M. W. Travers, *How to make achievement tests* (New York: Odyssey Press, 1950).

17

The A B C's of Assigning Grades

Grading is currently in the news.* Grade inflation, contract grading, mastery grading—all of these stimulate heated discussion and cries of dismay. My own ideas of grading have become somewhat clearer as I have talked to my teaching assistants about grading policies and thought through why some of the new grading systems make me uneasy.

First let us agree that grades are fundamentally a method of communication. Through the grade a professor is presumably trying to communicate something to someone else. The question then becomes, "What does the professor intend to communicate to whom?"

When one puts grading into this context, three things become apparent:

---

* The following section is largely derived from my article in the *AAUP Bulletin*, 1976, *62*, 320–322.

1. What professors communicate by a grade depends upon the meaning of the grade to the person reading it—the effect that it has on that person.
2. Evaluation is a great deal more than giving a grade. In teaching, the major part of evaluation should be in the form of comments on papers, responses to student statements, conversations, and other means of helping students understand where they are and how to do better. A professor giving a grade is communicating to several groups—the student, professors teaching advanced courses, graduate or professional school admissions committees, prospective employers, and so on.
3. Professors cannot change the meaning of grades unilaterally. While the grade may have a new meaning for the professor, those reading the grade will interpret it in terms of the meanings they have traditionally assigned to grades, unless the professor specifically interprets for them the new meaning he or she wishes to assign to a grade. Even if he asserts, "The grade means what I mean it to mean," the readers' interpretations will be colored by their previous experiences with grades, and they are likely to be disturbed, or to feel that they are being misled, when the professor uses grades in new ways. This explains the strong emotional reaction to "grade inflation," "all A" grading, or other practices deviating from the traditional meaning.

What is that traditional meaning? What are grades used for? I suggest that the person reading a grade typically wants information with respect to some decision involving a judgment about the students' *future* performance. Mastery systems of grading, pass-fail grading, and other alternative systems are resisted because they are not efficient conveyors of the information useful in predicting future performance.

What Do Students, Professors, and Employers Want from Grades?

Students want to be able to use grades to assist them in decisions such as the following:

1. Will I do well if I take additional courses in this field?
2. Should I major in this field? Does it represent a potential career in which I'm likely to be successful?

3. Do I have the skills and ability necessary to work independently in this field—learning more, solving problems, able to evaluate my own work?
4. What kind of person am I?

Professors advising the student or determining admissions expect the grade to tell them:

1. Does this student have the motivation, skills, knowledge, and ability needed to do well in advanced courses (insofar as the type of problems dealt with in the earlier course are relevant to the demands of the advanced courses or program)?
2. What kind of person is this? What does the pattern of grades tell us about this student's ability and work habits?

Similarly, prospective *employers* want to use grades to assist in decisions about whether or not the student will do well in their jobs.

1. How well will the student be able to solve problems on jobs related to the area of his or her coursework?
2. Does the overall pattern of grades indicate that this is the sort of person who will do well in our organization?

From this analysis it seems evident that grades are used not just as a historical record of what has happened, but also as information about what the student can do in situations outside the class for which the grade was awarded. For the users the grade is not so much historical as potentially predictive.

Do Grades Provide Information Useful for Decision Making?

One of the arguments against conventional grading is that grades are invalid; that is, they do not provide useful information for the major purposes for which they are usually used.

Most critics would grant that grades are useful for decisions about whether a student is likely to be able to succeed in an advanced course or in a further academic experience such as graduate or professional school, but they do not believe that they provide useful information for students or for potential employers.

Teachers assume that grades have some informational and motivational value for students. Critics argue that punishment and failure are not likely to be conducive to achieving the goal of continued enjoyment of learning, and that the threat of low grades is a crutch used to help inadequate teachers. I think that there is much truth in this argument. Yet uniformly positive feedback is not necessarily the most effective method of motivating all students. In fact there is much evidence that such a pattern of reinforcement sometimes diminishes motivation. Psychological research has demonstrated that human beings seek information about their competence and then will choose activities that give information upon which to build a sense of competence and self-esteem. While the research on grading is not conclusive, it does suggest that conventional grading is conducive to achievement.

What about information for employers? Probably most personnel psychologists would agree that the best predictor of success on a job is successful performance on a similar job. For a young person entering the job market, there is often no record of previous performance on comparable jobs. The employer must then make a decision on the basis of other information such as interviews, letters of recommendation, biographical data, family background, and test scores. Each such source is only partially adequate. Insofar as the new job involves at least some expenditure for training, it seems likely that grades, representing the result of skills applied in study, learning, and problem solving, will add some information, albeit incomplete, that will be useful for making the decision.

Because grades are commonly used in combination with other variables, however, one should not expect them to correlate with success for those selected. This is not simply a problem that only the top students were selected; it is a simple mathematical truism that when one uses several selection criteria, each of which has some validity, one should expect low positive, zero, or even negative correlations between any one selection variable and the ultimate criteria of performance. This occurs because one will select some people low in other important attributes because they have high grades. Thus the common criticism that grades don't predict later performances is largely invalid since most of the studies cited have been carried out in situations where grades have already been used in selection.

Special Grading Methods: Contract Grading, Behavioral Objectives, Mastery, and Optional or Repeated Tests

With respect to the contract system of grading, it seems to me that the problem basically is that students often gain points, not for achievement, but rather for carrying out those activities, such as writing papers or reading books, that *should* be conducive to achievement. Thus, rather than measuring learning, you assess whether the student has engaged in activities that are the means to learning. I suspect that this means that in many cases there is a considerable gap between the points the student has earned and the points a similar student would earn if the student's achievement in the course were assessed.

Assigning grades on the basis of the quantity of work done rather than the degree of competence achieved is not a problem restricted to contract grading. Many instructors subtract points for absences, tardiness, or other things they dislike. In psychology classes, points are sometimes added for participation in research studies, a very dubious practice unless it involves some assessment of what the students learned from research participation.

The real core of the problem may be in the use of the word "mastery." The mastery concept essentially emphasizes reaching a particular finish line. In fact, however, most educational purposes in higher education have no end point, but are extensive in breadth and depth of their possibilities. An achievement examination in a course is ordinarily designed to *sample* a domain of problems, concepts, or generalizations that the students can be expected to solve or to sample concepts the students will be able to generalize to a larger domain. The more limited your definition of those achievements that the students should "master," the less valid a test or grade is in terms of its ability to assess the students with respect to other problems, other concepts, or other generalizations in the total domain. For example, suppose I give my students a list of five problems at the beginning of the semester and say, "My objectives are that you should be able to solve these five problems." In this situation most students will master the problems but differ substantially in their ability to solve other problems within the same general categories. Five problems that have *not* been specifically studied during the course would be more likely to be a reasonable sample of future problems students might encounter than five problems the students have already memorized, and a larger sample of problems from the domain would be likely to be even better. Similarly, giving students the option of choosing among several test questions or problems on a test means that one is not getting an unbiased sample of what the students can do.

Letting students turn in book reports over and over again until they do them correctly is a fine teaching technique, but not a good assessment device. The student who writes an acceptable book report after ten trials is probably less able to write a new report acceptably than the student who does it right in the first place. Thus the grade on such a rewritten paper is *not* likely to be a valid predictor.

Posting Grades

Now let us turn to the question of telling the students what their marks are. Ordinarily you will be returning grades on student papers in class, but in very large classes you may wish to post scores rather than returning papers individually. Here, my first point is that the students' marks are as much their private property as their bank accounts, just as it is their right to keep their credit rating a secret if they want to. This means that if marks are posted, they should be reported anonymously. In posting grade lists, post the individual's score by a number rather than by initials. If your students do not have student numbers, the most convenient way to assign numbers is in the same order as the names appear on your class roll.

In posting grades, you will save yourself a considerable amount of time if, in addition to the score on a particular quiz, you also give the students some way of evaluating their work in the course to date. If you use a system involving a cumulative total of test scores, this is rather simple. Your grade list will include these columns: 1) the student's number, 2) the score on the examination taken most recently, and 3) the cumulative total of this score plus the scores on all examinations taken previously. A fourth column could include a letter grade. This, however, takes time and is unnecessary. You can accomplish the same thing by appending to the grade list a schedule that tells the students how to interpret their marks either in terms of percentiles or in terms of letter grades.

In giving these letter grades, two general approaches are sometimes advocated. One of these is to make these grades lower than those one intends to give at the end of the course. This should reduce the number of complaints about final grades. The other approach is to use these grades to motivate students to work harder. This means that you use many plus and minus grades. This indicates to the students that the grade may be shifted either way and presumably reduces the chance that they'll coast. You may also ask students to hand in their own estimates of their grades as an aid to knowing how to motivate them, and also in order to develop their abilities for self-evaluation. Atkinson's theory of motivation suggests that highest motivation to achieve occurs when the probability of success is moderate. This probably explains the finding of Means and Means (1971) that low grade-point-average students achieved more when told that they had done well on an aptitude test while, high grade-point-average students did better when told that they had done poorly.

Whatever your grading strategy, being more generous in assigning grades to tests and papers than in the final distribution of grades guarantees visits from aggrieved students. One way in which you get yourself into this position is by providing opportunities for students to omit questions on an exam, to throw out the lowest test grade, or to submit extra work for a higher grade. Any of these procedures can have some educational justification, but if you expect to finish the course with grades representative of those for similar courses at your college, you need to devise a system of grading in which the constituents of the total grade will come out at an appropriate level.

Professors sometimes devise systems of grading that allow students to drop out any test scores below A and are then surprised that their grade distribution is not comparable to that of other courses. And even psychology professors are disconcerted to find that their colleagues are not convinced that the students' level of achievement has improved so greatly that they all deserve A's.

In keeping students informed as to where they stand, you probably are also aiding them to control much of the anxiety they feel when the grading system is indefinite and unstructured. Sometimes it may seem easier to fight off grade-conscious students by being very indefinite about grades, but I feel that student morale is better when the students know the situation with which they must cope.

Because grades represent to many students a fearsome, mysterious dragon, anxiety can sometimes be reduced by encouraging the students to participate in planning the methods by which grades will be assigned. Students usually can recognize the need of the instructor to conform to college policy in grade distribution, but the dragon seems less threatening if they have helped determine the system by which they are devoured (or rewarded).

Some instructors have gone as far as to let students determine their own grades or to have groups of students grade one another. I like the idea that students should develop the capacity for self-evaluation, but I recognize that many students resist this procedure, either through modesty or fear that they'll underrate themselves. If you use it, I'd suggest thorough discussion of the plan with students and an agreed-upon, well-defined set of criteria that all students should use. Even if student participation is not possible, anxiety seems to be reduced if you explain the system you use and give your reasons for using this system.

Grading on the Curve

One of the persisting controversies in college teaching is whether to grade "on the curve" or in terms of an absolute standard. In fact, these two positions are probably not as far apart as the argument would indicate. Even teachers who grade on the curve are influenced in setting their cutoff points between grades in terms of their feelings about whether this was a good or poor class. And similarly, teachers who proclaim they do not grade on the curve set their standards in terms of what previous experience leads them to regard as reasonable accomplishment in the course. In essence, they grade on a curve, but set the curve on the basis of all the students they have taught, rather than the particular class taught in a given semester.

The use of an absolute standard requires that teachers formulate their major and minor objectives and then devise some means of telling when a student has achieved them. Travers (1950) has proposed one set of absolute standards:

—A   All major and minor goals achieved.

—B   All major goals achieved; some minor ones not.

—C   All major goals achieved; many minor ones not.

—D   A few major goals achieved, but student is not prepared for advanced work.

—E   None of the major goals achieved.

Even though instructors concede that grades are somewhat relative, strict grading on the curve seems to me likely to be damaging to morale and learning. Not only does it encourage a competitive situation that reduces the chance for students to learn from other students, but it also seems to encourage cheating.

What Do You Do With the Student Who Wants His Grade Changed?

If students are worried about their grades in connection with their admission to a specialized school or because they are on probation, you may offer to write a letter to their advisor or other authorities describing their work in detail and pointing out any extenuating circumstances that may have influenced the grade. This may serve to cushion your refusal to change the grade.

In addition, of course, you may try to explain to the students the rationale of grades. Usually this doesn't seem to do much good. Both students and faculty sometimes confuse two possible criteria upon which grades may be based. One of these is the relative amount of *progress* the student has made in achieving the goals of the course; the other is achievement of the goals of the course at the end of the course (usually relative to the achievement of other students). In most classes, research has demonstrated a relatively low correlation between these two criteria. If you were to mark solely on progress, the students who came into the course with the least background might still be the poorest students in the class at the end of the course and get an A for their progress. Most employers, registrars, and professors interpret a grade in terms of achievement of course goals; hence, professors who grade solely on the students' progress may send the students into advanced courses or jobs for which they lack the requisite skills and knowledge. However, most instructors find it difficult to assign a failing grade to students who have made much progress in the course, even though they remain the poorest students in the class. My own solution is to give all but failing grades in terms of final class standing. I usually give failing grades only to those students who not only demonstrate low achievement, but have also made little progress.

No matter how you grade, some student will be unhappy. The student who has just missed Phi Beta Kappa may feel just as bad as the student who has been asked to leave school. Be sympathetic, but beware! If you begin changing grades, the jungle drums of the campus will soon spread the word.

Don't finish reading this chapter with your own anxiety aroused by the dangers of grading. It is proper that good teachers should be humble as they see how great is the power they have over the happiness of their students by printing a simple A, B, C, or D. Nevertheless, one of the real satisfactions of teaching is giving a good grade to an ordinarily average student who has come to life in your course.

How to Lose Friends and Alienate Students*

1. Never give students any idea of what their grades are before the final examination. The shock of seeing an E as the final grade will so stun them that they'll be incapable of protest. Or better yet tell them they had A's all the way through the course and got an A on the final, but you have too many A's, so you're giving them B's.

2. Tell students that you really think they deserved a higher mark, but that you had to conform to department grading policies and hence had to grade them lower.

3. Tell students that their grades on the final exam were higher than their final grades in the course. (Of course they'll understand that the final examination is only one part of the total evaluation.)

4. Even though your school doesn't record pluses, tell a student that his grade was D+, C+, or B+, rather than a straight D, C, B. He'll gladly accept the fact that the C−, B−, or A− was only three points above him, and will be proud that he did better than anyone else who got a D or C or B.

5. If you make a distribution of total points earned on tests during the term, use large intervals, such as 80 to 90, 90 to 100, etc. When you show a student his position on the distribution, he'll readily

---

* These may look absurd, but they have all happened.

see that the person in the next interval above was really much superior.

6. Tell a student that grades are really very arbitrary, and that you could have split the B's from the C's in many different places, and that grades are so unreliable that you really can't distinguish your top B student from your low A student. He'll appreciate the aesthetic value of your choice of a cutting point.

Relevant Research

Not only do instructors control the pleasantness or unpleasantness of a good many student hours, but because of their power to assign grades they can block or facilitate the achievement of many important goals. The importance of this aspect of the teacher's role is indicated by studies of supervision in industry. In one such study it was discovered that workers were most likely to ask a supervisor for help if the supervisor did not have responsibility for evaluating his subordinates (Ross, 1957). This implies that as long as students are anxious about the grades the instructor will assign, they are likely to avoid exposing their own ignorance.

The students' anxieties about grades are likely to rise if their instructor's procedures make them uncertain about what they must do in order to attain a good grade. For many students, democratic methods seem unorganized and ambiguous. In an ordinary course students know they can pass by reading assignments and studying lecture notes, but in a student-centered class they are in a course where the instructor doesn't lecture, doesn't make assignments, and doesn't even say which student comments are right or wrong. The student simply doesn't know what the instructor is trying to do. Thus, if your teaching or grading procedures differ from those your students are used to, you need to be especially careful to specify the procedures and criteria used in grading.

Some instructors have thought that the grade problem might be licked by using a cooperative system of grading. Deutsch (1949) found no differences in learning between students in groups graded cooperatively and those graded competitively, although the cooperative groups worked together more smoothly. Following up Deutsch's work, Haines and McKeachie (1967) also found no significant achievement advantages for students working cooperatively vs. those working competitively for grades, but did find marked differences in group morale. Haines' work suggests that cooperative grading in the discussion can be successfully combined with individual grading on achievement tests. In an experiment in which a "teamwork" class using group incentives was compared with a lecture class, however, Smith (1955) did not find differences in satisfaction comparable to those of Haines and Deutsch.

Complicating the problem of grading is the probability that low grades produce different effects upon different students. As indicated earlier, Atkinson's theory suggests that low grades should be damaging to the motivation of students with low to moderate expectations, but should increase motivation of those with high expectations. Waterhouse and Child (1953) found that frustration produced deterioration in performance for subjects showing high interference tendencies (or anxiety) as measured by a questionnaire, but produced improved performance for those with low interference tendencies.

Pass-Fail Grading

During the 1960s there was a good deal of push toward the use of "pass-fail" grades rather than the conventional A, B, C, D, E. While the arguments for some such change seem persuasive, there is as yet little evidence that pass-fail grading has positive effects (Lempert, 1972; Bronfenbrenner, 1972).

Considering the importance of grading for both students and instructors, it is regrettable that there is so little empirical research. How do students learn to evaluate themselves? How do they learn to set goals for themselves? Do differing grading procedures facilitate or block such learning? To these questions we have no answers.

Conclusion

To sum up:
1. Grades are communication devices. Instructors cannot unilaterally change their meaning without distorting the communication process.
2. Grading standards differ from college to college and department to department, but there is some shared sense of the meaning of grades.

3. Grades are typically wanted by users to aid in predicting future performance.
4. Grades are not perfect predictors, but probably can contribute as much as the alternatives to grades.
5. Grades are typically based on a sample of achievement in the domain of the course goals. The better the sample the more useful the grade. Limiting or decreasing the sample reduces the usefulness of the grade.

The ultimate criterion with respect to a grading system should be the student's education. Grades are means to the end of education, not ends in themselves. Thus, instructors should be free to experiment with methods of increasing their educational value, particularly helping students learn how to evaluate their own work. But at least be aware of what is involved.

SUPPLEMENTARY READING

For another view, see S. Erickson, Grading $\neq$ evaluation, *Memo to the Faculty*, No. 46, 1971. University of Michigan, Center for Research in Learning and Teaching.

18

Morale, Discipline, Order

The topic of marks and grading leads rather naturally to the topic of morale, discipline, and order. This sequence unfortunately results because, to a very large extent, problems of morale often turn out to be problems of grading. I hope that the use of some of the techniques discussed in the preceding section will make these problems less difficult. At the same time, it must be admitted that the things under consideration here are mainly practical problems of the social psychology of the classroom. For this reason, no single set of recommendations will work for any particular instructor or for any particular classroom situation. What is considered good discipline will vary from instructor to instructor and from one situation to another. What I recommend is based on the philosophy stated in the introduction of this book.

Order in the Classroom

I now turn to some specific considerations. The first of these concerns order in the classroom. A certain degree of quiet and attention seems to be almost essential to the effective running of the educational enterprise. How can this end be achieved? There seem to be two ways to go about it. The first is to insist upon strict attention, set up strict rules on the point, and enforce them. This is not, however, a method I recommend in spite of its rather common adoption. One difficulty with such a method is that order, when it is achieved in this fashion, is dictated to the students. It has a way of putting the instructor into perpetual conflict with the students. The general upshot appears to be that, in such a classroom, the students try, in the numerous ways at their disposal, to beat the game. Whether or not this involves basic needs for revolt against authority, it seems that any interest that they may have initially had in cooperating with the instructor in an attempt to accomplish certain purposes is at least partly supplanted by a feeling of revolt. Furthermore, this policing technique contradicts two basic considerations. As I have already indicated, education, pursued in this manner, is a noncooperative enterprise. Students get to play a much less active part in the classroom than they might. Their enthusiasm is dampened; their tendency to ask questions is reduced; even if they are cooperative, their behavior seems to be directed less toward a real understanding of materials than toward an effort to parrot the wisdom of the instructor. Their learning thus becomes learning by rote, which minimizes understanding and thus defeats part of the purpose of being in the class in the first place. This rather common disciplinary procedure is also one of the major contributors to the perpetuated adolescence of the college student. Instructors who use this method set themselves up as parent figures. By doing this, they may elicit the submissive, unthinking obedience that is characteristic of children's behavior toward their parents. There were probably Freudian reasons that this method worked better with women than with men.

Having to some extent discredited the austere schoolmaster method of handling a class, I turn now to the positive side of my argument. I want to suggest a method that will give you almost as good order in the classroom without sacrificing education itself. To accomplish this, three procedures that parallel the basic considerations just discussed seem to be useful:

1. Give the students the notion that the accomplishment of course objectives is partly their problem.
2. Give the students the notion that they have certain responsibilities and, at the same time, certain rights. More of this later.
3. Give the students the notion that you are willing to entertain reasonable suggestions, objections, and questions in connection with course materials.

Unfortunately these ideas are new to many students and cannot be accomplished in a single day. They are ideas that mean the students will have to learn what may be a new adjustment to the classroom situation. If you use these ideas, you will have to be willing to put up with a certain amount of disorder in the class for a short time. They mean that you sometimes suppress your own aggression and prestige needs and maintain a constant awareness of student needs.

I try consistently to use this method in classes where enrollment may run as high as 500. The class is permitted to operate on an informal basis. Questions and comments from the floor are allowed. (In a class this size, questions from the floor should be repeated for the benefit of the class as a whole before they are answered. Avoid the entirely informal discussion with a single student that smacks of favoritism and, thus, defeats your purposes.) The result of this informality may be an initial unruliness in the class. It does not, however, interfere to a very important extent with a well-planned lecture, and it disappears after five or six lectures. The students placed in an informally run class of this sort seem to be in a situation analogous to that of the boys in the Lewin, Lippitt, and White investigation (1939) who shifted from the autocratic to the democratic group atmosphere, and their behavior is much the same. There is the initial outburst of horseplay (and occasionally aggression) and finally the settling down to a more cooperative, objective, and efficient level of performance.

Whether I am correct in recommending the democratic as opposed to the authoritarian group atmosphere in a *particular* class is a question of fact; it can be decided by experimentation. (For evidence see Chapter 5.)

I want to now consider some typical problems of discipline and order and attempt a few concrete suggestions of methods of handling these problems. Several specific problems follow.

● *Questions and answers in a large class.*   The lecture section is sometimes not regarded as the place for questions and discussions from the floor. Instructors often try to have the questions handled by an assistant in a quiz or discussion section. Potentially this solution is a good one; actually, it often leaves much to be desired for two reasons:

1. Handling a discussion section is sometimes more difficult than giving a lecture. A more reasonable arrangement than the one that is commonly used might be to have the assistants give the lecture and the instructors handle the quiz sections. The difficulties in discussion sections are apt to be that the assistants are not well enough acquainted with the materials the lecturers have covered and have difficulty keeping the discussion going. This can be surmounted if the assistants attend the lectures, participate in lecture planning, and receive help and supervision in planning the discussion, but the discussion-leader role should be one of developing skills in application and problem solving rather than interpreting the lecture. If senior professors have any advantages over teaching assistants, it presumably lies in their knowledge of the field. Thus, to the extent feasible, questions of fact and interpretation are best answered in the lecture itself.
2. Whatever its potential usefulness, the discussion section does not provide for the prompt answering of questions that arise in connection with specific lecture materials.

In most classes (even large ones) I believe that it is possible to answer such questions. If you also believe this and want to try to handle such questions, keep some of the following relevant considerations in mind.

The students must know that such questions are permitted. This is usually not difficult because certain students try to ask questions in almost any class. If you find yourself with a particularly inhibited group, questions written out and passed to the front of the room may handle the situation. In any event it is important to repeat the question before answering it.

One of the problems in large-group question answering and discussion is that a student's question may, in a group where several hands are raised, refer to something that was covered several questions back. By writing all questions on the board before beginning to answer them, you may save time and confusion since some groupings and relationships are apparent. Also such grouping of questions enables you to better apportion your time to those questions that are most significant or troublesome.

Experience in teaching a particular class will give you an understanding of the sort of questions that are apt to be asked on particular topics. Thus, you can be ready for the typical questions. Occasionally, however, you will be asked an atypical question; and it can happen that, for some of them, you will not know the answer. In this event, about the only course open to you is to admit that you do not know, promise to look up the answer and report on it at a later class meeting. If you use this method, *try to find the answer*. I do not recommend the technique of telling students to look up the answer for themselves. The students usually will not take the trouble, and they are apt to discover that this is simply a way of hiding your own ignorance. So far as finding the answers is concerned, remember that your colleagues are a good source, probably more useful than text materials.

Irrelevant questions may sometimes prevent important points from coming out. One way of handling such questions is to write the question on the board to answer later. By writing it down you indicate that you've heard the question and remove the necessity for the student to keep thinking about it. Frequently the question will have been answered by the end of the hour.

A somewhat different situation arises in the case of the student who flatly disagrees with you. Such disagreements are apt to be presented with at least the suggestion that anyone's opinion is as good as anyone else's. In such cases, factual evidence for your point of view would appear to be in order. In cases where the question is a controversial one, you may have to admit the possibility of the student being right. If this is necessary, you can turn the situation to your advantage, by showing the kind of experimental test of the question that is implied. My own discipline, psychology, is in a particulary vulnerable spot in this connection. Students come to the psychology class (and sometimes leave it) with the notion that everyone is a psychologist. A part of the purpose of the elementary course is to demonstrate that this is the case, but that there are still characteristics of rational scientific thought that make some hypotheses more tenable than others. But the task is not an easy one. The reason for this seems to be that since everyone has experiences and observes behavior, students seem to think that everyone in his right senses is qualified as a psychologist. And they demand of the psychologist something they demand of no other scientist—namely, that the psychological account of emotion, perception, or what not, corresponds to their own naive experience of them. This is to be contrasted with the position of the physicist. Physics also presents the students with an account of the nature of a part of the world. The tables and chairs of the physicist are not solid objects, but are actually made up of minute whirling particles. It is a tribute to the maturity of physics that this non-sense view of the world can be made reasonable. And it will presumably sometime come about that psychology will be able to describe its subject matter in this way. For some students, it may be useful to point out this sort of thing. For many it will not. While psychology is particularly vulnerable on this point, I have the notion that instructors in other disciplines face some of the same problems. Certainly in the arts and literature there is something of the "I know what I like" syndrome.

If I were asked how to summarize my ideas about handling questions, disagreement, and discussion in the classroom, I might put my argument this way: There are two stock formulas that seem to go a long way toward handling these problems. One is "This is the evidence." The other is, "You may be right."

● *Interference with the course routine by other "interests."* Here I refer to the students who knit, sleep, read comic books, draw pictures, gossip, or do any of the other things that students are apt to do instead of taking notes. As a general rule, the desirable way in which to eliminate these practices is by making it important to the students to listen to your lectures. This can be accomplished in one of two ways. Probably the most satisfactory from your point of view would be to discover ways of making your presentation interesting enough to command the attention of the student. If you are convinced that you are already doing everything that you can in this connection, it may be worthwhile to look at your examination procedures. If you do not include lecture materials on your examinations, from the point of view of some students there is very little to be gained in listening to you or in making notes on anything you say. This can be true of the most interesting lecturer. Since a large part of the students' motivation is directed toward passing examinations, you can make use of this in getting a class to pay attention and at the same time probably improve your teaching. There is nothing wrong, as I see it, in telling the students that certain materials of the lecture will probably appear on an examination.

Preparing for a Class Period

Disciplinary problems sometimes are a reflection of student dissatisfaction with your teaching. The time college teachers spend in specific preparation for their classes varies from none at all to many hours. Those who are low on the scale usually rationalize that the most effective illustrations and problems are those that arise spontaneously from the class. This may be true, but instructors who make effective use of them are usually those who have thought through their goals and procedures so well that they no longer have to worry about whether or not the class is going to fall apart.

Thus, I do advocate preparation for each class and suggest that the following steps be included:

1. Consideration of specific goals for the day in the light of overall course goals.
2. Review of previous work and especially of the previous day's discussion.
3. Review of the day's assignment.
4. Reading background materials related to the day's lesson.
5. Looking at work ahead and future assignments. As in most matters, students like to know where they stand in relation to assignments. They appreciate a schedule of future assignments passed out early in the semester. In courses without laboratories, students are conventionally expected to do two hours work outside class for each hour in class. In a freshman or sophomore course, the average students seem to be able to master up to a hundred pages a week for a three-hour course. This figure, of course, will vary depending upon the difficulty of the reading, the accessibility of the books, and the amount of written or committee work required.
6. Choosing the teaching methods or techniques to be used in terms of the goals to be attained and remembering that it pays to "throw a change of pace" now and then.
7. Working out an estimated budget of time for each activity in the class period, remembering that it is to be a guide, not a strait-

jacket, and allowing time for a summary and lead-in to the next day's work.

What to Do When You're Not Prepared

Unless you are exceptional, there will be some classes where you arrive without preparation, despite your dedication to good teaching. This can provide an exciting learning experience for you, but it can also be educational for the class. Here are some techniques to use when your car has broken down, your wife gave birth to a baby, you were called before the President for an unexpected honor, or you simply overslept:

1. Use the technique of Problem Posting described in Chapter 3.
2. Ask students to spend the first five minutes reviewing the assignment and previous lecture notes before writing down the one question each would most like to have you discuss. Collect the questions. Answer one or more yourself, but throw one out to the class, and while a student is answering, do a quick sort of the questions to group them more logically.
3. Split the class into buzz groups (see Chapter 6) and ask each buzz group to come up with one question to be discussed. Ask the first group for its question, discuss it, and ask if any other group had a question related to the first. Answer that and go on in a similar fashion.
4. Ask the class to spend the first ten minutes reviewing a particular part of the assignment so that they have it clearly in mind. While they are reviewing it, think of a discussion problem involving the material they are reviewing. Then break the class into buzz groups to discuss the problem. Use the remainder of the time to get reports from the discussion groups or start a second cycle by asking each group to discuss the advantages or disadvantages of two of the groups' solutions to the problem.
5. Admit that you're unprepared and ask the class how the time can best be spent. (Don't spend so much time discussing what to do that there's no time left to do it.)

Counseling Students

An additional factor affecting student morale is the instructor's willingness to counsel students individually. It is difficult for students to believe that you are interested in them if you avoid individual discussion of their work in the course. One of the most important factors in the student's relationship with the instructor is the instructor's availability and willingness to help. Chapter 19 is devoted to this topic.

However, at this point I would like to point out that, bothersome as regulations and scheduled office hours may be, they are useful in handling certain kinds of problem students. Most instructors have encountered students who want a great deal of personal counseling, or who express their conflict about independence of authorities by dropping in at odd times to complain about an assignment. While you should be sympathetic, intensive personal counseling or involvement with students may hamper your effectiveness rather than increase it. The formal barriers set up by the academic culture may thus sometimes be useful in controlling behavior that should be treated by a professional counselor rather than by an instructor.

SUPPLEMENTARY READING

R. D. Mann et al., *The college classroom* (New York: Wiley, 1970).

19

Counseling and Individual Instruction

Some of your most effective teaching may occur when students come to you with a problem with which they want help. I have already suggested that instructors should establish and keep certain regular office hours for meeting students. In this chapter I would like to discuss some of the problems that arise in those hours.

First of all, I should warn you that the students' ostensible reasons for coming to you may be quite different from the real reasons. Often students ask about a study problem when their real desire is to know the instructor better. They complain of inadequate study habits when underneath there may be difficulties with their home life. I do not mean that you should disregard the problems the students actually present, but if you are aware of possible underlying factors, you may be more understanding and more effective as a counselor.

Second, you should remember that you do not need to restrict your sources of information to the students' performance in your own class. Often, helpful information can be gained from the files of the student personnel office. By learning something about the students' backgrounds, you can better understand their problems.

In addition, remember that counseling need not be restricted to the office. In the classroom the teacher can do much to help individuals by rewarding their contributions, by helping them become accepted in the group, and by developing cooperative activities in which they can participate with other class members. Out of the classroom you may be able to get to the real problem more easily over a Coke in the student union than in a more formal office visit.

The most common of student problems is worded something like this, "I study harder for this course than for all my other courses, but I just can't seem to pass the tests." In handling this problem I usually encourage the students to express their own ideas about their difficulties. Sometimes their diagnosis and plans for improvement will be much more accurate than any you can give them. Frequently, simple information on budgeting time, on how the students can ask themselves questions about the assignment, or on getting an overview of a chapter before reading it can be of much help.

In general, the key is to get the students away from reading passively or trying to memorize and instead to questioning, relating, and thinking more actively about the assignment and lectures. Sometimes you can help by getting the students to really use the student workbook often published as an adjunct to the textbook. Even better may be to encourage peer teaching. In Chapter 9 we found that even poor students can learn by trying to explain something to a peer. For the theory underlying these suggestions see Chapter 23.*

Educational Counseling†

The term educational counseling has been used to refer to three distinctly different types of activity. All of them are inevitable accompaniments of an educational enterprise, but not all of them are

---

* For further help you might suggest Virginia Voeks, *On becoming an educated person*, Rev. ed. (Philadelphia: Saunders, 1964); D. E. P. Smith et al., *Learning to learn* (New York: Harcourt, Brace and World, 1961); or Francis P. Robinson, *Effective study* (New York: Harper & Row, 1946).

† Much of this section was written by Professor Edward S. Bordin, The University of Michigan.

equally accepted by faculties as part of their responsibility. The three activities included in educational counseling are 1) program planning, 2) remedial work, and 3) individualized teaching.

Program Planning

The modern university is a complex organization. The student's path through this organization is supposedly mapped by handbooks and catalogs. Unfortunately, most of these documents are, at best, forbiddingly dull and confusingly written. In too many instances they are less than adequate road guides because almost every curriculum has its unwritten requirements. These are preferences for certain sequences of courses or for the choice of one of several alternatives which are so strongly adhered to by the department or college that they become, in effect, requirements for graduation. At the same time, because they are not formal requirements, they exist as part of the folklore rather than as part of the written law.

This state of affairs means that where students are left on their own to select courses, there is great danger of having to extend the normal four-year program because of mistakes in curricular planning. This has given rise to the faculty counselor who is given the responsibility for guiding the students through the intricacies of their chosen curriculum. Often this faculty counselor is expected to double as an amateur professional counselor, one to whom the students can turn for help with any of the other problems that may arise—problems of vocational decision or problems of even more personal import.

The university usually places on this faculty counselor the responsibility for the enforcement of various other regulations governing the students' curricular activities—for example, the number of credits students may elect in a given period, the fulfillment of prerequisites, and the meeting of general requirements for graduation where they exist. The result is that these kinds of relationships between students and faculty are often strained, for the students going to see the faculty members become a part of a bureaucratic, impersonal processing that they are impatient to pare down to its irreducible essentials. To the faculty members, these duties loom as demeaning, much-to-be-avoided tasks comparable to KP in military service.

The result of all this is that though many catalogs will carry ambitious statements about faculty counseling, conjuring up an image of the wise, genial, pipe-smoking academician in leisurely discussion with the eager, respectful student who avidly gathers up the words of wisdom that are dropped in the course of this conversation, the stark reality of the relationship is too often that of a meeting between a rebelliously impatient student and a harried and disgruntled faculty member.

Remedial Work

As education has become more individualized in its treatment of the student, educators have become more concerned with special learning problems. Consequently, provision is made for specialized individualized help in removing blocks to learning and in improving such varied kinds of skills as reading, spelling, arithmetic, and well-articulated speech. In many universities there are specialists to help students overcome deficits in their methods of study or in the basic skills necessary to academic learning. This remedial work is not intended to compensate for an inadequate level of intelligence, but rather to allow for inadequacies in the students' prior preparation for college work.

University faculties are not of one mind about the appropriateness of providing this kind of educational service. Many of them see these inadequacies as reflections of the failure of primary and secondary schools to perform their functions adequately and reject any responsibility for helping rescue the unfortunate victim. One is tempted to designate this as a Malthusian philosophy because it is so frequently joined with the attitude that too many unqualified students are coming to college anyhow, so that any influences that will decimate the numbers are to be accepted rather than counterreacted. Where remedial counseling is carried on, there may be considerable variation in the amount of attention devoted to emotional factors in these learning difficulties. There are differences of opinion as to the extent to which emotional and motivational factors are at the roots of learning difficulties or are simply their concomitants. There seems no real need to choose between these two views of the role of emotion in motivation. One can assume that persons with these learning difficulties will demonstrate symptoms in varying degrees from the one extreme where the difficulties arise primarily from the mechanical sources or cognitive defects, to the other extreme where the difficulty arises because the particular skill has become invested with certain of the emotional conflicts of the individual. To the extent that remedial work is aimed at rectifying what must have been defects in the learning sequences by which a skill was acquired, remedial work is a form of educational counseling, and is close to the work of a teacher. To the extent that remedial work deals with the emotional and motivational factors as sources of the difficulty, it becomes a form of psychological counseling.

At some point you will recognize that a student needs psychological counseling. How do you get the student to the help needed? The first step may be to get the student to talk to you. Usually this can be handled by asking the student to come in, perhaps to discuss a paper or test. Typically the student will be aware that things aren't going well, and you can talk about what the student might do. One alternative, obviously, is to seek specialized help such as the reading clinic or counseling service. If the student agrees that this might be a good idea, I've found that it helps to pick up the phone and say, "I'll call to see when they can see you." In fact, most such agencies will at least carry out an initial interview with any student who walks in. But the sense of commitment involved when a faculty member has called seems to make students more likely to follow through than if they simply agree that they'll go in.

Individualized Teaching

The potentially most fruitful and most appropriate interpretation of educational counseling is the one least frequently explicitly defined and most neglected. When colleges and universities were small communities of a few hundred students and mature scholars, learning and teaching were naturally relatively individualized processes. The size of even the smaller major colleges and universities is such as to no longer make this individualized learning automatic. Even in classes of forty to sixty students, it is difficult for the learning process to include the meeting of a maturing and a mature intellect. Too frequently students must be content to listen to lectures and pursue readings aimed at some abstracted image of a student.

Educational counseling as individualized teaching can represent a method by which this more personalized learning can be preserved even in a large institution. It is particularly necessary to freshman students to whom new intellectual spheres are being opened, usually at a time when they have taken a big step away from their family and community roots. This is likely to be a time when a great many new assumptions and new ways of dealing with important ideas need to be digested. Educational counselors, because they have no commitment to covering a specific subject matter, can provide the students with an opportunity to digest and integrate the intellectual experiences they have been having. Far from being a chore to be assigned to the least successful faculty member, such a demanding responsibility is best undertaken by persons of broad intellectual interests and foundations who, at the same time, have strong pedagogical commitments.

This time, when students are making big strides toward greater independence from family and are trying to search out models who can represent innovations of the adult role to which to aspire, is a time when there should be opportunities for close relationships with faculty members. The very characteristics of the large university throw obstacles in the way of such an experience. Educational counseling is one of the important media for achieving it. It seems probable that the most effective pattern for doing this would be for counselors to plan small group meetings with the students assigned to them for counseling to provide an opportunity for the groups of new students coming from different parts of the state and country to exchange with each other and with a person of fully developed intellectual maturity the impacts of their initial university experiences. As colleges grow larger, more and more explicit plans for the sort of exchange that could be taken for granted in the smaller colleges are needed.

SUPPLEMENTARY READING

Edward S. Bordin, *Psychological counseling* (New York: Appleton-Century-Crofts, 1968).

20

Class Size,
Large Classes,
and Multiple Sections

As budgets decrease, more and more college teachers are going to be involved in dealing with large numbers of students enrolled in a single course. Typically, increases in enrollment or decreases in the number of faculty members are handled by simply increasing the size of classes, unless available rooms are too small.

Such changes give rise to at least two questions:

1. What is the optimum class size for effective teaching?
2. How can courses with large enrollments be most effectively organized?

In writing this book, I originally began with the topic, "Class Size." I concluded that section by stating that more meaningful research on class size must take into account the methods in teaching the classes of differing sizes. I though this was a pretty insightful statement, but now I think that it was naive, for size and method are almost inextricably intertwined. Thus the research on class size and that on lecture vs. discussion overlap. Large classes are most likely to use lecture methods and less likely to use discussion than small classes.

Research on Class Size

The question of class size was probably the first problem of college teaching approached by research. Are small classes really more effective for teaching than large classes? The professor's answer has generally been "yes." But the refreshing empiricism of the 1920s looked hard at many "self-evident truths" about human behavior; among them was the assumption that class size had something to do with educational effectiveness.

Among the first investigators were Edmondson and Mulder (1924), who compared the performance of students enrolled in a 109-student class with students enrolled in a 43-student class of the same course in education. Achievement of the two groups was approximately equal, with a slight edge for the small class on an essay and the mid-semester tests, and for the large class on quizzes and the final examination. Students reported a preference for small classes.

The Edmondson and Mulder results at Michigan encouraged the Committee of Research of the University of Minnesota to begin a classic series of studies of class size. In 59 experiments which involved such widely varying subjects as psychology, physics, accounting, law, and education, the results of 46 favored the large classes. Although only eight differences were large enough to be statistically significant at the 5 percent level, six of the eight favored large classes.

Support for small classes, however, came from studies in the teaching of French conducted by Cheydleur (1945) at the University of Wisconsin between 1919 and 1943. With hundreds of classes ranging in size from nine to thirty-three, Cheydleur found a consistent superiority on objective departmental examinations for the smaller classes. Mueller (1924) found similar results in an experiment comparing elementary psychology classes of twenty and forty students. More recent experiments are also favorable to small classes. Nachman and Opochinsky (1958) found a small class to be superior to a large on surprise quizzes, but the two classes were not significantly different on the final examination for which students prepared. Differences were also revealed in the more subtle and persisting results of Feldhusen's (1963) study showing that a small class in educational psychology produced more change in attitudes toward teaching than a large class.

The Macomber and Siegel experiments at Miami University (1957, 1960) are particularly important because their measures included, in addition to conventional achievement tests, measures of critical thinking and problem solving, scales measuring stereotype of attitudes, tests of student attitudes, and tests of student attitudes toward instruction. Statistically significant differences favored the smaller classes (particularly for high ability students). Significant differences favoring small classes were found on measures of change in misconceptions in psychology, on a case test of problem solving in a course in marketing, and on the measures of student attitudes toward all the courses. When retention of knowledge was measured one to two years after completion of the courses, large classes did not prove to be significantly inferior to small classes in any one course. However, in eight of the nine courses compared, small differences favored the small class (Siegel, Adams, and Macomber, 1960).

Few instructors are satisfied with the achievement of knowledge if it is not remembered, if the students are unable to use it in solving problems where the knowledge is relevant, or if the students fail to relate the knowledge to relevant attitudes. If one takes these more basic outcomes of retention, problem solving, and attitude differentiation as criteria of learning, the weight of this evidence clearly favors small classes. Moreover, in almost all studies, students and faculty members tended to prefer small classes. Other things being equal, then, one would opt for high student and faculty morale.

Class Size: Theory

Most college professors believe small classes to be superior to larger ones in many respects. For example, the Miami professors involved in the experiments reported by Macomber and Siegel felt that large classes were about equal to small classes in covering content but inferior in achieving other objectives. Is this simply academic featherbedding, or are there good reasons for the professors' distrust of the research results?

Let us briefly return to theory. I have stressed the role of the lecturer as an information communicator. Insofar as information is a one-way process, size of group should be limited only by the audibility of the lecturer's voice. In fact, as Hudelson suggests, a large class may have sufficient motivational value for instructors to cause them to spend more time in preparation of their lectures, resulting, I would hope, in better teaching and in greater student achievement. But if, as I suggested in my discussion of automation, the effective lecture involves interaction between instructor and students, the large class may be inferior even for lectures, for experiments suggest that fewer students raise questions or interpose comments in large classes than in small (Gibb, 1951).

But it is economically impractical to teach entirely in small classes. If educators are to make wise decisions about when and where small classes are most important, we need to analyze more carefully the changes in educationally relevant variables associated with changes in size. One lead comes from social psychologists Thomas and Fink (1963), who have reviewed research on face-to-face groups—not only classroom groups, but laboratory, business, and other groups also. They suggest that two types of input increase with increasing group size—*resource input* (skills, knowledge, and so on) and *demand input* (needs). It is clear that the larger the number of group members, the greater the likelihood that some members will have resources of knowledge, intelligence, or other skills needed for the educational purposes of the group. It seems likely, however, that there is a limited amount of relevant knowledge and skills, so that beyond some point additional students contribute little that is not already part of the group's resources. A group's utilization of resources is constrained by the simple facts that, 1) in a large group a smaller proportion of group members can participate orally, and 2) the larger the group, the less likely it is that a given person will feel free to volunteer a contribution.

Determining When Small Classes Are Needed

In order to apply these general propositions to teaching, educators need to ask the following questions:

● *In what teaching situations is the amount of information in the group important?* One might, for example, hypothesize that in most courses in which knowledge is the primary goal, the relevant information is contained in books and the instructor's mind, and the amount added by students is likely to be inconsequential; thus class size should be unimportant for this goal. On the other hand, if application is an important goal, varied knowledge of application situations contributed by students may well be significant; thus, if Thomas and Fink's principles are valid, there may be groups too small, as well as too large, to be maximally effective for this goal.

● *What kinds of students benefit most from small sections?*   Both Ward (1956) and Macomber and Siegel report results suggesting that the ablest students are most favorably affected by being taught in small classes. Siegel and Siegel (1964) report that personal contact with the instructor was particularly important for acquisition of concepts by three types of students: 1) those with low motivation, 2) those unsophisticated in the subject-matter area, and 3) those predisposed to learn facts rather than to apply or synthesize.

● *Is class size important for other types of students?*   Unfortunately, there has been little research on such problems. As the size of the class increases, the number of different demands or needs of members also increases. It is unlikely that the ability of the instructor and class to meet different student expectations increases proportionately, since class time is not expandable. As Stephan and Mishler (1952) have shown, larger groups are more likely to be dominated by the leader, and the teacher can give less individual personal attention to each group member. The research of McKeachie, et al. (1966) indicates that women and men high in need affiliation achieve well for teachers who take a personal interest in students; it might then be expected that such students would do better in small classes than in larger classes.

Educational Goals, Class Size, and Teaching Methods

In most courses there are several levels of goals—knowledge, critical thinking, attitudes toward learning, and so on. The teacher's task is to find methods that will achieve an optimal balance of all of these. If different methods are effective for different objectives, teachers need to be able to use an optimal combination of these methods. Unfortunately, most teaching research has studied the effect of one method vs. another when both are repeated day after day for a semester; thus, few data exist on the relative effectiveness of differing combinations or degrees of flexibility in teaching methods.

While many teaching methods could be used in large groups, it is probable that more time is devoted to lecturing than in smaller classes. The large class often reduces the teacher's sense of freedom in choosing teaching methods, assigning papers, or testing to achieve varying objectives. Assuming that teachers have some repertoire of relevant skills, anything that handcuffs instructors is likely to be educationally damaging, and this may be the major way in which large classes are likely to sabotage education.

What goals are most likely to be sacrificed in large classes?

As Table 20–1 indicates, large lectures are not generally inferior to smaller lecture classes when traditional achievement tests are used as a criterion. When other objectives are measured, large lectures are on shakier ground. Goals of higher level thinking, application, motivation, and attitudinal change are most likely to be achieved in small classes. Moreover, both students and faculty members feel that teaching is more effective in small classes.

Probably of more significance than class size per se is its relation to the teaching method used. For example, one would expect class size to be of minimal relevance in television teaching, of slight importance in lecturing, and of much importance for discussion. We have already seen in Chapter 4 that discussions are superior to lectures for achieving problem solving and motivational goals.

Class Size: Conclusions

It is commonplace to suggest that the effect of class size depends upon the method used, and it is probably true that the size of the group is less critical for success of lecture, for example, than for that of discussion (Attiyeh and Lumsden, 1972). Moreover, class size interacts with student characteristics; that is, small classes are educationally more important for some students than for others. But most important, analysis of research suggests that the importance of size depends upon educational goals. In general, large classes are simply not as effective as small classes for retention of knowledge, critical thinking, and attitude change.

TABLE 20–1   *Class Size*

REFERENCE	COURSE	CRITERIA		
		Factual Exam	*Higher Level Retention and Thinking*	*Attitude, Motivation*
Nachman & Opochinsky (1958)	Psychology	*S		
Mueller (1924)	Psychology	S		
Elliott (1951)	Psychology			S
De Cecco (1964)	Psychology	S	L	S
Feldhusen (1963)	Educational Psychology			S
Casey & Weaver (1956)	Human Development			*S
Macomber & Siegel (1957, 1960)	Psychology, Marketing		*S	*S
Siegel, Adams, & Macomber (1960)	Psychology, Marketing		*S (8 out of 9)	
Hudelson (1928)	Psychology, Physics, Accounting, Law, Education	L (46 exp.) S (13 exp.) *L (6 exp.) *S (2 exp.)		
Attiyeh & Lumsden (1972)	Economics	*S L = S		
Edmondson & Mulder (1924)	Education	L		
Cheydleur (1945)	French	S (1240 classes)		

L = Large Class Superior
S = Small Class Superior
* = Difference significant at .05 level or better. All other results are the actual direction of the difference in the experiment.

Multi-Section Courses

Unfortunately, there are seldom enough funds to teach all courses in small groups. As a compromise solution, I have scheduled large courses for two hours of lecture (in large sections) and two hours of discussion (in small sections). The assumption here is that lectures are valuable for certain purposes, such as communicating information, and that the effectiveness of the lecture method is not greatly affected by class size. Furthermore, certain large-group class meetings are economical for test administration, guest resource persons, and some films. By teaching the students in large sections part of the time, it becomes economically feasible to keep the discussion sections small enough to permit wide student participation. Thus, rather than offering 5 sections of 45 students each, you might consider the possible advantages of a 225-student lecture section and 9 sections of 20 to 30 students. As we saw in Chapter 4, the effectiveness of such a procedure is supported by research.

Coordinating Multi-Section Courses

In any multi-section course taught by several different instructors problems of coordination inevitably arise. In some courses this problem is resolved by enforced uniformity of course content, sequence of topics, testing, grading, and even anecdotes. Such a procedure has the advantage that students who later elect more advanced courses can be presumed to have a certain uniform amount of background experience. It also is efficient in that only one final examination must be constructed, only one course outline devised, and students can transfer from section to section with no difficulty in catching up.

The disadvantage of this approach is that such uniformity often makes for dull, uninteresting teaching. If the teaching assistants are unenthusiastic about the course outline, they are likely to communicate this attitude to the students. If the course can be jointly planned, this may make for greater acceptance, but may also take a great deal of time.

A second approach to this problem is to set up completely autonomous sections, with all the instructors organizing and conducting their sections as they wish. While this means that Psychology 1 from Smith may be quite different from Psychology 1 from Jones, proponents of this solution point out that transfer students who are accepted for advanced work are likely to differ even more from local students than local students differ from section to section under this plan, and that the difference in student learning between instructors is relatively small when compared with the total range of differences between students at the end of a course.

In the general psychology course at the University of Michigan we have used a plan that is in many ways a compromise between these two positions. We worked out together a set of objectives we all strove to accomplish. Half of the final examination was based on these objectives and given to all sections. In addition we agreed that the average grade given by each instructor would fall within a limited range determined by the average ability of his students. This grading restriction is not a minor matter, for one of the most common sources of friction in multi-section courses is the complaint from students that they got "C's" in Mr. Jones' section, but if they'd been in Mr. Smith's they would have made "A's" for the same work.

This plan often results in frustration for teachers who feel that the common section of the final is trivial or unfair. Such complaints may be valid, for it seems difficult to agree on test items other than those that test for specific facts or definitions.

Whether or not variation between sections is permitted, a frequent sore spot in multi-section courses is the tendency for students to leave or avoid sections taught by certain instructors and to jam others. Some instructors intentionally depict their sections as being more difficult in order to drive away less motivated students. If this produces large disparities in the numbers of students taught by "popular" and "unpopular" instructors, the cohesiveness of the instructional staff is likely to be threatened. On the other hand, both from the standpoint of student learning and instructor satisfaction, it would seem wise to give students some opportunity to select the section they feel will be most valuable (or pleasant) for them.

My experience is that conflict is minimized and education enhanced if certain sections are specifically labeled as being for a particular purpose. For example, certain sections may be labeled Honors sections or for graduate students; certain sections may be labeled sections placing greater emphasis upon theory; certain other sections may be taught entirely by discussion and so labeled. One of the advantages of a multi-section course is the opportunity it provides for homogeneous groupings, extra stimulation for the superior student, and taking advantage of students' backgrounds.

Some Tips for Teaching Large Classes

Often one assumes that a large class simply requires skills in lecturing and writing objective tests. These are important, but one can do more. Large classes need not constrain you as much as you might expect.

Getting Student Participation in Large Classes

While sectioning is preferable to the large class without sections, most teachers will at some time be faced with the necessity of teaching an unsectioned large class. In this situation my first advice is to try learning cells or student-led discussions as described in Chapter 9. If this is impractical, you can still get the advantages of student participation if you plan for it. Some techniques such as buzz groups were discussed in Chapter 5 on discussion methods; problem posting and the two-column method of large discussions were discussed in Chapter 3. The technique of role playing, discussed in Chapter 13, can be used for multiple role playing, with all students involved as role players. Maier (1971) gives examples of the use of such techniques.

Lumsden (1976) gives each student in his section a large square card with the letters A, B, C, and D printed so that one of the letters is visible at the top when each edge of the card is held up. For example, if A is first on the top side, B will be visible at the top when the card is rotated 90 degrees. Lumsden interjects questions into his lecture either orally, on the blackboard, or by use of a transparency, and then asks students to answer all at once by raising their cards. This enables him to get student participation and feedback on whether his points are understood.

Giving Tests in Large Classes

In classes of 200 or more, unwary instructors are likely to run into problems they would never dream of in teaching classes with an enrollment of 20 to 30. Most of these problems are administrative ones. For example, course planning almost inevitably becomes more rigid in a large class because almost anything involving the participation of the students requires more preparation time.

Perhaps you're used to making up your tests the day before you administer them. With a large class this is almost impossible. Essay and short-answer tests that take relatively little time to construct take a long time to score for 200 students; so you must spend long hours trying to devise thought-provoking objective questions. But once you've made up the questions your troubles are not over, for secretaries require a good deal of time to run off several hundred copies of a test. Thus, spur-of-the-moment tests are almost an impossibility, and by virtue of the necessity of planning ahead for tests, other aspects of the course also become more rigid.

With an objective examination, it is almost impossible to prevent students' gazes from passing over the answer sheets of their neighbors. An honor system, which may work well when students know the instructor and one another, may become less effective in a larger, more-or-less anonymous group. Hence you will either want to schedule the examination in rooms large enough to permit empty spaces between students or you will want to provide alternative forms of the test so that students in adjacent seats will have different forms. Such alternative forms can be constructed simply by changing the order of alternatives and of questions and hoping that this doesn't seriously affect the difficulty of the items.

Assuming that you've planned the test well in advance, and it is now mimeographed and stapled to an answer sheet, your problems are still not ended. With several hundred students even the mechanics of distributing the test may become difficult. If you're using alternate forms, you'll want to have the tests already stacked with the forms alternating, and you'll want to control distribution. Probably the simplest system if the classroom is vacant before the test is to place the tests in the seats before the students arrive. An alternative is to seat the students coming in first in the front rows in the order in which they have come in, distributing the tests as they enter. A third alternative is to distribute the tests after everyone has arrived, and be prepared for the complaint from students receiving their tests last that other students had much more time. This complaint may be just, for in a large class a quarter of the class hour can easily be consumed simply in distributing the test.

As indicated in Chapter 16, there is some evidence that essay examinations are superior to typical objective examinations in their effect on student study and learning. Thus you are likely to regret the loss of the opportunity to give essay tests in a large group. But this loss is not inevitable. To some extent it can be compensated for by greater care in the construction of objective test items. But it is also possible to use essay items without increasing your load beyond reason. In one of my large lecture courses I regularly included an essay item on the final examination with the stipulation that I would read it only if it would affect the student's letter grade for the course. Since the majority of the students were fairly clearly established as A, B, C, or D students on the basis of other work and the objective part of the final, the number of essays I needed to read was not excessive. My subjective impression was that knowledge of the inclusion of an essay item did affect the students' preparation for the exam.

Outside Reading

The testing problem is just one of several factors structuring the conduct of large classes. Another is the assignment of readings in the library. With a small group you can assign library work with little difficulty, perhaps only making sure that the materials needed are available and, if necessary, reserved for the class. With a class of several hundred students a library assignment without previous planning can be disastrous. The library's single copy of a book or journal is obviously inadequate, and will probably be stolen within a few hours by some student who wants to assure time enough to study the assignment thoroughly. The librarians are then faced by hordes of desperate students begging for the book. Thus a library assignment must be conceived far enough in advance (usually several months) that enough copies of the book can be obtained, and the librarian can prepare for the fray.

Teaching Large Classes: Conclusion

Large classes are probably generally less efficient than small ones. In any case, it is clear that many of the teaching problems are different. I have touched on only a few of the most salient ones. If you become involved in a large course, you'll also bump into such problems as whether or not to encourage individual contacts between yourself and students, how to use assistants effectively, what to do about meeting the educational needs of a wider range of students whom you usually know less well, and how to amplify your voice, gestures, facial expressions, and writing in order to communicate to the back rows. This is a challenge, but teaching stays interesting because of challenges!

SUPPLEMENTARY READING

Kenneth E. Eble, *The craft of teaching* (San Francisco: Jossey-Bass, 1976), chapter 13.

21

How to Win Friends and Influence Janitors

The beginning instructor's teaching may be greatly facilitated or hampered by relationships with other personnel of the college or university. You will occasionally wish to recommend or assign readings in library references. Sometimes instructors make such assignments without informing the librarian. The unhappy librarians are then deluged with students demanding a book that has already been taken out for two weeks or that is not even listed in the catalog. After a few such experiences, the librarian may not greet requests for special favors with great enthusiasm. Thus, one of the essentials of pre-course planning is giving the library a list of books in which reading will be required, perhaps with a description of the nature and time of use, and making sure that students are given the correct authors and titles.

Often, too, instructors ask the library to order many copies of books they plan to use. The next year they decide to use different sources, and the library is left with twenty copies of a book of which only one or two copies have ever been used. Usually librarians are happy to advise an instructor how many copies of a supplementary book should be ordered in terms of the number of students and the extent of the readings required.

Similar problems may arise in scheduling movies and audiovisual aids. It should be obvious that instructors cannot expect films and projectionists to be available the day they decide to fill in class time with a movie. As pointed out previously, effective use of visual aids requires planning. Moreover, if you have scheduled a movie, it is not conducive to good relations with projectionists to tell the operator when he or she appears loaded with projector and screen that you have decided not to use the film.

Relationships with janitors are also important. Instructors sometimes complain of lack of chalk, messy rooms, or broken seats, but fail to recognize their own responsibilities in building maintenance. You can hardly blame janitors for getting discouraged when they enter a classroom to find the floor littered with bits of paper, chalk, cigarette ashes, the blackboard smeared with scrawling, and the room in general disorder.

In beginning work in a different college, instructors may find that the rules, the traditions, the usual channels to go through for a particular service are not the same as they are accustomed to. If they ask with humility for information rather than attempt to order conformity to their expectations, they will have a much easier time in learning the ropes.

Important problems also arise in relationships to the administration, colleagues, and the student body. For example, the records and deadlines required by the registrar's office and other administrative offices often seem unimportant to instructors, and consequently they are apt to feel that a slight delay is of no consequence. However, an office that processes hundreds or thousands of records must have scheduling as rigorous as that of a factory production line. Laxness on the part of a few instructors may ruin a beautiful schedule.

Instructors also sometimes fail to remember that their courses may have relevance for the course of their colleagues. If the faculty members teaching coordinate and more advanced courses know what you are doing, they can shape their own courses accordingly. Because they have an interest in the course, they are usually pleased if they are consulted when any drastic changes are to be made. Certainly the department chairman should be kept informed.

It should be evident that students, too, have an interest in your teaching. One of your first obligations is to make sure that the course description in the college catalog is adequate. The academic counselors should have a more detailed description of the course if they are to counsel students wisely.

Periodic student evaluation of their teaching and of the course is helpful to most instructors. I have found that it is helpful simply to have students write "Things I Like," "Criticisms," and "Suggestions." A more highly structured form for obtaining student opinion is included in Appendix B. Often it is helpful to get evaluations not only from students taking the course, but also from students who took the course at an earlier date.

Most college instructors are asked at some time to sponsor a student group, to give an informal talk at a student meeting, or to meet with a student committee. My only words of advice here are "Act naturally." Don't try to knock yourself out trying to prove that you're a human being, and don't fear that the proper barriers between students and faculty will be breached. Occasionally, you will meet a student who aggressively calls you by your first name. This probably won't annoy you unless you're already worried about your position, but even if it does, it seems to do little good to reprimand the student. He or she will simply express resentment of authority in some other way.

There is one exception to my advice to act naturally—when college regulations prohibit certain activities that are condoned in your own circle of society. The most common issue is that of student drinking or use of drugs. Whether or not you approve or disapprove of the college's regulations, I see no great gain in achieving popularity as a faculty member who winks at such violations.

SUPPLEMENTARY READING

Kenneth E. Eble, *The craft of teaching* (San Francisco: Jossey-Bass, 1976), chapter 6; pp 163–172.

22

Ethical Standards in Teaching

As part of the code of ethics for psychologists, the American Psychological Association has published a code of ethics for teachers of psychology. Those portions relevant for all college teachers make up the rest of the text of this chapter.*

"The psychologist should encourage students in their quest for knowledge, giving them every assistance in the free exploration of ideas. Teaching frequently and legitimately involves a presentation of disquieting facts and controversial theories, and it is in the examination of perplexing issues that students most need the guidance of a good teacher. Disturbing concepts should not be withheld from students simply because some individuals may be distressed by them. When issues are relevant, they should be given full and objective

---

* Reprinted by permission of the American Psychological Association.

discussion so that students can make intelligent decisions with regard to them. However, presentation of ideas likely to be difficult for some students to accept should be governed by tact and respect for the worth of the individual.

"Differing approaches to psychology should be presented to students in such a way as to encourage them to study the relevant facts and draw their own conclusions. Free expression of both criticism and support of the various approaches to psychology is to be encouraged as essential to the development of individual students and the field of psychology. In dealing with an area of specialization other than his own, a psychologist should make it clear that he is not speaking as a specialist. In attempting to make an understandable and interesting presentation of subject matter to students, an instructor should not sacrifice adequacy of treatment to considerations of popular appeal.

"A teacher of psychology should respect the student's right to privacy and not require him to give information which he may wish to withhold; neither should the teacher reveal information which a student has given with the reasonable assumption that it will be held in confidence.

"A psychologist should require of his students only activities which are designed to contribute to the student in the area of instruction. Other activities not related to course objectives and not having secondary values should be made available to students on a voluntary basis. Exploitation of students to obtain research data or assistance with the psychologist's own work is unethical.

"Psychologists advising students electing psychology as a major field of study with the intent of entering the profession should be sure that students understand opportunities and requirements in the field, e.g., that few positions as psychologists are open to those with only a bachelor's degree, that there is considerable screening of candidates at the graduate level, and that the doctorate is required for many positions. Students with personality problems so severe that they are unlikely to be effective in graduate study or in later professional work should be discouraged from entering areas of psychology in which effective interpersonal relationships are crucial.

"A teacher of psychology who becomes aware of an adjustment problem in a student who might profit by counseling or psychotherapy should assist the student to find such help if it is available. When a student requests assistance, and counseling facilities are not available, the non-clinically trained instructor may offer help as an immediate expedient. In doing so he should indicate to the student that he is acting not as a trained counselor or clinical psychologist but simply as a teacher interested in his welfare. Private clinical work with a student, for a fee, is considered an unwise practice, since it may confuse the relationship between the student and the instructor in other activities."

23

Motivation, Learning, and Cognition in the College Classroom

If I were following a purely logical approach to the organization of this book, a chapter on learning would certainly come early, for decisions about teaching techniques should be based upon the principles of learning. In trying to help young teachers, however, I have found that most beginning teachers have too many immediate problems to solve to worry very much about general questions of educational theory. It is only after you have mastered some of the day-to-day problems that you are able to sit back and wonder why some things work and others don't. The next two chapters deal with more basic psychological material relevant to these broader concerns.

Motivation

Instructors know that student learning and memory are closely tied to *motivation*. Students will learn what they want to learn and will have great difficulty in learning material in which they're not interested. Students are not poor learners; nor are they unmotivated. They are learning all the time—new dance steps, the status hierarchy on campus, football strategy, and other more or less complex things —but the sort of learning for which students are motivated is not always that which contributes to attaining the goals of our courses. Too often teachers think of learning only in terms of formal instruction. It might be more realistic for teachers to think of themselves as individuals who facilitate certain kinds of learning. They can neither learn for their students nor stop them from learning.

A primary problem, then, is motivating students toward course goals. Usually the learning psychologist stops with this point, but to be useful the principle of motivation needs to be accompanied with information about dependable motives of college students. Teachers know, for example, that many of their students are taught by their parents to want to do well in school. Thus we can count on some motivation for achievement.

Curiosity

Psychology has a good deal more to contribute on the subject of motivation for learning than it did a few years ago. There has been a revolution in thinking about motivation, and like most revolutions, the seeds had been planted for a long time. A decade or two ago psychologists would have talked about reward and punishment and would have asked you to look at the rewards for learning in the classroom. This is still worth considering. Rewards and punishments often influence learning. But the revolution in research and theory lies in new evidence that people are naturally curious. They seek new experiences; they enjoy learning new things; they find satisfaction in solving puzzles, perfecting skills, and developing competence.

Thus, one of the major tasks in teaching is not how to scare students into doing their homework, but rather how to nurture their curiosity and to use curiosity as a motive for learning.

Fortunately, I can do more than point to curiosity as an important motive for learning. A good deal of research suggests that people seek and enjoy stimuli that are different from those they are used to —but that these stimuli must not be too different. When stimuli are totally incongruous or very strange, students develop anxiety instead of curiosity.

How does this generalization apply to learning in college? It is tempting to answer this question in vague phrases like "varied teaching methods," "posing new, but soluble problems," or "setting realistic standards of achievement." But I believe it is possible to go a little beyond this. One hint comes from studies by Berlyne (1954a and b). He found that asking students questions, rather than presenting statements of fact, not only improved learning, but also increased interest in learning more about the topic. Questions were particularly effective in arousing curiosity about things that were already familiar. But the most successful questions were those that were most unexpected. This agrees with the finding that National Merit Scholars describe the classes that influenced their choice of field as ones where they didn't know what to expect next (Thistlethwaite, 1960). Probably one of the points where much programmed learning has been weak is in this respect. The interplay between familiar and novel may be very significant in the development of curiosity.

How do instructors bring students into contact with novelty? Meaningful laboratory experience may be one answer. For example, outstanding scientists report that their motivation for science resulted from early participation in research. This has implications for social science. Perhaps instructors offer too few opportunities for students to experience the thrill of discovery.

Complexity can also arouse curiosity. Chapter 10 reviewed evidence that study questions requiring thought produce greater learning from reading. This is not only because of the cognitive result of greater meaningfulness, but also because "deep processing" questions make studying more interesting (Entwistle, In press; Svensson, 1976).

Competence

One of the reasons curiosity is important to nurture is that it is a motive intrinsic to learning, and thus continued learning is not dependent upon a teacher to reward learning.

Another intrinsic motive for learning is competence or self-efficacy. Human beings receive pleasure from doing things well. To the degree that teachers can help students develop a sense of standards that will enable them to see that they are developing increasing skill, teachers can also contribute to the goal of continued learning after the class has been completed. Bandura (1977) has developed in some depth a theory of self-efficacy. This theory suggests that while teachers are important sources of information about self-efficacy, students will interpret the same information in differing ways depending upon the context of the information and their previous experience. Thus, seeing the teacher or other students perform a task will not help students who see themselves as so different that another's success bares no relationship to their own chances to perform the task. Even their own success may be misinterpreted as luck. For such students teachers need to link success with the perception that the success was due to the student's own ability and effort. Success alone is not enough. For students who lack a sense of efficacy teachers must not only provide situations where success occurs, but also give students opportunities to undertake the task on their own to prove that they have themselves mastered it without special help. The importance of nurturing curiosity is not only for its value in learning the material of a particular course, but also for its importance in motivating learning after the course. As you saw earlier I think that nurturing curiosity, developing increased interest, is probably the most important goal of almost every college and university course.

But there are other motives of students that are also relevant to learning.

The Affiliation Motive

Most students want to be liked. This motive may work against instructors as well as for them. The teacher's friendly approval can be an important reward for learning, but the "average raiser" is not always well liked. Thus, in some colleges students who want acceptance by their classmates may avoid any conspicuous display of academic achievement. Many students suffer from conflict between the need to get good grades and the need to be well liked. One of the symptoms of this conflict is the ostentatious neglect of study by some bright students and their apparent surprise when they get good grades. This ploy is so well known that its techniques have been analyzed carefully by Stephen Potter in his scholarly volume, *One-upmanship* (1955). This conflict has in the past been particularly a problem of women. Horner (1968) termed it the "fear of success."

Many students have conflicting motives. One common conflict is between independence and dependence. This means that students are likely to resent the teacher who directs their activities too closely, but they also are likely to be anxious when given independence; so that teachers have the neat trick of finding ways of simultaneously satisfying both needs. As a result of this conflict some students disagree with their teachers not on rational grounds but simply as a way of expressing emotions. Similarly, student apathy in a required course may be irrational expression of resentment about being required to do anything.

Grades as Incentives

Let us consider the case of the most important motivational device—grades. Whatever students' motivations for being in college, grades are important to them. If students are really interested in learning, grades represent an expert's appraisal of their success; if they're interested in getting into professional school, good grades are the key that will unlock graduate school doors; if they want to play basketball, grades are necessary for maintaining eligibility. Most students are motivated to get at least passing grades, and much as instructors resent record keeping, the grades for which they are responsible are a powerful motivational tool.

Many teachers are a little embarrassed by this, regarding grades as one of the necessary evils of teaching. They try to discount grades in discussion of the organization of the course and try to arrive at grades in such a way that they can avoid trouble with disappointed students. But they frequently fail to use grades to bring about the sort of learning they desire.

Because grades are important to them, many students will learn whatever is necessary to get the grades they desire. If instructors base grades on memorization of details, students will memorize the text. If they believe grades are based upon their ability to integrate and apply principles, they'll attempt to do this.

As far as speed of learning goes, it probably doesn't matter what motives instructors use, but this doesn't mean that the type of motivation used is unimportant. A good deal of evidence has accumulated to suggest that negative (fear) and positive (hope) motives affect behavior differently. Teachers usually use mixtures of positive and negative motives. When negative motives predominate, students will work hard, but only if this is the only way to avoid undesirable consequences. If there are ways out of the situation, they'll take them. The result frequently is that students do the least they can get away with or spend their time devising elaborate methods of cheating.

Negative motives are not as effective outside the learning situation as are positive motives, because fear is a more effective motivational device if the threatened danger is close than if it is distant. Students who are afraid are likely to want to avoid being reminded of the possibility of failure. Hence they may avoid study until the pressures are so great that they simply have no alternative. Thus, teachers who motivate their students by fear of bad grades need to use frequent tests if their threats are to be effective.

The striking difference in behavior between students motivated by fear and students motivated by hope is illustrated in their behavior during examinations. A study by Atkinson and Litwin (1960) showed that male students who were high in anxiety about tests were among the first to complete the course examination and tended to do more poorly on the examination than in their work during the course. Students with positive motivation to succeed tended to stay in the examination room longer. Note that this illustrates the tendency of the fearful person to avoid the situation that arouses anxiety. Heckhausen (1974) showed that students who fear failure improve in performance when they were helped to attribute failure to lack of effort rather than to lack of ability and to set reasonable standards for themselves.

To sum up my argument thus far, motivation is important in learning. Curiosity and competence motivation are the most important and lasting motives for learning. We can use student motivation for success, approval, and so on to produce learning. Grades are important incentives for many kinds of motivation. Thus it's important to make sure that grades are not separate from the kind of learning desired. Using grades chiefly as a threat may produce avoidance rather than interest.

Achievement Motivation

Atkinson has developed a theory of motivation from which he derived the hypothesis that students with high achievement motivation would be more highly motivated in situations in which they perceived their chances of success as about fifty-fifty. Laboratory research supported the hypothesis. Atkinson and O'Connor (1963) then hypothesized that grouping by ability would be particularly effective for students with strong desires to achieve, since the homogeneous class should provide an achievement situation in which the students' judgments of their own success as compared to their peers should be more likely to be intermediate. The Atkinson and O'Connor results showed that the high-achievement motive students not only made greater academic gains in homogeneous classes, but also reported greater interest in school work.

The Atkinson and O'Connor results are relevant not only for the problem of ability grouping, but also for the general problem of motivation for learning. From Berlyne we have the suggestion that motivation is highest in situations of moderate novelty; from Atkinson we learn that for students with basic motivation for success, motivation is highest when chances of success are moderate. Both of these findings point to the value of pacing learning so that each step offers some newness and only a moderate risk of failure.

One of the first steps in teaching may be to stimulate doubt about what has previously been taken for granted. I've never really studied the teaching role of the "devil's advocate," but this may be an important way to stimulate motivation.

The Teacher as Model

One of the major sources of stimulation of motivation is the teacher. Your own enthusiasm and values have much to do with your students' interest in the subject matter. Probably nonverbal as well as verbal methods are used to communicate such attitudes; that is, facial expression, animation, and vocal intensity may be as important as the words you use.

Organization

A teacher's job isn't done when he or she interests the class, for the amount students learn depends upon the amount taught, and this is not so simple as it may at first appear. It may well be that the *more* instructors teach the *less* their students learn! Several years ago some teaching fellows were arguing furiously over how to teach about the nervous system. One group argued that since students wouldn't remember all of the details, they might better omit them and teach only the basic essentials which we want everyone to learn. Another group argued that students would forget much of what they learned. "But," they said, "if they're going to forget a large percentage, we need to teach much more than we expect them to remember. Otherwise they'll forget even the important things."

To a psychologist such an argument is simply an invitation to an experiment, and consequently the combatants agreed that they'd try out their ideas in their own classes and compare the results on the final exam questions covering the nervous system. The outcome was clear. The students whose instructor had omitted details were clearly superior to those whose instructor had given them the whole story. This result would not have been surprising to David Katz (1950), the German-Swedish psychologist who devised a number of unique experiments demonstrating that, beyond a certain point, adding to the elements in an intellectual task causes confusion and inefficiency. Katz called this phenomenon "mental dazzle."

Fortunately, teaching is an area where you can have your cake and eat it too, for it is possible to teach more and have it remembered better. The magic formula is *organization*. As Katona (1940) demonstrated in a series of experiments on organization and memory, people can learn and remember much more when their learning fits into an organization. If I give you a series of numbers chosen at random, like 73810547, and ask you what the fourth number was, you probably have difficulty remembering, but if I give the numbers 12345678, you can remember immediately what the fourth number was. Teaching that helps students find a framework within which to fit new facts is likely to be more effective than teaching that simply communicates masses of material in which the student can see no organization.

The successful teacher is one whose students see meaningful problems. The ideal class would begin with a problem so meaningful that the students are always just a step ahead of the teacher in approaching a solution. If students can develop their own ways of structuring the material, it is likely to be recalled and used better than if the structure is provided by the teacher. My own research suggests that students often dislike and do not necessarily learn well from teachers who are highly organized—you can have too much organization as well as too little. The important thing is that students find some way of structuring the material. Students with more background and ability can do this even in relatively unstructured situations, but in courses where the material is new to the students it is probably important that the teacher provide ways of organizing the material at least in the conclusion of the lecture. There is an old maxim, "Tell them what you're going to tell them. Tell them. Tell them what you've told them." Like many old maxims, this one is not true—or at least is oversimplified. Giving a summary in advance sometimes helps, but it is detrimental for some students (for example, extroverts, Leith, 1974a), and its effectiveness depends not only upon the type of organization provided, but also upon the succeeding content and previous background of the students. Questions are likely to be better than statements, and questions requiring thinking are generally better than those simply calling attention to main points.

Variability and Verbalization

How can instructors help students develop principles and concepts they can apply much more broadly than answering a problem requiring only a memorized answer? I suppose all instructors have been disheartened by having a student answer a routine problem perfectly and then fail to use the same knowledge in solving another problem where it is relevant. There have been a number of educational attempts to solve this problem. One of the early slogans was, "Learning by doing," a theory that if people learned something in the situation where the learning was to be used they wouldn't have the added step of learning when to apply it. This is perfectly reasonable and makes sense psychologically. The only problem is that the number of situations in which one must use knowledge is infinite. If each human being had to learn everything by doing it, civilization would still be in the Stone Age.

Our whole civilization is based on the fact that people can use *words* to shortcut the long process of learning by trial and error, but direct experience may be useful at certain stages of learning. If one is to learn to apply a principle in new situations, we need to develop it from experiencing specific instances in varying contexts. A number of experiments have demonstrated that repetitive drill is much less effective than varying problems which help to develop principles that can be applied to new situations (for example, Wolfle, 1935). Verbalization can help us identify the common elements in these situations and shorten the learning process. In fact research suggests that even such a complex skill as learning to solo an airplane can be learned in much shorter air time if the learner practices the skill mentally and verbally.

Among the most interesting research programs have been the studies of learning by monkeys carried out by Harlow and his colleagues at Wisconsin. Harlow was studying discrimination learning in monkeys. The monkey was rewarded with food whenever he chose the correct one of two objects, such as a cube or sphere. Psychologists have long known the course learning follows in such situations, and Harlow's monkeys displayed the usual pattern of beginning with virtually chance responses and gradually becoming more consistently accurate. Harlow, however, did not stop with one problem as most learning experimenters have done. Rather, his monkeys were kept at work learning one problem after another, and the monkeys' learning curve gradually changed. With more and more experience the monkeys learned the problems more and more quickly until eventually they needed only one trial to learn which was the correct object. Harlow's monkeys had learned how to learn.

If these experiments are relevant to college teaching (and I think they are), instructors may be able to teach students how to solve problems in their fields by giving them a series of related problems to solve, so that they learn the critical dimensions and most likely approaches.

Feedback, Contiguity, and Active Learning

If instructors expect students to learn skills, the students have to practice, but practice doesn't make perfect. Practice works if learners *see the results* of their practice and gain information from the results about what to do.

A number of experiments suggest that active learning is usually more efficient than passive learning. One reason for this may be the improved opportunities for feedback in active learning. Discussion techniques may help develop critical thinking because students do the thinking and there is an opportunity to check their thinking against each other. But one of the dangers of "student-centered" or "nondirective" discussions is that the results are not apparent. Students may make comments, express opinions, and participate actively, but this doesn't guarantee that their opinions are any more informed at the end of a semester than they were at the beginning. Of course not all feedback has to come from the instructor—students can learn much from other students or from books—but in order to learn, students need to test out their ideas in a situation in which they can get the results of the test and see examples of better thinking.

Nevertheless, instructors need to go a step beyond the principle that students learn what they practice with knowledge of results. It's not always easy to get students to practice critical thinking in the classroom. After all, why stick your neck out? The student who remains quiet in class avoids the risks of disagreement, criticism, and embarrassment. To develop critical thinking, students must learn to want to think.

This brings us back to motivation. Curiosity and competence are powerful motives, but a smile, a nod of encouragement, an excited, "Good. Let's follow that idea through"—these are also tools that teachers can use, not only to provide knowledge of results, but also to develop the motivation to continue intellectual activity.

To maintain motivation instructors need to pose problems that are within the range of their students' abilities. Studies of the development of achievement motivation in children indicate that parents develop this motivation by encouraging the child to do well and by setting standards that the child can achieve. Other parents who orient their children toward achievement fail because they set unreasonable goals. Both for the purposes of motivating students for critical thinking and for developing the ability to think critically, experience in solving problems within the students' ken is essential. This by no means implies that students should not experience failure or criticism, but it does mean that they should be faced with problems that will, as often as not, be soluble.

One of the misconceptions of educators who have recognized the importance of motivation is that they've stopped with the motives students already have. Teachers have assumed that students will learn only those things in which they're interested; so that you need only turn students loose in an environment that contains possibilities for learning. But students' motives are not fixed. Teachers can create new motives. They can help students to enjoy learning for its own sake. While they must make use of existing motives to create initial satisfactions in learning, they need not be limited by them.

Cognition

Psychology has been undergoing a revolution in theory during the past two decades.* The older associationist-behaviorist approaches have been superseded by and incorporated into newer information-processing approaches, derived in part from computer analogies and in part from a long tradition of cognitive theories. These approaches, called cognitive psychology, seek to explain behavior in terms of mental processes. Methodological and theoretical advances have enabled psychologists to make precise tests of theories about the processes human beings use in learning, memory, problem solving, and decision making.

As compared with earlier research on human and animal learning, cognitive approaches place more emphasis upon meaningful human learning. They thus have more potential applicability to problems of education than earlier theories had.

Learning, Semantic Memory, and Retrieval

Until the past few years the basic construct of learning theory was "reinforcement." For many years psychologists believed that stimulus-response connections were stamped in by rewards or "reinforcements." Memory was the reactivation of these connections. Now theorists go beyond simple reinforcement analysis of learning and memory. They think of memory as consisting of different types of storage. For example, an *image* store enables us to recognize a face or familiar opera recording; a *semantic* store enables us to reconstruct the meaning of something you have read or heard. Instead of a telephone switchboard metaphor of the mind, these theorists now think of semantic learning as more like the building up of files, networks, or maps. When we learn, we may add more details to the maps, or we may add more connections between points on the map, or we may even construct alternative maps that are more compact and useful for certain purposes, much as a map of the Interstate Highway system omits details, but is useful in planning long auto trips. But even these metaphors are inadequate; they imply a static

---

* The remaining section of the chapter is derived in large part from a paper I wrote as a partial summary and afterthoughts from a seminar held at the Exxon Educational Foundation in October, 1976.

storage. The current view is rather that memory refers to some properties of an information-processing system—a system involving nerve cells in activity—activities having to do with learning and retrieving meaningful relationships. Learning and remembering are active processes.

Donald Norman of the University of California at San Diego (1977) suggests differentiating three processes of complex learning:

1. Accretion.
2. Restructuring.
3. Fine tuning.

Accretion is adding knowledge to existing cognitive structures. *Restructuring* implies reordering knowledge into new patterns or extending and making connections between existing patterns. *Fine tuning* is the process involved in adapting a cognitive structure so that it can be used more efficiently and appropriately for particular purposes. Much higher education involves developing a more specialized form of a structure than most students already have. Often teachers fail to help students see the link to the general schema they already know.

Students differ not only in how they fit what instructors teach into their existing structures, but also in how readily they develop appropriate new structures. The task of the teacher differs depending upon which kind of learning is involved. Accretion may be achieved simply by referral to a previously learned principle or use of a familiar example; restructuring may require challenges to old structures and much student activity in trying out new understanding.

Instead of thinking of learning and memory in terms of tighter and stronger associations between stimuli and responses, with the associations strengthened by reward, psychologists now think of storage as being influenced by attending to things and interacting with them in such a way that they are related to existing memory structure. We store memories in terms of their potential uses—their meanings. What we store is not just what was said, read, or observed at a particular time; rather what is stored depends also upon previous experience.

Collins and Quillian (1972), who have proposed one model of memory, give as an example the sentence: "The policeman held up his hand and the cars stopped." We accept this statement matter-offactly and probably remember it as a policeman standing in an intersection directing traffic. Had an earthquake started parked cars rolling down a hill, the sentence becomes surprising.

The image of driverless cars rolling down the hill helps you retrieve from memory the sentence about the policeman read a few sentences earlier. Moreover if I ask you sometime later to recall the main ideas of this article, Kintsch's work suggests that you will be more likely to recall the example of the policeman holding up his hand to stop traffic than many of the more substantive points.

In any case, the point here is that we store the sentence about the policeman not just in terms of the dictionary meanings of the words in the sentence, but also in terms of other things we know, such as that policemen often direct traffic, and that moving cars normally have drivers. We process and store meanings without thinking about the process consciously until something does not fit with our previous experience.

Because understanding and learning involve adding previously learned relationships of meanings, students differ in what and how they learn in a particular lecture or assignment. Often teachers have an inadequate comprehension of what students have learned and what is blocking understanding.

Analysis of Tasks and Cognitive Processes

Up to this time cognitive theorists have worked primarily on sentences and simple stories less complex and lengthy than the material involved in college learning. For application to education, instructors need detailed analyses of bodies of college instructional material.

Reviewing the recent history of attempts to apply learning theory to instruction in the Exxon seminar Estes pointed out that the teaching machine movement had involved first, task analysis, and second, development of technology using an existing theory or set of concepts with respect to learning. Teaching machines worked when material could be: 1) broken down into small units, 2) presented in a sequential order, and 3) be used in the same form in which it was presented in training. Unfortunately, the theory on which teaching machines were based had limited applicability to most educational purposes. Computer-assisted instruction (CAI) represented a somewhat more sophisticated attempt to analyze school learning and assess learning theory for possible applications. It is more successful than teaching machines, but again has been limited in its applicability because of limitations of the theories upon which CAI has been based.

The kind of education involved in higher education is more general purpose than that involved in teaching machines and previous CAI. It needs to be more modifiable and more transferable to situations remote from the training situation. Thus the problem of task analysis is much more complex than that involved in the simpler types of training that were relevant for teaching machines or previous CAI. It should not be necessary to analyze every task for which education is carried out. If education is general, it should be possible to define general kinds of tasks cutting across situations. One way of identifying generalizable task characteristics might be to look at process-oriented aptitudes. The sort of analysis Estes made of the subtests of intelligence measures represented exactly this sort of movement; that is, if educational psychologists can define intellectual factors in terms of the cognitive processes demanded, they probably have a good start at defining generalizable task characteristics. They can then analyze learning tasks such as studying a textbook or listening to a lecture, both with respect to the cognitive processes involved and the structure of the content.

Even a relatively simple analysis of an educational task may be useful. For example, one might ask, "Why does a student fail an essay question on an exam?"

1. She does not understand the question.
2. She has not learned the material.
3. She lacks cues for retrieval.
4. She lacks an appropriate strategy for retrieving the material.
5. She lacks words needed for an answer.
6. She lacks a conception of the required solution; for example, when asked to "explain," she lacks an adequate conception of what is involved in an adequate explanation.
7. She cannot hold the required material in active memory while writing the answer.

When long-term memory is unorganized, a big load is placed on short-term memory during the task of writing an appropriate answer. For example, Cole et al. (1971) found that nonliterate African children seemed deficient on free-recall tests, but when they were led by special techniques to respond in meaningful *categories*, recall was similar to that of American children. Some college students may have similar difficulties in organizing course material into meaningful categories.

The point of such an analysis of an essay test is that rather than simply telling a student to study a particular chapter more thoroughly, instructors can look for common threads of difficulties in processing exemplified in several questions; they can even design tests laying bare different possible sources of difficulty, so that remedial action can be taken.

Teachers should not expect to make big improvements in education. Norman (1977) suggested that good lecturers and good textbook writers today are probably close to the best that is achievable; similarly, good students probably learn about as efficiently as they can. But many teachers and learners are probably not very efficient. When preparing a course, teachers may simply update a set of lecture notes; when told to learn something, students may simply repeat and rehearse materials—using methods not very effective for learning, remembering, and using meanings. Analyses of the processes students use in reading an assignment, answering a question, or in other aspects of education may be useful in locating difficulties and suggesting more effective learning and teaching strategies.

Can Teachers Be Helped Now?

Granted that teachers lack the research needed to apply cognitive theory to higher education today, are there any suggestions that might be helpful to them right now?*

What psychologists have to say is really different in nature as well as content from earlier psychological approaches. The difference is that the newer information-processing, cognitive approach is not as *prescriptive*—not as oriented toward *behavioral control*. As James Greeno (1976) wrote:

> As we get deeper into the analysis of what human beings actually do in cognitive tasks, we become more appreciative of the adaptive quality

---

* A useful paper on this topic is George Leith, "Implications of cognitive psychology for the improvement of teaching and learning in the universities." In B. Massey, ed., *Papers of the Third International Conference on Improving University Teaching*, University College, University of Maryland, 1977.

of cognitive processes. General laws of the kind needed for *control* of behavior in Skinner's sense do *not* characterize the science of psychology, because the interesting features of cognitive systems are not context-free. What we seem to be developing, rather than a set of general laws, is a set of rather specific descriptions. As our knowledge is translated into application, I think it will have much more the character of permitting individuals to achieve their potential, based on capabilities that are understood because of scientific study, rather than of laws that determine what people will do.

Yet faculty members, administrators, and even students *want* prescriptions: "What can I do to get better results?"

I do not think psychologists can any longer simply say, "Reward correct responses." But I think some statements may be helpful in analyzing the problems and suggesting possible solutions. I would like to suggest some such statements based on my own limited understanding of cognitive psychology and previous research in college teaching:

1. Human beings are learning organisms—seeking, organizing, coding, storing, and retrieving information all their lives; building on cognitive structures to continue learning throughout life (certainly not losing capacity to learn); continually seeking meaning.

2. Human beings can remember images; they can remember transcriptions of the exact words that were used in a lecture or textbook; or they can remember meanings depending upon the demands of the situation.

3. In our society, at least, there is a strong tendency to store and retrieve meanings rather than exact reproductions of what we experience. What meaning a student gets depends not only upon the student's past experience, expectancies, and set but also upon the student's learning strategy or style.

Marton and Säljö (1976b) differentiate among students in terms of depth of processing, a concept current in cognitive psychology (for example, Craik and Lockhart, 1972). The difference between deep-level processing and surface-level processing is in some ways comparable to the difference between literal interpretations of the Bible and the interpretations of scholars using formal criticism.

Probably the easiest way to communicate Marton and Säljö's distinction is to quote an actual example from their study. Their students read chapters from Coombs, *The World Educational Crisis: A Systems Analysis* (1971, Swedish edition). They were then asked,

"What is meant by the output of an educational system?" Answers going from surface to deep processing were the following:

—Level 1: What Comes Out of the Educational System (Surface). "Something to do with . . . well . . . you know, the result of." "The product . . . I think."

—Level 2: Those Who Leave the Educational System with a Completed Education.
"It's the trained work-force that the educational system produces. It's, well, for example . . . well, simply the trained work-force."

—Level 3: The Effects of Education on Society and on Individuals Produced by Knowledge and Attitudes Acquired Through Schooling (Deep).
"Mm, it's the knowledge that . . . and values . . . yes, the knowledge and values that students have acquired. That is, whatever it is that influences them and makes them read this or that and do this or that."

Surface-level processors tend to study as if learning were something that happens to the learner; deep-level processors act much more as if learning is something the learner *does*. (Dahlgren and Marton, 1976.)

4. Instructors teach students not only the *knowledge* of history, biology, or psychology, but also structures, modes of thought, and strategies for learning (Olson, 1976). The important thing taught is form, not content. Different means may produce the same knowledge but not the same broader understanding for different learners or different uses. Comparisons of college teaching methods typically find no significant differences in tests of knowledge. There are, however, differences between teaching methods in retention, application, transfer, and other outcomes (McKeachie and Kulik, 1975).

Mayer (1974), for example, taught students binomial probability by two methods. One group was taught calculating with a formula; the second group was taught the meaning of the variables in the formula. After training, the formula group was better able than the meaning group to solve problems of the sort they had been trained on; the meaning group, however, was superior on creative problem solving involving general knowledge of the concepts.

Can "meaning" learners also find new principles in new problems better than rule learners? If so, they have learned the sort of general cognitive skill teachers need to aim for.

At the very least, the cognitive approach indicates that teachers need to be aware of several kinds of outcomes—not just *how much* was learned, but also *what kinds of learning* took place. (Accretion? restructuring? fine tuning?) They can look at transfer of learning in terms of near transfer (internal connectedness) and far transfer (external connectedness).

5. Learning something in the classroom may have different consequences from learning it from peers, from books, or learning it from one's own experience.

This does not mean that all learning should be experiential. Written language is very powerful and much used in our culture. Science is largely based on written, rational discourse.

6. In addition to the differentiated effectiveness of different methods for different outcomes, methods are differentially effective for different learners.

Egan and Greeno (1973) found that some learners learned most readily by the formula, or algorithmic, method, while others learned more effectively by the meaning method. The optimal method of training involved a combination of methods. For learners who did well with algorithms, additional training on the meaning of the variables after the normal training resulted in good performance on both criterion measures, while for the meaning group, additional drill on problem solving brought their performance on routine problems up to that of the other group. Thus, adaptation of instruction to individual differences in cognitive abilities or styles can result in greater effectiveness.

Greeno (1976) suggests that general cognitive structures not only are taught along with content, but are also prerequisites to understanding content. Students who have no general structures for understanding science may be as lost in a biological science course as an American attempting to use our conventional narrative structures to understand an Indian folk-tale using a different kind of narrative structure. Thus, teachers have to consider structures not only as results of instruction, but also as prerequisites for instruction. In addition, teachers must find ways of getting from the structures in students' minds to the desired structures. It may be that sometimes inadequate, and even incorrect, simple concepts or analogies are the quickest way to bridge the gap. Summaries and reviews also help (Leith, 1971).

7. Because of interactions among student characteristics, teacher characteristics, goals, subject matter, and methods (Cronbach and Snow, 1977), flexibility and variability of approaches is more likely to be effective than a single method. Any given method is likely to be effective for some students and ineffective for others.

8. If learners are given options, can they choose the method most suited to their own abilities? Research on giving students options between different methods of learning, such as independent study, lecture, or discussion, suggests that students realize little benefit from such choices (Pascal, 1971).

Perhaps one of the problems is that many students are unable to identify their own most effective style. Pask and Scott (1973) taught elementary concepts of probability theory by a system in which the computer carried on a tutorial conversation with the student in order to learn the student's idiosyncratic method of problem solving. Adaptive teaching systems are designed to present material at increasing levels of difficulty as students become more proficient. Pask and Scott argue that such systems will not be effective if the student's problem solving strategy makes a difference. Thus their CASTE (Course Assembly System and Tutorial Environment) is designed to interact with the student in such a way as to externalize normally unobservable learning or problem solving strategies.

Pask and Scott studied two strategy classes—serialist and holist. Students using a serialist strategy break problems into subproblems, taking one step at a time. They assimilate data from specific relations of low order. Students using a holist strategy solve problems *in toto;* they assimilate data widely from high-order relations without certainty about particulars. Holist students tended to come from philosophy, history, and the social sciences; serialists were more likely to come from natural science and mathematics.

Pask and Scott developed a test to identify serialist vs. holist dispositions of students and developed teaching heuristics to match the serialist and holist strategies. When students were matched with the appropriate teaching treatment, they learned and retained material well; those who were mismatched learned very little. Unfortunately, students given their choice of treatments did not consistently choose the method optimal for their own strategy.

9. In addition to teaching students to identify their own most ef-

fective learning strategies, can instructors teach students to be able to use a larger repertoire of strategies? If this were achieved, instead of adapting teaching methods to students, students could adopt the learning strategy most effective for whatever teaching method they encountered.

10. Testing practices may influence students' learning strategies. The classic study in this area antedates information-processing approaches by three decades (McCluskey, 1934). It was concerned with the practical problem of the relative advantages of essay vs. objective tests. One group of students expected to be tested by an objective test; another group expected to be tested by an essay test. Each group was tested with both objective and essay questions. The groups made equivalent scores on the objective test, but the group preparing for an essay test did better than the objective test group on the essay questions. The results suggest that the strategy used by students preparing for an essay test is superior to that used when studying for an objective test.

In a more recent study Marton and Säljö (1976b) showed that students' depth of processing of a given chapter was influenced by the type of questions asked following the reading of an earlier chapter. Rote memory questions such as, "According to the author the shortage of teachers depends on three factors. Which three?" produced surface-level processing, while deep-level processing was induced by questions such as, "Explain the meaning of the following quotation—'Too many poor teachers will drive good ones out of the market.'"

Does a course using essay tests have different effects on students' later approaches to similar subject matter than a similar course using objective tests? Does the type of questions used produce an effect lasting beyond the particular course? My guess is that the breadth of effect of essay testing may well depend upon the sort of comments or questions written by the instructor on the test. Comments may help students learn new strategies or skills for learning and *using* a particular subject matter—and perhaps several types of courses taught in this way may produce effects generalizing across subject matters.

How do you teach such general skills or strategies? So far as I know there are no systematic rules; yet I suspect that good teachers do it intuitively. Probably helpful comments not only indicate errors and inadequacies, but also ask questions or make suggestions steering students to a more sophisticated, or deeper, approach. Johnson (1975) has shown that creativity of answers is influenced by marginal comments. Probably most teachers have some implicit models of how they can influence student learning and such models probably contain much truth. If psychologists can help teachers become more explicit, there should be a better chance for the model to improve with experience.

11. The cognitive structure of each student is different from that of the teacher. Thus, the paradox arises that the teacher must learn from students the students' structures if the teacher is to be effective in helping students learn from the teacher.

12. Talking, writing, doing, interacting, and teaching others are important means for learners to restructure their learning.

If teachers are to make bridges between: a) structures in the subject matter, curriculum, or course design, b) structures in the teacher, and c) structures in learners, they need to carry on discussions in which students have an opportunity to externalize their problems and progress. Since such interaction becomes increasingly difficult as class size increases, teachers need to provide at least some opportunities for small-group discussion, dialogue, writing, explaining, or doing something to which the teacher, other students, and the learner, herself, can respond (for example, Leith, 1974b).

13. Teachers are important as models for students. Personal, warm encouragement from a fellow human being has important effects upon motivation to learn and upon the degree to which students attempt to follow the example of a model. As Bandura (1976) and Eelen and D'Ydewalle (1976) have shown, learning from observing a model may be very effective.

14. In the classroom three levels of processes are going on. The figural aspect is:

a. the subject matter content, but as Olson suggests, inseparably linked with content is
b. the level-of-thinking, method, or cognitive structure. And in the background of these cognitive aspects of teaching-learning is
c. the interpersonal level of emotional relationships of students to teachers.

Psychologists know little about how to integrate these three levels in such ways as to optimize education, but it is clearly a dynamic, ongoing process involving much adaptation on the part of both teacher and students.

15. A teacher may not only teach a student the subject matter and how to learn that subject, but also how best to learn from that teacher.

16. Increases in effectiveness of education may come as much, or more, from helping students understand their own learning processes as from varying your teaching (Norman, 1977).

SUPPLEMENTARY READING

Richard E. Mayer, *Thinking and problem solving: an introduction to human cognition and learning* (Glenview IL: Scott-Foresman, 1974).

24

Personalizing Education

For almost one-hundred years the image of the ideal education has been Mark Hopkins on one end of the log and James Garfield on the other. Whether or not such a faculty-to-student ratio is optimal might be questioned, but whatever the case, it is clear that most faculty members have to work with larger groups in which personalization of education depends upon sensitivity to individual differences among students. But there is an infinite variety of differences among students. What sorts of differences are most important to teachers as they strive to make the learning experience most valuable for each class member?

It is not enough to know that certain variables affect learning gen-

---

Parts of this chapter are based on my chapter in W. J. Minter, ed., *The Individual and the system* (Boulder, Col.: Western Interstate Commission for Higher Education, 1967). Footnotes have been omitted.

erally. Intelligence, for example, has an obvious influence upon student learning, but knowing student differences in intelligence is not important to a teacher unless highly intelligent students need to be taught in some way different from students of less intelligence. Of concern here are interactions, that is, characteristics differentiating students for whom different kinds of teacher behavior are differentially effective.

Basically, this chapter questions the assumption that the ideal educational situation is one in which all students have personal attention from their instructors. Rather, my thesis is that the goal is to educate all students to the best of their and our capacities. Personal attention is one means to that goal, but not an end in itself. Different students need different things. Some may need individual personal attention from instructors, but some don't. For some students at some times really personalized education may involve opportunities for independent study, for work in student-led groups, or for other types of learning involving *less* rather than *more* individual contact with faculty members. Moreover teachers should keep in mind that students are survivors of twelve years or more of formal education. They have been selected and trained for certain kinds of academic achievement. While they differ in many ways, they are not nearly as diverse as people in general. They have well-practiced ways of learning and coping with different kinds of instruction. Instructors are not likely to produce major changes in their achievement, but they can do some things if they have some ideas about what differences are worth paying attention to.

Now, what can research to date tell instructors?

Student Characteristics

● *Intelligence.* Intelligent students do better than less intelligent students in most educational situations. But it does make a difference how students of differing intelligence are taught. Remmers (1933), in three experiments comparing varying combinations of lecture and recitation, found fairly consistent results favoring a greater proportion of recitation for abler students and a greater proportion of lecture for the less able students. Ward's study (1956) indicated that the ablest students, more than other students, are favorably influenced by small classes. Calvin, Hoffman, and Harden (1957) found in three experiments that *less* intelligent students consistently did better in group problem-solving situations conducted in an authoritarian manner than in groups conducted in a permissive manner. The same difference did not occur for bright students. Hansen, Kelley, and Weisbrod (1970) found that TIPS, a system involving frequent testing, was most effective for less able students. All of these probably indicate that less structured methods, such as discussion, are more appropriate for bright students than for less able students.

Siegel and Siegel (1964) found that low-ability students performed better on a test of conceptual acquisition if they had been previously tested with an emphasis on factual rather than conceptual learning. High-ability students were affected by the difference in methods based on their previous knowledge; high-ability students with high previous knowledge benefited from emphasis on conceptual learning, while the unsophisticated high-ability student, like the low-ability student, performed better on conceptual acquisition if previous emphasis had been on factual learning.

These results fit well with the wisdom of college faculties who have generally urged smaller classes, greater use of discussion, and a higher conceptual level in honors classes. Bright students will generally be able to handle a greater information-processing load than less able students; that is, the able students can figure out things better for themselves and provide their own organization. The less able students are more likely to benefit from attempts to simplify and organize the material for the students, organization that may be detrimental for the better students (see Snow, 1976). Siegel and Siegel, however, inject a cautionary note—being bright is not enough. The naive bright student is perhaps more like the less able student than is sometimes recognized by college honors committees, a point also illustrated in the research of Mayer, Stiehl, and Greeno (1975).

● *Cognitive style.* Some students are predisposed to learn facts; others are disposed to apply and synthesize facts. In an experiment at Miami University the former type of student was particularly helped by personal contact with the instructor. In addition, students with little prior knowledge in a subject matter area also benefited particularly from personal contact with the teachers (Siegel and Siegel, 1964).

In a later publication (1966), however, Siegel and Siegel point out that the effect of personal contact with instructors depends upon what the instructor does. In research on the personal contact variable ,they compared the performance of students enrolled in television courses who had the television teacher as instructor for a discussion or laboratory section with the performance of students who had other faculty members or teaching assistants as teachers in these sections. Some instructors used the period for clarification of the lectures; others for further exploration. In the Siegel and Siegel research, the high-ability student benefited from personal contact when the contact involved exploration, but the low-ability student benefited from clarification. It is clear from these results that getting to know the instructor personally is not the answer to the student's problems. The effect of personal contact depends upon the sort of interaction, the sort of student, and the match between student orientation, instructor goals, and method used.

The match between cognitive style of student and instructor was also illustrated in Runkel's (1956) finding that students who thought like their instructors, using the same dimensions to organize concepts, received better grades than students using other dimensions. What psychologists don't yet know is how instructors develop students' abilities to use new dimensions, or, in other words, to see their subject matter from new perspectives.

That students' cognitive styles can be affected by instruction is indicated by Heath's (1964) and Wish's (1964) evaluation of the Physical Science Study Committee's high school science course. PSSC students were more likely than students having had conventional courses to prefer questioning and principles rather than memory of facts and applications in a test of cognitive preferences.

● *Independence, responsibility, and flexibility.* A pioneering step in the direction of relating personality and response to teaching methods was taken by Wispe (1951), who used TAT-like measures to differentiate three types of students: the "personality-insecure" student (51 percent of the sample), the "satisfied" student (26 percent of the sample), and the "independent" student (23 percent of the sample). The "insecure" student had unfavorable attitudes toward permissive teaching. The "satisfied" student had favorable attitudes toward instructors, fellow students, and both directive and permissive teaching methods. The "independent" student was highly verbal and wanted more permissive teaching no matter what method the instructor used. The "independent" student had moderately favorable attitudes toward fellow students and instructors, but was likely to direct aggression against the instructor in directive classes. While other studies have suggested that favorable attitudes are likely to be associated with improved learning, the Wispe study does not give direct evidence that teaching and student characteristics interacted in affecting learning.

Patton's results (1955) are clearer. Comparing students in conventionally taught classes with those in which students were given major responsibility for the course, Patton found that the degree to which students accepted responsibility in the latter class was positively correlated with gain in ability to apply psychology, rating the value of the course, and interest in psychology. But what sort of student accepted responsibility in such a course? Patton found that the students who liked his experimental class and assumed responsibility were likely to be independent of traditional authority figures and high in need for achievement. Similarly, in the Oberlin studies (McCollough and Van Atta, 1958) students who were less rigid and less in need of social support profited more in measured achievement from independent study than those students who were not as independent. Domino, using the Achievement via Independence and Achievement via Conformity scales of the California Psychological Inventory, found in two studies (1968, 1971) that independent students did better with teacher styles stressing independence, while students high in Achievement via Conformity did better with more structure.

Despite the variety of measures used, the studies cited in this section show some consistency in finding that a certain type of student, characterized as independent, flexible, or high in need for achievement, is happy and achieves well (at least on a test of application of concepts) in classroom situations that give students opportunity for self-direction.

● *Authoritarianism.* Authoritarianism was one of the most intensively studied research variables of the 1950s. Research on this variable fits with the preceding research.

Watson (1956) studied the effect of permissive and restrictive teaching and testing methods upon students differing in authoritarianism and permeability (extraversion). The methods were not differentially effective as measured by achievement tests, but student satisfaction was affected by testing methods. Highest satisfaction resulted when students were tested in an atmosphere appropriate for their needs; that is, permissive for permeable, restrictive for impermeable. This finding is in line with the finding of Bendig and Hountras (1959) that authoritarian students prefer a high degree of departmental control of instruction.

Students high on a variable akin to authoritarianism were found to gain more when taught in a homogeneous group. The instructor who taught this section found that he had to resist pressures from the students for lectures. He secured his good results by using many direct questions, encouraging student responses, and by vigorously defending absurd positions which even authoritarian students would argue against (Stern, 1962).

● *Motivation.* Let us turn to some specific motives for learning.

As I noted earlier, Patton's students who accepted responsibility for their own learning tended to be high in the achievement motive. Koenig and McKeachie (1959) similarly found that women high in need for achievement preferred independent study to lectures.

Our studies at Michigan have shown that need for affiliation is an important determinant of student reactions to differing styles of teaching. Men who are high in need for affiliation do better work in classes where the teacher takes a personal interest in students; conversely, men who are low in need for affiliation tend to do relatively poorly in these classes (McKeachie, et al., 1966).

Beach (1960) studied the personality variable of sociability as a predictor of achievement in lecture and small-group teaching methods. In the lecture section the nonsociable students (as measured by the Guilford Inventory of Factors STDCR) achieved significantly more than the sociable students; in the small-group sections the results were reversed.

These studies reinforce the point I made earlier. Personal contact with the instructor is valuable for some students, but not for all. Those likely to be favorably affected are those with low motivation and those high in sociability or need for affiliation. There are many students who fall in these groups, but also many who are not positively affected and may even achieve less when personal contact with the instructor is increased.

● *Anxiety.* What is the effect of anxiety upon learning? How can you best teach anxious students?

The answers to these questions turn out to be less obvious than one would expect. Generally, psychologists assume that anxiety is detrimental to learning. The research evidence suggests that the relationship is more complex, depending equally on the level of anxiety, the difficulty of the material, and the ability of the student. Generally speaking, anxious students do less well under high levels of stress, but what is stressful may differ for different students.

Since anxiety is generally believed to be increased by uncertainty, the anxious person should work most effectively in a highly structured situation. This hypothesis is partially supported by the research of D. E. P. Smith and his co-workers (1956), who found that anxious students who were permeable (sensitive to stimuli, impulsive, socially oriented, and low in ego strength) made optimal progress in a remedial reading course when taught by directive methods. Impermeable anxious students, however, were unaffected by differences in teaching methods. H. C. Smith (1955) found that students with high anxiety and low initial achievement gained more on achievement tests and were more highly satisfied in a "teamwork" class than in a conventional lecture. Dowaliby and Schumer (1973) found that anxious students did relatively better with directive teaching. Domino (1974) replicated this finding, but Peterson (1976) shows that the situation is more complicated. Highly anxious, high-ability students and nonanxious, low-ability students need structure; others do not.

• *Anxiety and testing.* The relationship between anxiety and performance on classroom examinations administered under varying conditions has been the subject of several experiments. To test whether the anxiety created by tests might be dissipated by permitting students to write comments on tests, half of the students in a University of Michigan experiment were given answer sheets with spaces for comments and half were given standard answer sheets. Measures of students' feelings about the tests failed to show any difference between the two groups, but the students who had the opportunity to write comments made higher scores on the test. These results held up in a series of experiments (McKeachie, Pollie, and Speisman, (1955). These findings suggested that student anxiety during classroom examinations builds up to such a point that it may interfere with memory and problem solving. Reducing the stress of the examination by permitting students to write comments resulted in improved performance.

This interpretation is supported by the work of Calvin, McGuigan, and Sullivan (1957), who found that students who were given a chance to write comments on an achievement test were superior to control students in their performance on the second half of the test, and that the students who made the greatest gain were the highly anxious students as measured by the Taylor Manifest Anxiety Scale. Similarly, W. F. Smith and Rockett (1958) found that instructions to write comments significantly interacted with anxiety, helping the performance of high-anxiety students but hurting the performance of students low in anxiety.

The experimental results on interaction of anxiety and teaching variables are tantalizing enough to stimulate further work, but they are not consistent enough to lead to any stable generalizations. It does look as if anxious students react badly to failure and are helped by chances to express themselves. But the fact that differences in sex and in other personality variables, such as permeability, interacted with anxiety in the experiments above suggests that multivariate designs are necessary to explore this area adequately.

● *Introversion—extroversion.* Leith (1974a) has carried out and reviewed a number of studies on differential effects of various educational situations on introverts and extroverts. For example, as noted in my discussion of the "learning cell," extroverts learn better when studying with another extrovert than when working alone. Leith also found that extroverts learned better by a discovery method, while introverts learned better by reception. Similarly, extroverts learned better with less feedback, while introverts learned better with more feedback.

● *Sex.* Our coeducational institutions may have a vested interest in the assumption that the best education for men is also best for women. In any case, until recently very little research has dealt with the differences in learning styles of men and women.

Carrier (1957) investigated the manner in which individual differences in four personality variables affected performance in more and less stressful testing situations. He found that one of the most important variables determining reaction in his experiment was sex. Women were much more detrimentally affected than men by his stress situation.

In a later experiment (McKeachie, 1958) half of the students in a large class received a tranquilizing drug, meprobamate, while the other half received a placebo just before an examination. If students tend to be too anxious, such a drug should improve test scores. The results did not confirm this hypothesis. Students who had the drug reported experiencing less anxiety during the examination than did the placebo group, but they did not make better scores.

The really interesting result of the experiment was the sex-drug interaction. Women benefited from the drug more than men. Thus sex once again turned out to be an important variable. The results make sense if a curvilinear relationship between anxiety and performance is assumed, with women too anxious and men less than optimally anxious. Thus, reduced anxiety should result in improved performance for women, but poorer performance for men. Once again teaching techniques have different effects on different types of students.

We have found in our research at Michigan that instructors who assign much difficult work are particularly effective with women. Men do well in a class in which the instructor compliments students when they have done well.

With the current interest in Women's Studies and changing images of "proper" sex roles, one would expect interest in research on the differences in college learning between men and women. The results cited above suggest that the methods most effective in teaching men have not necessarily been those most effective with women. At least at Michigan, women students have tended to be somewhat more concerned about achievement, more willing to do what the instructor demands, and more responsive to personal interest from instructors. Nevertheless, a good deal more research is needed before we can talk confidently about what personalization of education means for both men and women.

● *Student–discipline interactions.* The characteristic learning problems differ somewhat from discipline to discipline, and the general student characteristics I have discussed in this chapter may be far less important in individualizing instruction than student characteristics related to hang-ups in particular disciplines. Research is needed to identify these, but I would guess, for example, the religious background might be a very important characteristic of both student and teacher in certain courses in philosophy and behavioral science. The combination of a fundamentalist student with an instructor who is still rebelling against his own religious training may result in the sort of conflict that interferes with, rather than facilitates, learning. Similarly, in mathematics a relevant characteristic may be the student's attitude toward mathematics, previous success in it, and for women, perhaps the degree to which mathematics is seen as a masculine activity.

Instructor Characteristics

Even less is known about instructor characteristics affecting personalization than about student characteristics. We do know that faculty members who are attentive to individual students are more likely to be effective teachers than those less attentive to students (McKeachie et al., 1966).

The instructor has a major effect on personalization through influence on group norms in the classroom and college. Some student groups stifle individuality, chop down creative contributors, and are insensitive to members' needs. How do you create groups in which individual students can feel respected, free, and motivated to make the maximum contributions of which they are capable? One relevant factor is almost certainly the degree to which the course is structured along competitive or cooperative lines. As Haines and McKeachie (1967) showed, students in classes stressing competition for grades show more tension, self-doubt, and anxiety than those in classes structured for cooperative achievement.

Faculty members find it is easier to accept the possibility that students may have personal barriers to learning than to recognize that we as teachers often defend against real changes in ourselves. If we accept Roger Heyns' definition of college as a community of learners, every teacher-student interaction carries potential for learning of both teacher and student. One of the barriers to student learning is that many professors see themselves as handing down learning from a celestial throne. We know very little about professors' views of themselves and their roles and the effect of different role concepts upon personalization of instruction. We need to follow up on recent research on college professors with studies of such characteristics as, 1) ability to see subject matter from the perspective of a student, 2) flexibility in ways of conceptualizing subject matter, 3) commitment to the field, 4) nurturance, and 5) willingness to listen and learn from students.

Educational Strategy

If the "Mark Hopkins on the end of a log" ideal is impossible in these days of soaring enrollments, is there any real hope of individualization? I believe there is. Too often teachers have carried the academic lock step into each individual course, meeting classes faithfully three times every week, giving the same assignments to every student, treating each student exactly the same in the interest of fairness. But even large universities and large classes can provide for individuality. Couldn't instructors, in a large class, for example, permit some students to gain information from reading in the library rather than from attending lectures? Might not some students be encouraged to do laboratory work, while others gain direct experiences in field settings? Could instructors provide small group discussions for some and computer consoles for others? At present no one knows much about which students best achieve which goals with which experiences, but I would bet that the mere presence of several alternatives would result in educational gain.

Students themselves have opinions about how they can best learn. Although these opinions are not always accurate, giving students some opportunity to determine their own conditions of learning, to suffer the consequences of bad choices, and to learn from these consequences may be the most important way in which education can be personalized.

There is evidence that students are fairly good judges of when they have been taught effectively, and my guess is that most teachers are fairly accurate in their estimates of which students they are most effective with. This, however, should not be taken to mean that learning is always pleasant and satisfying. When teachers really touch students deeply, the students may face a painful reorganization of their definitions of themselves and of their relationships to others. Their methods of thinking, their conceptions of the universe, even their values, may be challenged by the mode of thinking of a discipline taught in a way that reaches them as people. They have the choice of incorporating the learning and reorganizing themselves or compartmentalizing the content in such a way that it has minimal effect upon them. In the struggle between compartmentalization and reorganization, teachers and the other students can be important allies of growth if they are able to respond to feedback from the affected students about the problems they are having in incorporating the learning.

One implication of the data on interactions of student characteristics and teacher characteristics in affecting learning might be to feed all the data into a computer to assign students to the classes of those teachers who best fit their needs. But this seems to me an unlikely and possibly undesirable consequence. Not only is the information too unreliable to guide decisions for individuals, but also it may well be that on the basis of this information instructors might better teach students to learn from a variety of teachers than to restrict them to teachers to whom they can adjust most easily. Similarly, teachers might be trained to identify and teach effectively those students who are not normally "turned on" by their style of teaching. This latter alternative is particularly attractive to me because sensitive teachers can respond to feedback from students, modifying their tactics from week to week and day to day as they observe their effects. Teaching should be a two-way process in which both students and teachers learn from one another; as long as teaching conditions facilitate two-way interaction, the good sense of teachers and students can be substantially relied upon.

The studies I have cited are really only the first toddling steps necessary for understanding how to personalize education. They give instructors some clues about what kind of relatively permanent differences in students to look for, as well as some leads about what kinds of procedures may be helpful to them. But such categorization is only a beginning. While it is an improvement over the attitude that students are all about the same, categorization of students may be a disservice if it leads teachers to forget that students are living, growing, changing individuals and need different things from teachers at different times. My colleague, Richard Mann, points out that students whose motivation is low, who mistrust the teacher, and who seem rigid and anxious early in a term may, after some resolution of their relationships with the teacher, have an enormous in-rush of energy and now be much more flexible and creative. Mann's own research has been directed toward understanding the development of student-teacher relationships over a term, and this research seems to me at the heart of the problem of personalizing education. Mann suggests that particular teachers can be characterized not so much as having a hard time with a particular type of student as having trouble with a particular type of feeling—such as dependence, depression, hostility, or even affection. While certain students may be the articulators of this feeling, it may be more important for the teacher to note that the feeling characterizes the whole group at this time than to note the particular students who lead in expressing the feeling. It may be just as important to teach teachers how to cope with these feelings, or to wait them out, as to teach them how to deal with particular students. Mann suggests that difficulties with particular students often are the result of responses to the mood of the entire class, which are so defensive or inappropriate as to permanently alienate those students who feel this mood most strongly. A teacher may, for example, become so angry or punitive in response to a rebellious class that the most rebellious students simply are "turned off" from then on. (See Mann et al., 1970)

As classes become larger, the opportunity for two-way communication and moment-to-moment shifting of educational strategy is reduced, and teachers are more and more likely to misperceive student needs and feelings. Knowledge of the student characteristics I have discussed can be helpful in formulating an initial educational strategy, but real educational success depends upon continual re-evaluation and modification of your teaching plans as you observe student responses. As financial pressures increase, there is danger that instructors will abandon all pretense of two-way interaction and subvert teaching into one-way communication of information. If this occurs, there will be an increasing pressure to "technicalize" the communicator's role. Just as teachers have turned student counseling over to professional counselors, they may turn large lecture and television teaching over to "master teachers" or actors. But for effective education, colleges need to preserve student-teacher interaction as the central aspect of higher education and to preserve opportunities for teachers to get satisfaction from teaching. Rather than letting the teaching technologies substitute for teaching, teachers can use them to preserve small-group, person-to-person interactions in the face of large enrollments.

Supplementary reading

Samuel Messick et al., *Individuality in learning* (San Francisco: Jossey-Bass, 1976).

25

Doing and Evaluating Research on Teaching

Determining which of two teaching methods is more effective looks like a simple problem. Presumably all that is necessary is to teach something by both methods and then compare the results. This is essentially the research design of many of the studies that are widely quoted to show the effectiveness of the Keller Plan, television, discussion, independent study, or other methods. Unfortunately, there are some hidden traps enthusiasts for one method or another are likely to overlook.

Suppose, for example, that a group of students is given an opportunity to take a class taught by some method quite unusual in their college. The very fact that the method is different gives it excitement. Sometimes the reaction may be one of enthusiasm; in other cases it may be one of outraged hostility. The latter reaction seems to be particularly likely when students taught by a new method know that they are competing on examinations with students taught by the tried and true traditional methods. In any case it is difficult to know how much of student improvement (or loss) in learning may be accounted for by the emotional reaction to a new and different method and how much can be expected when the new method is routine. This "Hawthorne effect" affects not only students but also professors. How many new curricula, new courses, or new teaching methods have flowered briefly and then faded as the innovators' enthusiasm waned or as new staff members replaced the originators? Unfortunately, relatively few studies have made comparisons over a period longer than one semester. Students who have experienced a semester of instruction by a new method (except television) are generally more likely to choose a section by this method than are students without previous experience. This difference in motivation, as well as added skill in the requisites of "Studentship" in a new method, might result in greater advantages for a new method after two or more semesters of trial than after a single semester.

A second methodological problem is establishing a suitable control group. In some experiments a single instructor uses both teaching methods. Here the obvious problem is that it is difficult to determine how much the instructor's own personality and skills have influenced the outcome. It is impossible to know whether or not other teachers would obtain similar results. The obvious remedy for this defect is to persuade several professors to use both methods. Leaving aside the salesmanship necessary to institute such a research design, the effort involved in trying to teach by two methods, keeping strictly to each, is tremendous. As a result, the methods either tend to coalesce or, in an overzealous attempt to avoid this, the experimenter institutes artificial and additional constraints to accentuate the differences.

Another problem in establishing controls is that the conditions of the experiment may introduce special factors that interfere with normal results. For example, the experiment may require extensive testing, the presence of observers in the class, or other interferences with normal classroom routine. A class in which a "live" professor is talking to television cameras is probably not a suitable comparison group for classes watching the lesson on television receivers.

A fourth problem is biased sampling. According to newspaper reports, studies of educational television have demonstrated that students taking the course at home learn as much as those on campus. The obvious problem is that people who sign up for a television course and come to campus to take the exam are probably somewhat different in motivation and background from typical college sophomores. As Greenhill points out (1959), efforts to equate such groups are never successful.

A fifth problem is in the statistical methods used to analyze the results of teaching-methods experiments. Ordinarily experimenters are concerned about avoiding the type of error involved in concluding that one method is more effective than another when in reality they do not differ significantly. However, they are less likely to be sensitive to another type of error that may be just as damaging—the error of concluding that there is no difference in effectiveness when two methods are not found to differ significantly. In addition to the logical fallacy involved in accepting failure to disprove the null hypothesis as proof of no difference, there is the problem of choice of methods of analysis. The chance of obtaining such results depends upon the type of statistical analysis used. With "weak" statistics, a difference is less likely to be detected than with "strong" statistics. The true effect of a variable may be beclouded if no effort is made to remove other sources of variance. As I suggest later, the application of multivariate statistics, such as analysis of covariance, might, by taking out other sources of variance, reveal more clearly the true effects of varying methods. Further, when several tests of the same hypothesis are made with different groups, experimenters might well use combined tests of significance. For example, if ten groups come out in the same direction, it is extremely unlikely that the methods are not differentially effective even though no one difference would be statistically significant.

But even with better statistical methods, large, consistent effects are not likely. Education is a tremendously complex effort affected by many variables. No one thing, or group of variables, is likely to stand out clearly amidst the noise of the other variables not under study.

A sixth problem is the interaction among teaching methods, student characteristics, teacher characteristics, or other variables. What is effective for some students may not be for others.

The Criterion Problem

The major problem in experimental comparisons of teaching methods is the criterion problem. Stuit and Wilson's (1946) prediction studies in naval training showed that as the criterion was increasingly well defined, prediction of success improved. Undoubtedly one of the reasons for the many nonsignificant differences in studies of teaching is poor criterion measures.

The criterion problem is illustrated by the experiment of Parsons, Ketcham, and Beach (1958). In order to determine the effectiveness of various methods, they took the brave step of setting up some groups in which students didn't come to class at all. The groups who didn't come to class did *best of all* on the final examination. The catch is that the examination was based entirely upon the textbook. As Parsons and Ketcham point out, their results with the other groups suggest that as more and more new ideas and points of view are introduced, students become less likely to remember what the textbook says. This points to the problem of evaluation of effectiveness. If the instructor's goal is that students remember the textbook, a test on the textbook is appropriate; but one cannot conclude that a particular method is superior in achieving all goals, if only one outcome has been measured.

Few professors complain that students are too highly motivated. Yet for purposes of research, the degree of student motivation for good grades may actually make it very difficult to evaluate the effectiveness of two teaching procedures. Because passing or excellent grades are so important to students, they may compensate for ineffective teaching by additional study in order to pass the course examination at the level to which they aspire. Thus, the effects of ineffective procedures may be masked or even misinterpreted when course examinations are used as criterion measures. Nachman and Opochinsky (1958) provided a neat demonstration of this when they found differences between a small and large class on surprise quizzes, but no difference on a final examination. When significant differences in achievement are found in an experiment, the difference may simply reflect the degree to which students in differing classes were able to find out what the examination was to be and the degree to which it would determine their course grade.

All too often, studies of teaching effectiveness have confused different goals of evaluation. Course examinations are typically intended to aid teachers in determining student grades. For this use fairness requires that the examination give each student an equal opportunity to obtain a good score. Thus the content of the examination is ordinarily that studied by all students. But when comparing two methods of teaching, you want to know what each group learned that the other did not. Thus a comparison of the lecture method with a discussion method based on a common final examination from a textbook does not really compare what the two groups of students learned in their different classes, but rather what they learned from reading the text. Many of the early experiments on the Keller Plan not only tested only material covered in the Keller Plan course, but also actually used on the criterion test items students in the Keller Plan had answered on previous quizzes. The point here is that the criterion measure should sample progress on *all* goals, not just a small sample chosen for a particular method. If separate scores for different goals can be assigned, the researcher and the audience are then free to assign their own values to those goals well achieved vs. those poorly achieved.

The difficulty in arriving at an overall index of teaching effectiveness is complicated by the probability that a teacher effective in achieving one course objective is not necessarily effective in achieving others. Bendig (1955), for example, found a significant interaction between instructors and tests in an introductory psychology course. Some instructors' students did particularly well on certain tests during the course, but not well on other tests. Cross (1958) and McKeachie (1959a) found that instructors whose students did well on an objective test in psychology were ineffective when their students' achievement was measured on an essay test designed to gauge understanding and integration of the materials. In studies of teaching it is thus important to specify objectives and to use measures of each objective. Measures of retention after the end of a course can often add to your confidence in reported differences.

Because achievement measures have been so insensitive to differences in teaching methods, most experimenters stress the favorable student reactions to the new method they have introduced. Although the relationship between student satisfaction and learning is low, it can certainly be argued that, assuming equal learning between two methods, teachers would prefer to have students leave their classes with warm feelings about their experiences. Moreover, teachers would expect these feelings to be related to interest in learning more, and there is some evidence to support this (McKeachie and Solomon, 1958). However, when researchers use student satisfaction as a criterion, they should be aware of the fact that it is highly influenced by the role expectations students have of college teachers.

Marked deviations from these expectations almost inevitably will be rated lower than more conventional teaching behavior. Laboratory studies of problem-solving groups reveal that authoritarian leaders are rated by group members as being more efficient than democratic leaders (Haythorn, 1956). This makes sense both in terms of members' expectations for leaders and also because a leader who plays an active role is almost inevitably going to make a more vivid impression on a group than a leader whose behavior is more subtle. In evaluating student reactions, therefore, researchers need to be conscious of these role expectancies and determine what is a proper base line against which to evaluate the reactions.

As an aside here, let me also point out that new methods are not usually tested except by a teacher who is enthusiastic about them. Consequently the comparison may be between student reactions to a new method and an enthusiastic teacher vs. an old method taught unenthusiastically.

The prospective researcher also needs to be warned that even a careful definition of desirable outcomes does not end the criterion problem. In many cases, laudable attempts to measure attitudinal or affective outcomes have led to the conclusion that neither of two teaching methods was superior to the other in achieivng this or that goal, when there is no evidence that *any* teaching could affect the goal as measured by the tests used. At the very least, the experimenter needs to report some evidence that the measure is at least sufficiently sensitive to reveal significant changes from the beginning to the end of the semester. If there is no change on a variable over a semester, it is unlikely that two teaching methods will differ in the amount of the change they cause.

Finally, evaluation need not end with tests given to the students who are enrolled in the experimental classes. In a large university it is easy to assume that an experimental course is assimilated into the whirlpool of activity without even a ripple. Seldom, however, has this assumption been tested, and in smaller colleges or for large-scale innovations it is not a safe assumption. Researchers might gain much useful knowledge by looking outside their experimental classrooms to other effects of the experiment. Do students taught by one method rather than another make more use of their knowledge and skills in other courses they are electing? Is superior achievement in the experimental course won at the expense of achievement in other courses? What is the impact of the use of a particular teaching method upon other faculty members? How does the use of a new method like television change faculty perceptions of teaching and its value; how does it affect faculty-administration relationships? In short, what effects does a new method have upon the total culture of the college? *

SUPPLEMENTARY READING

Lee Cronbach and Richard Snow, *Aptitudes and instructional methods* (New York: Irvington, 1977).

---

* Morris Janowitz started my train of thought along this line.

26

Student Ratings
of Faculty

Everyone evaluates college teaching, but no one knows how to do it. Campus conversations often contain phrases like: "Professor Jones is great—absolutely great!" "Bill Smith is an excellent researcher but I'm afraid that he's not very effective in the classroom." "The staff of our college are unusual in their combination of high scholarship and superb teaching!"

Yet, whenever a program for rewarding good teaching is discussed it encounters the barrier, "But how can we evaluate teaching?"

The ultimate criterion of good teaching is education. Teachers whose students make good progress toward educational goals are effective teachers regardless of how they look or what techniques they use. But this straightforward statement makes the problem meretriciously simple. The plain fact is that it is only rarely that instructors have defined their educational objectives clearly enough to permit measurement. Even when objectives are relatively clear, they seldom have had the ingenuity and tenacity necessary to devise adequate measures. As a result, evaluation of teaching has been forced to rely upon expedients of less obvious validity.

No one has doubted that students have opinions about the quality of instruction they receive, but only within the past five decades have these ideas been systematically gathered. Numerous articles have been published, arguing for or against the use of student rating. However, the research in the area is scattered, and those contemplating the use of student ratings may not realize that there are empirical answers to some of the questions they raise. It is the purpose of this chapter to review these research findings.*

Validity

The validity of student ratings has been the chief bone of contention between those for and those against the use of student ratings. The problem seems to resolve itself into the question, "Validity for what?"

Almost everyone agrees that the aim of teaching is to produce changes in students. While the validity of a measure must be defined with respect to the purposes for which the measure is to be used, the major concern about validity with respect to student ratings lies in whether or not teachers who are effective in achieving educational goals are also rated highly. A substantial amount of research has been carried out on validity. While the results vary somewhat from study to study, the results typically are moderate correlations between student ratings of teachers and the average achievement of the teachers' students, and the only study that was adequately controlled through random assignment of students to sections found substantial positive correlations between ratings and achievement (Sullivan and Skanes, 1974). Moreover the correlations were higher in courses taught by experienced faculty members than by inexperienced part-time instructors.

Nevertheless certain standard arguments are still presented in faculty meetings discussing student ratings.

---

* The best summary of research on student ratings of teaching is Kenneth O. Doyle, *Student evaluation of instruction* (Lexington, Ma.: Lexington Books, 1975).

● *"Students can't really evaluate a teacher until they've left college and gotten some perspective on what was really valuable to them."* This common objection to the use of student ratings usually ends with the comment, "I just hated Prof. Jones, but now I realize that he did more for me than any other teacher I ever had!"

While such anecdotes are common, these sorts of changes of opinion are the exception rather than the rule. Drucker and Remmers (1951) showed that student ratings of instructors correlate well (.40 to .68) with ratings of the same instructors made by alumni ten years after graduation. Teachers whom students think to be good are still remembered as being effective years later, and vice versa.

● *"Students rate teachers on their personality—not on how much they've learned."* This common objection is only partially supported by the evidence. Students do seem to know when they are learning. Elliott (1949), in a study of thirty-six college chemistry teachers at Purdue, found that ratings on four of the items on the Purdue scale were significantly correlated ($P = .05$) with teaching effectiveness. They were:

1. Conduct during laboratory period (actively helpful vs. waits to be asked for assistance).
2. Attitude (liberal or narrow minded).
3. Educational effectiveness of recitation.
4. Rating as compared to other instructors at Purdue.

One of Elliott's most interesting discoveries was that certain instructors were relatively more effective in stimulating achievement in low-ability students than in high-ability students, while other instructors were more effective with high-ability students. While the overall ratings of these two types of teachers were not significantly different, the teachers who were more effective with high-ability students were rated higher by these students than by low-ability students. Teachers who were more effective with low-ability students were rated higher by those students. These data indicate that what students achieve in a course is to some degree reflected in their ratings of their instructors.

This conclusion is confirmed by Russell (1951), who found that as compared with underachievers, students who achieved more than would have been predicted in a psychology class rated the course higher on "contribution of text to course," "fairness of examinations," and "fairness of grades." Student ratings are affected by the teacher's personality, but those personality variables affecting student ratings also influence learning. Thus Williams and Ware (1976) found that teachers coached to show enthusiasm and activity were not only rated more highly, but also produced greater learning than in classes they taught with less enthusiasm and activity.

• *"Students can't tell whether or not the instructor is giving authentic information."* This is probably true. The Dr. Fox studies (Naftulin, Ware, and Donnelly, 1973; Williams and Ware, 1976; Ware and Williams, 1975) demonstrate that even professors, professionals, and administrators are unable to tell when a lecture not directly in their field of expertise is not authentic. It seems unlikely that freshmen are likely to be more critical. What freshmen can report is how they have been affected by what was taught. Thus, student ratings are highly valid for such goals of education as motivating students for further learning (McKeachie and Solomon, 1958), stimulating curiosity, and influencing more sophisticated attitudes (McKeachie, Lin, & Mann, 1971). For evaluating the adequacy of the content of a course, judges need to be experts in the field, typically other faculty members.

Factors Influencing Student Ratings of Instructors

• *What characteristics of students affect their ratings of instructors?* Doyle (1975), Costin, Greenough, and Menges (1971), and Kulik and McKeachie (1975) have reviewed the research on factors influencing student ratings. Probably the single most important variable is student expectations. Students who expect a course or teacher to be good generally find it to be so. Most demographic characteristics make no difference according to studies by Remmers and his associates at Purdue (1927, 1949). These include such variables as veteran–nonveteran, age, sex, and student's grade in the course. Whether a student is a freshman, sophomore, junior, or senior makes little difference in teaching ratings. Graduate students, however, rate teachers higher than do undergraduates.

• *What characteristics of instructors are related to student ratings of teaching effectiveness?* Sex of instructor makes no difference in the student ratings. Associate professors are rated higher than other ranks (Elliott, 1949). Instructors possessing only bachelor degrees are rated lower than those having M.A.'s or Ph.D.'s. Older teachers tend to be rated lower than younger teachers (Riley et al., 1950). General severity of grading does not affect overall ratings of instructors, although instructors who grade low are more likely to be rated low in the item, "fairness in grading" (Heilman & Armentrout, 1936).

One of the more interesting findings is that the instructor's knowledge is not important in determining his effectiveness in student eyes. Neither his knowledge of the subject matter nor his knowledge of correct teaching procedures is reflected in his ratings by students. Moreover, Elliott found a significant negative correlation between the instructor's actual knowledge of the subject he was teaching and student ratings of his effectiveness. Riley, however, found that professors with published research were rated higher than those without publications.

● *What characteristics of the class are related to the students' rating of their instructor?* Student ratings of effectiveness were not correlated with size of class at Brooklyn College (Goodhartz, 1948), but at Grinnell College classes over thirty were rated lower than smaller classes (Lovell and Haner, 1955). Required courses were not rated lower than elective courses at Brooklyn College, but were at Grinnell College. Other variables such as subject matter, method or homogeneity of group have not been studied.

Choosing and Administering a Scale for Student Evaluation of Instruction

When a faculty decides to inaugurate a program of student evaluation of instruction, it often fails to make use of the experience of other colleges and universities. For example, the Purdue rating scale has been in use for twenty years, and its users have available a rich supply of normative data. Similarly, the University of Washington (Wilson, 1932), Miami University, Minnesota, Michigan, Kansas State, the University of Wisconsin at Green Bay, Michigan State, Illinois, Northwestern, Cornell, and a number of other institutions have accumulated a good deal of data and experience in connection with their student rating scales.*

The advantages of utilizing such accumulated experience should be carefully considered by a college contemplating student evaluation of faculty. The Grinnell College form uses a forced-choice technique that should reduce bias. Some of the rating scales have been factor analyzed. In the Student Rating Form in Appendix B, items are grouped according to factors commonly found in student-rating forms.

Choosing Scales or Items for Scales

Establishing the Purpose of Collecting Student Opinion

Whether you plan to use one of the readymade scales or construct your own, a necessary prerequisite is to examine your goals in gathering student impressions. Different goals imply different items.

The three most common uses of student ratings are:

1. To assist an instructor in improving instruction.
2. To provide evidence relevant to evaluation of teaching effectiveness for promotion or salary decisions.
3. To provide information useful for students in choosing courses.

Using Student Ratings for Improving Instruction

The use of student ratings does not guarantee that instructors will improve. In other contexts I have argued that feedback results in improvement when:

1. It provides information.
2. The learner is motivated to improve.
3. The learner has better response alternatives available.

Centra (1973) and Pambookian (1972) demonstrated that new in-

---

* Some of these scales are copyrighted and have informative manuals about student ratings. One such is: James B. Maas and Thomas R. Owen, *Cornell inventory for student appraisal of teaching and courses: manual of instructions* (Center for Improvement of Undergraduate Education, Cornell University).

formation was important. Their research revealed that teachers whose self-ratings were higher than their students' ratings improved after receiving the student ratings; teachers who were accurate or underestimated the student ratings did not improve. In a study at the University of Michigan (McKeachie, et al., 1975) we attempted to meet the other conditions by providing counseling when student ratings were returned to teachers. This proved to be superior to a printed report of the results.

The principles governing feedback have implications for choice of items. Items chosen by the instructor because he or she wishes the information are more likely to be helpful to the teacher than items on scales written for more general purposes. Aside from an item or two to indicate general feelings of satisfaction, more specific items are likely to be more informative than general items.

It may also be helpful to choose one or two items from each of the factors commonly found to represent the half dozen or so major qualities students use in thinking about instruction.

In general, you are likely to learn more from items you have chosen because you want to know about certain aspects of your course or teaching than from more general items. Most standard forms give individual teachers the option of adding items. Take advantage of the option.

There is no reason to wait until the end of the course to administer a student-rating form. I've found it helpful to give the form after three to five weeks of the term.

Research also indicates that little improvement results unless the ratings are discussed with another teacher who can sympathize, congratulate, and make suggestions about other things to try. So pick someone you trust and respect as a teacher, and go over your ratings with that person.

Using Student Ratings for Personnel Decisions

The current press for teacher accountability is one of the factors that have led to attempts to mandate the use of standard, uniform student-rating scales for assessing teaching effectiveness. Student ratings of teaching are related to teacher effectiveness as measured by the achievement of the teacher's students. Nevertheless this does not mean that student ratings are sufficient evidence of teaching effectiveness. Ideally one would gather evidence from a number of sources, giving most weight to those sources most expert with respect to different aspects of teaching. For example, it is hard to conceive of anyone more expert than students themselves with respect to the degree to which the teacher has stimulated intellectual curiosity and interest in the subject matter field, an important educational goal; on the other hand one would expect peers to be most competent to judge the scholarly content of a course, assuming that they have examined syllabuses, examination papers, lecture notes, or other sources of evidence. Thus, personnel decisions inevitably involve value judgments using data from several sources with respect to teacher effectiveness in achieving a number of different goals.

As suggested earlier, a standard scale is not likely to be very helpful for improving teaching—nor is a lengthy standard scale likely to be helpful for personnel decisions since it is unlikely to be equally well suited for different disciplines or different courses within a discipline. Since comparisons between instructors in different courses can at best be only very general, one should probably not attempt much more than to determine whether students rate an instructor as excellent, adequate, or poor. An item or two on the degree to which a course stimulated interest or curiosity and perhaps one on general effectiveness should be sufficient for personnel purposes.

Moreover, ratings should be obtained over several courses and several semesters before being admitted as data in the faculty evaluation process. A rating of a particular course in a particular semester may be influenced by special circumstances that affect its validity. Even when ratings from several courses are available, they need to be interpreted by peers or administrators who know something about the nature of the courses and students involved.

Using Student Ratings to Assist Students in Choosing Courses

One of the first universities to collect student ratings was Harvard, where students began in the 1920s to publish a book reporting student opinions of courses and professors. Such books are now commonly found on college and university campuses. If this is to be the primary purpose of the scale, one would presumably want to include items that are likely to provide information that will make a difference for student decisions. While there has been no research in which use of ratings in student decision making has been studied, there have been a number of studies of qualities students believe to be related to superior teaching. Feldman's review of these studies (1976) lists the following qualities as being consistently reported:

1. Stimulation of interest.
2. Clarity.
3. Knowledge of subject matter.
4. Preparation.
5. Enthusiasm.
6. Friendliness.
7. Helpfulness.
8. Openness to other's opinions.

Summary

Student ratings of teaching can be useful for several purposes, such as:

1. Improving teaching.
2. Providing data relevant to judgment about teaching effectiveness.
3. Aiding student choice of course and instructor.

They are not automatically valid and useful for any of these purposes. Thus it is necessary to understand what student ratings can and cannot do before embarking upon large-scale institutional programs of student ratings.

SUPPLEMENTARY READING

Kenneth S. Doyle, *Evaluational instruction* (Lexington MA: D. C. Heath, 1975).

27

Improving Your Teaching

Is there really any hope that teachers can improve—and continue to improve—their teaching? Does successful teaching depend upon adopting a particular teaching method? Does it depend upon having a particular type of personality?

These are disquieting questions to those concerned about their teaching. Here are my answers: Teachers can improve; they don't need complete psychoanalysis; and not everyone can use the same methods equally successfully.

Let's take an example. Bob, one of our graduate students, was a brilliant theoretician. In all of his academic work he was outstanding. There was no question that he knew psychology, but when he began to teach it, his students almost revolted. After the first four

Adapted from W. J. McKeachie, Improving your teaching, *Adult leadership*, 1955.

weeks of the semester, his students were asked to evaluate his teaching.

Here are some of their comments:

—"Mr. Smith has convinced me that he knows his material, but he is way over my head."

—"I have no idea what we are supposed to be getting either from textbooks or lectures."

—"Mr. Smith does right by his material, but not by his students."

Naturally Bob was concerned about these reactions. It would have been natural for him to say, "These students are just stupid. If the material is over their heads, it is their fault for not studying more. I'll simply tell them they'll have to work harder."

Fortunately, Bob thought instead, "What can I do about this?" He came to me with some anxiety and a willingness to make any changes that would produce better results.

There was no doubt that he was spending enough time in preparation. His lecture materials were carefully worked out to insure complete coverage of the topic. However, it was obvious to him that he had to change the level of his lectures. How was he to know when he had reached the appropriate level?

In discussing this we decided that he needed more prompt and continuous feedback from the students if he was to keep the presentation on their level. Perhaps if the classroom atmosphere were less formal, if the students participated more, their discussion would provide clues to their understanding of the material.

"But," Bob said, "if I let the students talk, how can I cover the material? I'm crowded for time now. Still—I guess it doesn't do me much good to cover the material if the students don't get it. Maybe I shouldn't worry so much about covering everything."

Bob was particularly puzzled by the student's comment that he didn't know what he was to get from the course. "Why did he sign up if he doesn't know what he wants to get out of the course?" Bob asked. "I suppose this is a new field to the students, and I know it isn't what they expected, but what can I do?"

After some discussion we decided that he might work out study questions for the students to take home. He tried devising these questions to focus on major points in the assignments. He handed these questions out in advance. Frequently these questions came up again during the class period and often stirred up lively discussions. When student evaluations were collected six weeks later, Bob's students rated him a very good teacher.

The point of Bob's experience is not to suggest that everyone should use study questions. Rather, it is intended to indicate how improvement can result from getting feedback from the students themselves.

Student Feedback

This chapter is based upon the assumption that the purpose of education is to bring about changes in students. If instructors agree with this assumption, it is apparent that information from students is required to provide a basis for improved teaching. Student evaluation of instruction is a relatively direct method of obtaining this information. But there are other sources of feedback available to the instructor. What are they?

A venerable one is the classroom examination. Too often instructors simply check off errors automatically, with little thought of interpreting them to find out the general areas in which students did poorly and where they did well. Instructors thus lose a potentially valuable source of feedback. By asking a colleague to look over a few student papers you can get a check on whether or not your expectations are reasonable.

Another source of feedback, which is even more valuable because it is immediate, is the behavior of students in class. One of the most useful features of class discussion is that it reveals so well the misconceptions, biases, and emotional reactions of the students. Teachers who minimize student participation dam up one of their most useful channels of feedback.

Even in the lecture hall instructors can get many cues for improving their teaching. While few teachers can ignore students who are sleeping or reading newspapers, many of them fail to note restless shifting of position, blank stares, whispered asides, and other indications that the students are not with them.

As a third source of feedback teachers can use individual conferences with students outside of class. While these students are often not typical of the entire class group, their problems sometimes indicate possible inadequacies in instruction that teachers can use as cues for improvement.

More Sources of Feedback

My emphasis thus far upon feedback from students has undoubtedly raised some questions. Some readers may be saying, "Our job is to educate students, not to please them. Making students happy doesn't necessarily contribute to education."

This point is well taken. Research on teaching methods has not thus far shown a strong relationship between student satisfaction and student achievement. It seems obvious that students must give some interest and attention to their work in order to learn, and student reactions are therefore valuable, but it is probably fallacious to assume that what the students say they like is always what contributes most to their education. Hence, teachers should not rely upon the students as their only sources of help in teaching. Let's now turn to some other sources.

One of the most frequently neglected aids is the advice of colleagues. Sometimes teachers seem afraid to discuss their teaching methods with other teachers or to ask for advice in handling some teaching problem. Insecurity about teaching is so great that it is almost unheard of for a teacher to visit a colleague's class. Yet in our University of Michigan program for training college teachers, the trainees report that they gain much from discussing teaching problems with their colleagues, from observing other teachers, and from suggestions by observers of their classes. I suspect that all teachers dread having a colleague see them get tripped up on some simple question, but one of the things most difficult for the new instructor to learn is that other teachers get tripped up in the same way. Learning that one's problems are not unique is a wonderful remedy for the tenseness and anxiety that often characterize the new (and not so new) teacher.

New Ways in Teaching

Thus far we have been primarily concerned with the problem of spotting teaching weaknesses or of diagnosing difficulties. I have assumed that intelligent teachers who learn of their errors will be able to change their teaching techniques for the better. This, however, assumes that they know, or will be able to devise, other teaching techniques that will be more successful. Unfortunately, this is not always the case. There are teachers who think reading from lecture notes is the only teaching method possible for their subject matter. How then may you increase your working repertoire of teaching techniques?

First of all, of course, you may learn about techniques other teachers use. Talking about teaching, observing other teachers, and reading journals on college teaching are ways of becoming acquainted with the techniques other people are trying.

Have you tried PSI, buzz groups, role playing, nondirective discussion, directed discussion, field trips, or guest experts? These are some of the methods available to add variety to your teaching. But the problem then remains, "How can I put these into practice?"

As one of my trainees said, "I've read all about role playing. I'm convinced it would be useful in my class, but I'm scared to death to try it."

What are the barriers that keep teachers from trying new teaching techniques? One barrier is simply effort. Usually it is easier to teach a class as you've done in the past than to try something new. This barrier is probably not so hard to overcome if you have used the diagnostic information discussed earlier and are aware of weakness in your teaching.

A far more important barrier to change is fear of loss of status. To most instructors the status of the teacher is a cherished reward for years of study. To be an authority who dispenses crumbs of wisdom to the multitudes is a very satisfying role. Trying a new technique may involve a threat to your status. If the new method fails, the students are likely to feel that you don't know what you're doing. But even if it works, it may mean some change in your status. For example, permitting student participation means that more embarrassing questions are likely to be asked, that less emphasis will be placed on learning from the instructor, and that the instructor's leadership may be challenged by aggressive, intelligent students.

A third barrier is simply fear of failure. Teachers who try new techniques are not likely to be skilled in its use and are likely to imagine consequences far more catastrophic than any which are likely to occur. In using new techniques instructors may feel that they are losing control of the situation and that anything may happen.

Another barrier is fear of unfavorable reactions from colleagues. Even when a new teaching method is successful, experimenting instructors are likely to feel that other professors feel they are deserting the tried and true academic traditions in order to curry student or administration favor.

How Do You Make the Change?

Overcoming these barriers depends first of all upon being sure of the reasons for trying a new technique. Unless you have thought through the goals, you may miss any evidences of success in the use of a new method. This is particularly important because these evidences of success are among the most important rewards you can get.

A second aid in overcoming barriers is to try new techniques in a group in which you are secure and from which you can expect cooperation. This may mean making the first trial in your best class. In some cases it may even be worthwhile to ask for volunteers to join a special section of the class that will experiment with a new learning method. Those who volunteer thus will not be shocked by changes in your behavior and usually will give the method a fair trial.

A third aid in putting new methods into practice is to gain group support. In the Michigan teacher-training program we encourage formation of friendships among the teacher trainees; we encourage them to talk about methods and discuss experiences in trying them out. This furnishes the instructors with emotional support, enables them to express their anxieties, and gives them the rewards of approval by friends for their trials of new methods. Such support can be found by almost all teachers. Almost always you can find others who enjoy teaching and who like to talk about it. Such an informal group can serve the same functions as our training group.

Faculty Development Programs

When I wrote the first edition of this book, the term "faculty development" had not even been conceived. Now almost every college and university has a faculty development program. This means that on many campuses you can get professional help in improving your teaching. Most faculty development centers offer workshops to assist you in developing additional skills. In addition they will consult with you about specific problems and offer technical or financial assistance for changes you wish to make. They will suggest sources of additional information. Each of the suggestions made in this chapter can be facilitated by the faculty development (or instructional development) center. Moreover there is no opprobrium attached to consulting such a center. Their customers are predominantly good teachers trying to be better. Try it. It's free!

Student–Teacher Relationships

In discussing methods of diagnosing teaching weaknesses and improving methods, I have purposely avoided what is probably the basic problem in improving teaching. That is: "How do we build a different pattern of relationship with our students?"

The obvious way to write this chapter would have been to exhort teachers to understand student needs and to like and respect their students. These are the foundations upon which successful teaching methods are laid. But most teachers already like their students and try to understand them. The trouble is not that they don't try to obtain these fundamentals, but rather that they aren't able.

This chapter is intended to help you sneak around your own emotional blocks to different relationships with students. By focusing attention on teaching methods you can sometimes make discoveries about student needs that might have evaded you through years of worrying about them. By finding teaching methods that elicit increased student interest, you may gain that approval of students that will give you enough security to build new relationships. In any case, teachers who begin to improve their teaching will again discover that teaching is fun!

SUPPLEMENTARY READING

One way of improving is to try new approaches. Even if innovations don't work, they almost always broaden your skills and help you see aspects of teaching that you may previously have overlooked. An excellent source of innovations is the series of monographs published by *Change* magazine entitled *Report on Teaching*:

Report 1. Chemistry, History, Psychology
      2. Biology, English, Political Science
      3. Economics, Mathematics, Philosophy
      4. Geography, Music, Sociology

28

Faculty Attitudes and Teaching Effectiveness

What can I say about the work of the teacher? Clearly it is not possible to detail in a few summary statements the "best" methods of teaching. Nevertheless, a conclusion that it doesn't make any difference which methods are used is clearly unjustified. Rather, research suggests that decisions about teaching methods do have important consequences in terms of differential achievement of the varying objectives of a course, differential effects upon various types of students, and probable differential effects depending upon other factors such as the instructor, the course content, and the overall "climate" of the institution. To analyze such complexities would obviously be a task for a giant computer. In the absence of the data necessary for such an analysis, educators must, as in other frontier areas, depend upon expert judgment. Most of the reports of research on teaching neglect to report the reactions of the faculty involved (except in the case of television where they are generally negative). Yet until we gain more confidence in our evaluation tools, we are almost forced to weigh faculty judgment heavily.

I would argue, however, that faculty judgments of teaching methods are extremely important even aside from their possible validity as expert judgments.

As I pointed out earlier, we seldom know how well a particular method was used in experimental studies of teaching methods, but it seems very likely that the effectiveness of a method depends upon the competence and enthusiasm of the teachers in the study. If the teachers are important, their enjoyment of the method becomes a critical variable. Thistlethwaite (1960) finds that National Merit Scholars report that one of the critical variables influencing their choice of a field is the instructor's enthusiasm. It seems probable that such enthusiasm is unlikely to be communicated if instructors find teaching distasteful. Thus, even though studies found that a particular method when ideally used is superior to other methods, I would be dubious about urging its widespread adoption if teachers using it become bored or dissatisfied.

When one looks at teaching from the standpoint of satisfaction to the instructor, some of the problems considered here look a bit different. Some administrators and foundation executives seem to be annoyed by professors' stubbornness in not accepting larger classes or teaching by television, but if the rewards in teaching are considered, the attitudes of faculty members toward class and institutional size become more understandable.

What are the satisfactions in teaching? Certainly one is the pleasure of seeing a student develop. Another is the pleasure of intellectual interchange with young people possessing questioning minds and fresh ideas. Still another is the sense of satisfaction from pulling together ideas in a wide-ranging discussion, from asking the right question at the right time, and from finding the right example to clarify what was previously unclear. Perhaps a less laudable but nonetheless real satisfaction is that found in having disciples who respect and admire you. These satisfactions are difficult to secure without close sustained personal contact with students. If instructors are to know students well enough to see their progress, small classes are important, not only because they permit more individual interaction with students, but also because they permit instructors to use term papers, essay tests, and other evaluation methods that give them a greater understanding of what students are thinking. While objective tests might also be used to give a personalized understanding of each student's strengths and weaknesses, few teachers take the time to analyze the patterns of right and wrong answers that would be necessary for such understanding, and such an analysis becomes prohibitively time-consuming in a large class, whatever the testing methods used.

Moreover, if the satisfaction of observing student growth is important, opportunities for contacts between instructor and student over a period longer than a one-semester course need to be insured. One of the advantages of the small college over the large university is that students in a small college not only are more likely to come into contact with their instructors outside of the classroom, but they are also more likely to elect later courses from the same professors. In a community where professors know most of the students, professors are more likely to discuss students with each other. In a large university a professor may teach a student one semester and never see that student again. Professors are very unlikely to discuss the student with other professors because they don't know which colleagues know the student.

Many professors conscientiously attend some student teas or other social functions to promote contacts between students and faculty. In the small colleges it is likely that professors will meet at such functions some of the students they have taught and will have an opportunity to use this contact to gain greater understanding of the students and perhaps even to stimulate their thinking. But the larger the college the less the statistical chance that they will meet students they teach at a tea. This means that even professors who conscientiously devote a portion of their time to such "informal" contacts with students are unlikely to have significant encounters. Because they are nearly always dealing with strangers or near-strangers, the intellectual interchange is almost perforce limited to polite inquiry about the student's academic and vocational aspirations or conversation about the current film at the campus theater. In short, any satisfaction received from observing and contributing to a student's growth must ordinarily come during the semester (or at most two semesters) that the student is enrolled in your class. No matter how powerful your impact, it is asking a great deal to expect it to have noticeable effects in sixteen weeks.

Size of an educational institution has a very similar relationship to the quality of education students receive from one another. The large institution with a student body of heterogeneous background offers students an opportunity to gain breadth, tolerance, and new perspectives from their contacts with one another. But large size is likely to reduce educational values by reducing intellectual interchange between students. There is certainly no reason why students at a large college could not discuss with other students an interesting problem raised by one of their mutual professors. But they are probably more likely to do so if they are living near another student who is also familiar with the problem and concerned about it. In a large college the statistical chances that another student in the same class will be in the same living group are smaller than in a small college. Students in a large college with many courses, and even many sections of the same course, have few common intellectual experiences. Consequently, it is difficult for them to communicate about intellectual problems outside of class, and the common concerns that become the basis of social communication are football, the student newspaper, dating, and the dormitory food. With such barriers to inter-student education professors miss the good feeling that could be experienced if they found that their teaching has provided an intellectual stimulus reaching far beyond their classrooms.*

Of course there are also satisfactions in teaching by television or in a large class. You can gain a very satisfying sense of power from knowing that you are communicating your ideas to many students. The roar of laughter at a joke well told is music to a lecturer's ear. The satisfaction of carrying through without interruption a well-planned lesson is satisfying to the "Master Teacher" whose performance is televised.

Although these are valid satisfactions, they seem less directly related to the goals of education than the satisfactions associated with observing student development. What would a college be like if its faculty were largely made up of teachers whose satisfactions were primarily those of a good performer?

As colleges increase in size in order to cope with a growing student population, there is a natural tendency to routinize and automate educational processes in the interest of increased efficiency. In industry, assembly-line methods have long been effective. Yet, in recent years, industry has found that workers are even more efficient

_____

* As a professor at a large university, let me note that I don't consider our case hopeless if we recognize what problems we need to solve.

if, instead of performing one specific, repetitive task, their jobs are enlarged enough to provide variety and interest. While there is little likelihood that college administrators will intentionally insist upon uniform teaching methods, increasing class size indirectly limits the professors' choices of teaching methods, reducing their ability to select the methods best suited for their objectives and reducing their satisfaction in teaching.

Although I have emphasized the case of the faculty against such pressures, let me also point out that resistance alone will probably not be enough. If teachers expect their administrations to preserve their freedom of choice, they incur a heavy responsibility for analyzing more carefully the manner in which they spend class time. Do teachers really teach differently in small classes than in large? Are they making optimal use of the flexibility in scheduling and the teaching aids that remain within their control? Can teachers honestly say that a change would be less effective or enjoyable without trying it? Let's keep enjoyment in teaching, but let's not lose the enjoyment in a rut of convention.

Enjoyment of teaching is important not only for the enthusiasm professors communicate to their students, but also in determining their interest in continued improvement. Both of these important values are likely to be lost if teaching becomes so routinized and depersonalized that it is no longer fun. Motivated teachers are able to respond to feedback from their students in order to achieve better and better approximations to optimal solutions to the problems of teaching. As additional information from research accumulates and as better conceptualizations emerge, they should be able to do an even better job.

SUPPLEMENTARY READING

Donald Bligh et al., *Teaching students* (Dover, England: Exeter University Teaching Services, 1975).

Appendix A
Objectives of the
General Psychology Course*

What are the objectives of the general psychology course? In order to choose techniques of teaching, to establish the proper classroom atmosphere, and to know what tests or evaluation instruments to use, the instructor of the first course must answer this question. We hope that this paper, which describes our attempts at an answer, will be of service to other instructors facing the same problem.

A decision about objectives is a question of values rather than facts, but there are various factors that may weigh in the decision. We should note here that we feel that *the formulation of objectives should not be something which the instructor does alone and never changes, but rather that it should be a continuous, cooperative effort involving instructor,*

---

* Based on an article by W. J. McKeachie, R. L. DeValois, D. E. Dulany, Jr., University of Michigan; D. C. Beardslee, Wesleyan University; and Marian Winterbottom, Connecticut College. Reprinted from *The American Psychologist*, Vol. 9, No. 4, April 1954 with permission of the American Psychological Assn.

students, and other interested participants. However, we direct this article to the instructor, because we feel that the ultimate responsibility for the task is hers.

Perhaps the first consideration should be the objectives of the college and the place of this course in the curriculum. Is this course primarily for specialists, or is it intended to contribute toward a general education? In most colleges the committee or dean in charge of curriculum will be willing to help the psychology instructor in this phase of choosing objectives. In addition, books and articles on the goals of higher education may be useful.

The second step might be a job analysis of the role of college students and eventual citizens in our democracy in terms of the aims of higher education. What do these roles require? How can a psychology course be helpful to a person in these roles? While this way of establishing objectives would appear to be an obvious one, S. L. Pressey* has pointed out that it has seldom been attempted by builders of psychology curricula.

Third, what is the student's status in relation to the possible objectives of the course when he begins the course? What are his needs and expectations? Certainly it is not wise to spend a great deal of time teaching students the names of defense mechanisms if a great majority of the class already knows them. Hence, a pretest may be valuable. Any instructor who gives her final examination at the beginning of the semester will probably be surprised at the number of items most students get right without having had the course. Similarly, the instructor should consider the students' expectations of the course. While one may have changing expectations and preconceptions as a goal, one still needs to know what they are.

A fourth guide in the formulation of objectives is the function of the course in the eyes of the profession as a whole. We doubt that the complete uniformity of all comparable courses in institutions would be desirable, but the opinions of other experienced teachers may be helpful. Here we suggest a review of the literature.

Another possible factor influencing one's goals is the ease of producing change. For example, if one regards a positive attitude toward psychology as a relatively unimportant outcome of his course, he still might include it in his goals if it could be easily attained without sacrificing progress toward other goals. Conversely, the goal of a more positive attitude toward other ethnic groups might be considered important, yet not worth including if one can have relatively little success in achieving it.

Other sources of help may be implied in the guides already mentioned.

---

* S. L. Pressey, A personal communication in 1952.

We have consulted with faculty members in charge of courses in other departments to discuss methods of better integrating our efforts toward common goals. We have also been aided by faculty members of advanced courses for which our course is a prerequisite. They can tell what they expect as a basis for their courses. If there is a college examiner, she too will give valuable help. Students who have completed the course also may be of service in pointing out what they have gained and what in retrospect seems to have been lacking. We have utilized college seniors in this respect; we think we might obtain even more useful information from college graduates.

At the University of Michigan, the elementary psychology course is taught by several regular staff members and thirty to forty graduate student teaching fellows. Since each teaching fellow is given a great deal of freedom in organizing and teaching his or her own sections, it has seemed doubly desirable to agree upon certain objectives that would form the core of the course in all classes and could be relied upon as the basis for advanced courses. The sources just suggested were utilized by the staff of the course in formulating our objectives. We tried to think always of changes in students and to state the objectives as far as possible in terms of gains that might be measurable.

We recognize that our goals reflect our own biases and that other statements might be equally acceptable. In fact we find ourselves continuously redefining and clarifying them. We certainly do not propose that they should be adopted by all other departments. Rather, we present them because they have been of aid to new teachers doing initial course planning. We think other teachers may find it helpful to try to formulate their own objectives. We hope our example will be suggestive to them.

Objectives of the University of Michigan Course

Ideally, we would present our list of objectives on a large sheet of paper in which the spatial organization could be used to indicate relationships. Since this is impossible, some explanation of organization is necessary.

First, we have outlined our general objectives for the entire elementary psychology course.* In the full set of objectives we took each of

---

* While we give here only the general goals and an example of how we have developed them for one content area, the complete set of objectives suggesting related concepts and references has been deposited with the American Documentation Institute. Order Document No. 4205 from the ADI Auxiliary Publications Project, Photoduplication Service, Library of Congress, Washington, D.C., remitting in advance $3.75 for 35-mm microfilm or $2.00 for 6 x 8 in. photocopies. Make checks payable to Chief, Photoduplication Service, Library of Congress.

the major topic units of the usual course and tried to specify what aspects of the over-all objectives should be accomplished in the unit. Both the titles of the units and the order of units were arbitrary. We made no attempt to force the topics into a single theoretical framework. The outline of general objectives follows.

I. General Goals (to be aimed at throughout the course)
   A. Motives
      1. Desire to continue learning about behavior and experience.
      2. Interest in reading reports of psychological research.
      3. Curiosity about behavior—that observed or one's own.
   B. Scientific values and skills
      1. Attitudes.
         a. Respect for data and eagerness to get what is available with respect to a problem or decision.
         b. Appreciation of scientific methods, and readiness to apply them to problems of human behavior—with awareness of their limitations.
         c. A critical attitude toward generalizations about human behavior. (We are not trying to make our students complete scientists. What we are trying to do is to develop an appreciation of science, and of psychology, as an attempt to apply scientific method to the study of human behavior. We are faced with the problem of wanting our students to have faith in and support psychologists because psychologists attempt to use scientific methods, but not to have such faith that they blindly accept all the claims and generalizations of psychologists. We want them to ask, "What is the evidence?")
         d. Intelligent skepticism about the finality of our present state of knowledge. Ability to get along without absolute answers to every problem.
         e. Intelligent skepticism about the adequacy of methods used in arriving at conclusions, especially about human behavior.
         f. Recognition of the influence of needs and cultural values upon the acceptance of generalizations and upon the definition of research areas. Desire to separate values from observation.
      (We believe that some of these attitudes are learned through the influence of a teacher who makes his own attitudes evident, as well as by specific teaching.)
      2. Abilities.
         a. Ability to continue learning psychology after completion of the course.

(1) Skill in reading and evaluating popular accounts of psychology.

(2) Sensitivity/attentiveness to behavior and skill in observing and learning from it.

(3) Ability to evaluate one's own writing, discussion, or ideas.

b. Understanding of the elements of the experimental method in psychology.

(1) Recognition of the importance of control of variables in research.

(2) Knowledge of some of the important variables to control in research on human behavior; for example, motivation, past experience.

(3) Understanding of some of the terms used in describing experiments; namely, assumptions, hypotheses, variables, sample, control group.

c. Ability to discriminate between reasonable and unreasonable generalizations in terms of the evidence upon which they are based.

d. Awareness of some of the major tools and methods of psychology.

C. Knowledge of psychology

1. Awareness of major psychological approaches to human behavior (not necessarily by name).

2. Ability to see the operation and meaning of major psychological concepts and principles in everyday life.

3. Ability to describe behavior in objective terms (relatively independent of the students' own biases) and to gain emotional understanding of it. (In this area, we do not want our students to go around "analyzing" their friends and pointing out rationalizations, projections, and repressions, but we do want them to gain increased sensitivity to the feelings of others.)

4. Understanding of the principles and concepts of psychology that are basic for further study of psychology or for use in other areas of life (for example, knowing the psychological meanings of words that have wide use in our culture).

D. Attitudes toward people

Our goal here is to teach in such a way that our students will relate the principles we teach to their attitudinal structures and have greater ability to help and receive help from others.

We followed our general statement of goals with detailed specifications of goals for each topic of the course. Many instructors like to state such goals in behavioral terms. Although there is little empirical evidence that formulating such statements results in more effective teaching, it does help teachers become aware of possible ambiguities in their own thinking. A guide for formulating objectives is R. J. Kibler et al., *Objectives for Instruction and Evaluation* (Boston: Allyn and Bacon, 1974).

Appendix B

Student Perceptions of Learning and Teaching

W. J. McKeachie
The University of Michigan[*]

The items on this questionnaire ask you to comment on various aspects of your course.

The questionnaire has eight brief parts. The first part is intended to assess your perception of your own learning; the second part is your perception of characteristics related to instructor effectiveness. Other parts are not evaluative, but are intended to assess aspects of teacher style; for example, either a high or low degree of structure may be effective.

Thank you for taking the time to fill this form out thoughtfully. Your answers and comments will help your teacher improve the course.

Date: _____   Your Class Standing (Circle):

Course: _____   FR   SOPH   JR   SR   GRAD

Instructor: _____

---

[*] Teachers are welcome to use this form or items from it without requesting permission from the author.

Your GPA in all courses at this college:

3.5–4.0_____	2.0–2.4_____	Sex: Male Female
3.0–3.4_____	0–1.9_____	
2.5–2.9_____		

1–almost never or almost nothing   4–often or much
2–seldom or little   5–very often
3–occasionally or moderate   6–almost always or a great deal
     If not applicable, leave blank

Impact on Students

1. My intellectual curiosity has been stimulated by this course.
   Comments:

2. I am learning how to think more clearly about the area of this course.
   Comments:

3. I am learning how to read materials in this area more effectively.
   Comments:

4. I am acquiring'knowledge about the subject.
   Comments:

5. The course is contributing to my self-understanding.
   Comments:

6. The course is increasing my interest in learning more about this area.
   Comments:

Instructor Effectiveness

7. The instructor is enthusiastic.
   Comments:

8. The instructor gives good examples of the concepts.
   Comments:

9. The instructor goes into too much detail.
   Comments:

10. The instructor is helpful when students are confused.
    Comments:

11. The instructor seems knowledgeable in many areas.
    Comments:

Rapport

12. The instructor knows students' names.
    Comments:

13. The instructor is friendly.
    Comments:

Group Interaction

14. Students volunteer their own opinions.
    Comments:

15. Students discuss one another's ideas.
    Comments:

16. Students feel free to disagree with the instructor.
    Comments:

Difficulty

17. The instructor makes difficult assignments.
    Comments:

18. The instructor asks for a great deal of work.
    Comments:

Structure

19. The instructor plans class activities in detail.
    Comments:

20. The instructor follows an outline closely.
    Comments:

Feedback

21. The instructor keeps students informed of their progress.
Comments:

22. The instructor tells students when they have done a particularly good job.
Comments:

23. Test and papers are graded and returned promptly.
Comments:

Notice!!! This Scale Is Different!!!

Student Responsibility

1–definitely false
2–more false than true
3–in between

4–more true than false
5–definitely true
If not applicable, leave blank

24. I had a strong desire to take this course.
Comments:

25. I actively participate in class discussions.
Comments:

26. I try to make a tie-in between what I am learning through the course and my own experience.
Comments:

27. I attend class regularly.
Comments:

28. I utilize all the learning opportunities provided in the course.
Comments:

29. I have created learning experiences for myself in connection with the course.
Comments:

30. I have helped classmates learn.
    Comments:

Overall Evaluation

Indicate your evaluation of characteristics below, using numbers based on the following scale:

   1. Poor   2. Fair   3. Good   4. Very Good   5. Excellent

31. Rate the instructor's general teaching effectiveness for you.
    Comments:

32. Rate the value of the course as a whole to you.
    Comments:

Added Comments Below

Appendix C

Checklist of Teaching Techniques

TECHNIQUE	GOALS POTENTIALLY ACHIEVED
Books	Knowledge Critical thinking
Lecture	Knowledge Inspiration, motivation (a "cutting edge" lecture) Identification with a scholar Critical thinking (by example)
Discussion	Critical thinking Relating knowledge to student experiences Application Attitude change
PSI	Knowledge, application and other (depends upon type of tests and tutoring)
Student panel, student reports	Interest and motivation (at least for participants)

TECHNIQUE	GOALS POTENTIALLY ACHIEVED
Guest lecturer or resource person	Added interest and information
Films	Makes materials more concrete Facilitates learning materials involving motion or visual detail Interest
TV	Interest (greater involvement than film) Motion, visual details
Slides	Permit visual materials to be greatly enlarged and held in view while explained Interest
Bulletin boards, mock-up	Provide opportunity for learning at student's own pace May help student relate learning in classrooms to materials presented in mass media Provide concrete examples
Recordings	Provide concrete auditory experience Taped recordings can be made cheaply by instructor to bring situations outside the classroom to the class
Field trips	First-hand knowledge Interest
Laboratory	First-hand experience Scientific method
Role playing	Real-life experience Develops human relations skills Interest
Buzz groups	Create awareness of problems Practice in problem solving Increased involvement
Study guides, workbooks	Aid organization and learning of materials Promote application of knowledge
Periodicals	Bridge gap between classroom and other experiences of students
Teaching machines and programmed texts	Learning knowledge and skills, particularly those requiring repetition and immediate feedback
Computer-aided instruction	Potentially can achieve any of these goals when combined with other materials, but currently limited by availability of college-level programs

References

Abt, C. *Serious games*. New York: Viking, 1970.

Adams, J. C.; Carter, C. R.; and Smith, D. R., eds. *College teaching by television*. Washington, D.C.: American Council on Education, 1959.

Adult Education Association. How to use role playing. *Leadership Pamphlet #6*. Adult Education Association, 743 N. Wabash, Chicago, IL, 1955c.

Allen, W. H. Audio-visual communication. In C. W. Harris, ed. *Encyclopedia of educational research*, 3rd. ed. New York: Macmillan, 1960.

Anderson, J. R., and Bower, G. H. *Human associative memory*. Washington, D.C.: V. H. Winston and Sons, 1973.

Anderson, R. C. Learning in discussion: A resume of the authoritarian-democratic studies. *Harvard Educational Review*, 1959, *29*, 201–267.

Anderson, R. P., and Kelly, B. L. Student attitudes about participation in classroom groups. *Journal of Educational Research*, 1954, *48*, 255–267.

Angell, G. W. Effect of immediate knowledge of quiz results on final examination scores in freshman chemistry. *Journal of Educational Research*, 1949, *42*, 391–394.

Antioch College. Experiment in French language instruction. *Antioch College Reports*. Yellow Springs, OH: Office of Educational Research, Antioch College, October 1960.

Arbes, B., and Kitchener, K. G. Faculty consultation: a study in support of education through student interaction. *Journal of Counseling Psychology*, 1974, *21*, 121–126.

Asch, M. J. Non-directive teaching in psychology: an experimental study. *Psychological Monographs*, 1951, *65*, no. 4.

Ash, P., and Carlton, B. J. *The value of notetaking during film learning.* Pennsylvania State University Instructional Film Research Program, Port Washington, NY: U.S. Naval Training Device Center, Office of Research, Technical Report No. SDC 269-7-21, November 1951.

Ashmus, M., and Haigh, G. *Some factors which may be associated with student choice between directive and non-directive classes.* Springfield, MA: Springfield College, 1952.

Atkinson, J. E., and Litwin, G. H. Achievement motive and test anxiety conceived as motive to approach success and motive to avoid failure. *Journal of Abnormal and Social Psychology*, 1960, *60*, 52–63.

Atkinson, J. W., and O'Connor, P. A. *Effects of ability grouping in schools related to individual differences in achievement-related motivation.* Final Report, Office of Education, Cooperative Research Project 1238, 1963.

Atkinson, R. C. Ingredients for a theory of instruction. *American Psychologist*, 1972, *27*, 921–931.

Attiyeh, R., and Lumsden, K. G. Some modern myths in teaching economics: the U.K. experience. *American Economics Review*, 1972, *62*, 429–433.

Axelrod, J. Group dynamics, nondirective therapy, and college teaching. *Journal of Higher Education*, 1955, *26*, 200–207.

Bainter, M. E. A study of the outcomes of two types of laboratory techniques used in a course in general college physics for students planning to be teachers in the elementary grades. *Dissertation Abstracts*, 1955, *15*, 2485–2486.

Baker, R. G. Psychodrama in teaching scientific method in the social sciences. *Sociatry*, June 1947, *1*(2), 179–182.

Balcziak, L. W. The role of the laboratory and demonstration in college physical science in achieving the objectives of general education. Unpublished doctoral dissertation, University of Minnesota, *Dissertation Abstracts*, 1954, *14*, 502–503.

Banathy, B. H., and Jordan, B. A classroom laboratory instructional system (CLIS). *Foreign Language Annals*, 1969, *2*, 466–473.

Bandura, A. *Social learning theory*. Englewood Cliffs, N.J.: Prentice-Hall, 1976.

―――. Self-efficacy: toward a unifying theory of behavioral change. *Psychological Review*, March 1977, *84*(2), 191–215.

Bane, C. L. The lecture vs. the class-discussion method of college teaching. *School and Society*, 1925, *21*, 300–302.

Barnard, J. D. The lecture demonstration vs. the problem-solving method of teaching a college science course. *Science Education*, 1942, *26*, 121–132.

Barnard, W. H. Note on the comparative efficacy of lecture and socialized recitation method vs. group study method. *Journal of Educational Psychology*, 1936, *27*, 388–390.

Barr, A. S. et al. The measurement of teaching ability. *Journal of Experimental Education*, 1945, *14*, 1–206.

Bauer, R. The obstinate audience: the influence of process from the point of view of social communication. *American Psychologist*, 1964, *19*, 319–328.

Beach, L. R. Sociability and academic achievement in various types of learning situations. *Journal of Educational Psychology*, 1960, *51*, 208–212.

―――. Self-directed student groups and college learning. In W. R. Hatch and A. L. Richards, *Approach to independent study*, New Dimensions in Higher Education No. 13. Washington, D.C.: U.S. Department of Health, Education, and Welfare, 1965.

―――. *Student interaction and learning in small self-directed college groups*. Final Report. Washington, D.C.: Department of Health, Education, and Welfare, June, 1968.

Beard, R. M. *Teaching and learning in higher education*. Middlesex, England: Penguin Books, 1972.

Beard, R. M., and Bligh, D. A. *Research into teaching methods in higher education*, 3rd ed. London: Society for Research into Higher Education, 1971.

Beardslee, D.; Birney, R.; and McKeachie, W. J. *Summary of conference on research in classroom processes*. Unpublished manuscript (Mimeo), Department of Psychology, University of Michigan, 1951.

Becker, S. K.; Murray, J. N.; and Bechtoldt, H. P. *Teaching by the discussion method*. Iowa City: State University of Iowa, 1958.

Bendig, A. W. An inverted factor analysis study of student-rated introductory psychology instructors. *Journal of Experimental Education*, 1953, *21*, 333–336.

―――. Ability and personality characteristics of introductory psychology instructors rated competent and empathic by their students. *Journal of Educational Research*, 1955, *48*, 705–709.

Bendig, A. W., and Hountras, P. T. Anxiety, authoritarianism, and student attitude toward departmental control of college instruction. *Journal of Educational Psychology*, 1959, *50*, 1–8.

Berlyne, D. E. A theory of human curiosity. *British Journal of Psychology*, 1954a, *45*, 180–181.

———. An experimental study of human curiosity. *British Journal of Psychology*, 1954b, *45*, 256–265.

———. *Conflict, arousal, and curiosity.* New York: McGraw-Hill, 1960.

Berman, A. I. *Balanced learning.* New York: Harper & Row, 1973.

———. Media-activated seminar. *Educational Technology*, March 1974, 43–45.

Bills, R. E. Investigation of student centered teaching. *Journal of Educational Research*, 1952, *46*, 313–319.

Birney, R., and McKeachie, W. The teaching of psychology: A survey of research since 1942. *Psychological Bulletin*, 1955, *52*, 51–68.

Bligh, D. A. A pilot experiment to test the relative effectiveness of three kinds of teaching methods. *Research in Librarianship*, 1970, *3*, 88–93.

———. *What's the use of lectures?* 3rd ed. Hertfordshire, England: Penguin Books, 1972.

Bloom, B. S. Thought processes in lectures and discussions. *Journal of General Education*, 1953, 7, 160–169.

Bloom, B. S., ed. *Taxonomy of educational objectives, handbook I: cognitive domain.* New York: Longmans, Green, 1956.

Bork, A. *The physics computer development project.* Irvine CA: Department of Physics, University of California, 1975.

Born, D. G. *Student withdrawals in personalized instruction courses and in lecture courses.* Paper presented at the meeting of the Rocky Mountain Psychological Association, Denver, May 1971.

Bovard, E. W., Jr. Group structure and perception. *Journal of Abnormal and Social Psychology*, 1951a, *46*, 398–405.

———. The experimental production of interpersonal affect. *Journal of Abnormal Psychology*, 1951b, *46*, 521–528.

Bowman, C. C. The psychodramatic method in collegiate instruction: case study. *Sociatry*, March 1948, *1*(4), 421–430.

Bradley, R. L. Lecture demonstration vs. individual laboratory work in a natural science course at Michigan State University. *Dissertation Abstracts*, 1963, *23*, 4568.

Breland, N. S., and Smith, M. P. *A comparison of PSI and traditional methods of instruction for teaching introduction to psychology.* Paper presented at the National Conference on Personalized Instruction in Higher Education, Washington, D.C., 1974.

Briggs, L. J. Intensive classes for superior students. *Journal of Educational Psychology*, 1947, *38*, 207–215.

Bronfenbrenner, U. A Cornell study relating to grading conditions. *Center for Improvement of Undergraduate Education Notes*, 1972, *3*, 2–4.

Burke, H. R. An experimental study of teaching methods in college freshman orientation course. Unpublished doctoral dissertation, Boston University, *Dissertation Abstracts*, 1956, *16*, 77–78.

Burkhardt, S. M. *A study in concept learning in differential calculus.* Unpublished doctoral dissertation, Columbia University, 1956.

Burtt, H. E.; Chassel, L. M.; and Hatch, E. M. Efficiency of instruction in unselected and selected sections of elementary psychology. *Journal of Educational Research*, 1923, *14*, 154–161.

Calhoun, J. F. The combination of elements in the personalized system of instruction. *Teaching of Psychology*, 1976, *3*(2), 73–76.

Calvin, A. D.; Hoffman, F. K.; and Harden, E. L. The effect of intelligence and social atmosphere on group problem solving behavior. *Journal of Social Psychology*, 1957, *45*, 61–74.

Calvin, A. D.; McGuigan, F. J.; and Sullivan, M. W. A further investigation of the relationship between anxiety and classroom examination performance. *Journal of Educational Psychology*, 1957, *48*, 240–244.

Cantor, N. *The dynamics of learning.* Buffalo: Foster and Steward, 1946.

Carpenter, C. R. *The Penn State pyramid plan: interdependent student work study grouping for increasing motivation for academic development.* Paper read at 14th National Conference on Higher Education, Chicago, March 1959.

Carpenter, C. R., and Greenhill, L. P. *An investigation of closed-circuit television for teaching university courses.* Instructional Television Research Project No. 1, University Park: Pennsylvania State University, 1955.

————. *An investigation of closed-circuit television for teaching university courses.* Instructional Television Research Project No. 2, University Park: Pennsylvania State University, 1958.

Carrier, N. A. The relationship of certain personality measures to examination performance under stress. *Journal of Educational Psychology*, 1957, *48*, 510–520.

Carroll, J. B. Research on teaching foreign languages. In N. L. Gage, ed., *Handbook of research on teaching.* Chicago: Rand McNally & Company, 1963, 1060–1100.

Casey, J. E., and Weaver, B. F. An evaluation of lecture method and small-group method of teaching in terms of knowledge of content, teacher attitude, and social status. *Journal of Colorado-Wyoming Academy of Science*, 1956, *7*, 54.

Centra, J. A. The effectiveness of student feedback in modifying college instruction. *Journal of Educational Psychology*, 1973, *65*, 395–401.

Chance, C. W. Experimentation in the adaptation of the overhead projector utilizing 200 transparencies and 800 overlays in teaching engineering descriptive geometry curricula. *Audio-Visual Communications Review*, 1961, *9*, A17–A18.

Cheydleur, F. D. Criteria of effective teaching in basic French courses. *Bulletin of the University of Wisconsin*, August 1945.

Churchill, R. *Preliminary report on reading course study*. (Mimeo) Yellow Springs, OH: Antioch College, 1957.

Churchill, R., and Baskin, S. *Experiment on independent study*. (Mimeo) Yellow Springs, OH: Antioch College, 1958.

Churchill, R., and John, P. Conservation of teaching time through the use of lecture classes and student assistants. *Journal of Educational Psychology*, 1958, *49*, 324–327.

Coats, W. D., and Smidchens, U. Audience recall as a function of speaker dynamism. *Journal of Educational Psychology*, 1966, *57*, 189–191.

Cole, M.; Cay, J.; Glick, J.; and Sharp, D. W. *The cultural context of learning and thinking*. New York: Basic Books, 1971.

Coleman, W. Role-playing as an instructional aid. *Journal of Educational Psychology*, 1948, *39*, 427–435.

Collins, A. M., and Quillian, M. R. How to make a language user. In E. Tulving and W. Donaldson, eds., *Organization of memory*. New York: Academic Press, 1972.

Coombs, C. H. *A theory of data*. New York: Wiley, 1964.

Coombs, C. H.; Milholland, J. E.; and Womer, F. B. *The assessment of partial knowledge in objective testing*. Final Report, Engineering Research Institute. Ann Arbor: University of Michigan, February 1955.

Coombs, P. H. *The world educational crisis: A systems analysis* (Swedish ed.). Stockholm, Sweden: Bonniers, 1971.

Corey, J. R.; McMichael, J. S.; and Tremont, P. T. *Long-term effects of personalized instruction in an introductory psychology course*. Paper presented at the meeting of the Eastern Psychological Association, Atlantic City, 1970.

Corey, J. R.; Valente, R. G.; and Shamow, N. K. *The retention of material learned in a personalized introductory psychology course*. Paper presented at the meeting of the American Psychological Association, Washington, D.C., September 1971.

Corman, B. The effect of varying amounts and kinds of information as guidance in problem solving. *Psychological Monographs*, 1957, *71*, no. 2 (Whole No. 431).

Costin, F. Lecturing versus other methods of teaching: a review of research. *British Journal of Educational Technology*, 1972, *3*, 4–31.

———. Three-choice vs. four-choice items: implications for reliability and validity of objective achievement tests. *Educational and Psychological Measurement*, 1972, *32*, 1035–1038.

Costin, F.; Greenough, W. T.; and Menges, R. J. Student ratings of college teaching: reliability, validity, and usefulness. *Review of Educational Research*, December 1971, *41*(5), 511–535.

Craig, R. E. Directed vs. independent discovery of established relations. *Journal of Educational Psychology*, 1956, *47*, 223–234.

Craik, F. I. M., and Lockart, R. S. Levels of processing: a framework for memory research. *Journal of Verbal Learning and Verbal Behavior*, 1972, *11*, 671–684.

Creager, J. A. *A multiple factor analysis of the Purdue rating scale for instructors*. M.S. Thesis, Purdue, 1950.

Cronbach, L. J., and Snow, R. E. *Aptitudes and instructional methods: a handbook for research on interaction*. New York: Irvington, 1977.

Cross, D. *An investigation of the relationships between students' expressions of satisfaction with certain aspects of the college classroom situation and their achievement on final examinations*. Unpublished honors thesis, University of Michigan, 1958.

Cutler, R. L.; McKeachie, W. J.; and McNeil, E. B. Teaching psychology by telephone. *American Psychologist*, 1958, *13*, 551–552.

Dahlgren, L. O., and Marton, F. Investigations into the learning and teaching of economics. *Reports from The Institute of Education, University of Goteborg*, September 1976, No. 54.

Davage, R. H. *The pyramid plan for the systematic involvement of university students in teaching-learning functions*. Division of Academic Research and Services, Pennsylvania State University, 1958.

———. *Recent data on the pyramid project in psychology*. Division of Academic Research and Services, Pennsylvania State University, 1959.

Dawson, M. D. Lectures vs. problem-solving in teaching elementary soil section. *Science Education*, 1956, *40*, 395–404.

Dearden, D. M. An evaluation of the laboratory in a college general biology course. *Journal of Experimental Education*, March 1960, *26*(3), 241–247.

De Cecco, J. P. Class size and coordinated instruction. *British Journal of Educational Psychology*, 1964, *34*, 65–74.

Deignan, F. J. A comparison of the effectiveness of two group discussion methods. Unpublished doctoral dissertation, Boston University, *Dissertation Abstracts*, 1956, *16*, 1110–1111.

Della-Piana, G. M. Two experimental feedback procedures: a comparison of their effects on the learning of concepts. Unpublished doctoral dissertation, University of Illinois, *Dissertation Abstracts*, 1956, *16*, 910–911.

Deutsch, M. An experimental study of the effects of cooperation and competition upon group processes. *Human Relations*, 1949, *2*, 199–232.

Diamond, M. J. Improving the undergraduate lecture class by use of student-led discussion groups. *American Psychologist*, 1972, 27, 978–981.

Di Vesta, F. J. Instructor-centered and student-centered approaches in teaching a human relations course. *Journal of Applied Psychology*, 1954, *38*, 329–335.

Domino, G. Differential prediction of academic achievement in conforming and independent sections. *Journal of Educational Psychology*, 1968, *59*, 256–260.

———. Interactive effects of achievement orientation and teaching style on academic achievement. *Journal of Educational Psychology*, 1971, *62*, 427–431.

———. *Aptitude by treatment interaction effects in college instruction.* Paper presented at the meeting on the American Psychological Association, New Orleans, LA, 1974.

Doty, B. A., and Doty, L. A. Programmed instructional effectiveness in relation to certain student characteristics. *Journal of Educational Psychology*, 1964, *55*, 334–338.

Dowaliby, F. J., and Schumer, H. Teacher-centered vs. student-centered mode of college classroom instruction as related to manifest anxiety. *Journal of Educational Psychology*, 1973, *64*, 125–132.

Doyle, K. O., Jr. *Student evaluation of instruction.* Lexington, MA: Lexington Books, 1975.

Dreher, R. E., and Beatty, W. H. *An experimental study of college instruction using broadcast television.* Instructional Television Research Project No. 1, San Francisco: San Francisco State College, 1958.

Drucker, A. J., and Remmers, H. H. Do alumni and students differ in their attitudes toward instructors? *Journal of Educational Psychology*, 1951, *42*, 129–143.

Dubin, R., and Hedley, R. A. *The medium may be related to the message: college instruction by tv.* Eugene, OR: University of Oregon Press, 1969.

Duchastel, P. C., and Merrill, P. F. The effects of behavioral objectives on learning: a review of empirical studies. *Review of Educational Research*, 1973, *43*, 53–69.

Dukes, R. L., and Waller, S. J. Towards a general evaluation model for simulation games: GEM. *Simulation and Games*, 1976, 7, 75–96.

Ebbinghaus, H. *Memory: a contribution to experimental psychology.*

Trans. by H. A. Ruger and C. E. Bussenius. New York: Teachers College, Columbia University, 1913.

Eble, K. E. *The craft of teaching.* San Francisco: Jossey-Bass, 1976.

Edmondson, J. B., and Mulder, F. J. Size of class as a factor in university instruction. *Journal of Educational Research*, 1924, *9*, 1–12.

Edwards, J.; Morton, S.; Taylor, S.; Weiss, M.; and Dusseldorp, R. How effective is CAI?: a review of the research. *Educational Leadership*, 1975, *33*, 147–153.

Eelen, P., and D'Ydewalle, G. Producing or observing response-outcome contingencies in a two response alternative task. *Psychological Belgica*, 1976, 61–71.

Egan, D. E., and Greeno, J. G. Acquiring cognitive structure by discovery and rule learning. *Journal of Educational Psychology*, 1973, *64*(1), 85–97.

Eglash, A. A group discussion method of teaching psychology. *Journal of Educational Psychology*, 1954, *45*, 257–267.

Elliott, D. N. *Characteristics and relationships of various criteria of teaching.* Ph.D. Thesis, Purdue University, 1949.

———. Reported in D. Beardslee, and R. Birney. *Summary of conference on research in classroom processes* (Mimeo). Department of Psychology, University of Michigan, 1951.

Entwistle, N. *Personality, learning, cognition, and teaching.* London: Wiley, In press.

Entwistle, N., and Hounsell, D., eds. *How students learn.* Institute for Research and Development in Post-Compulsory Education, University of Lancaster, 1975.

Ericksen, S. C. *Motivation for learning.* Ann Arbor: University of Michigan Press, 1974.

Evans, D.; Roney, H.; and McAdams, W. An evaluation of the effectiveness of instruction and audience reaction to programming of an educational tv station. *American Psychologist*, 1954, *9*, 361–362.

Faw, V. A. A psychotherapeutic method of teaching psychology. *American Psychologist*, 1949, *4*, 104–109.

Feldhusen, J. R. The effects of small- and large-group instruction on learning of subject matter, attitudes, and interests. *Journal of Psychology*, 1963, *55*, 357–362.

Feldman, K. A. The superior college teacher from the students' view. *Research in Higher Education*, 1976, *5*, 243–288.

Feurzeig, W.; Munter, P. K.; Swets, J. A.; and Breen, M. N. Computer-aided teaching in medical diagnosis. *Journal of Medical Education*, August 1964, *39*(8).

Fisher, K. M. A-T science teaching: how effective is it? *BioScience*, November 1976, *26*(11), 691–697.

Flesher, W. R. Inferential student rating of instructors. *Educational Research Bulletin*, 1952, *31*, 57–62.

Friedman, C. P.; Hirschi, S.; Parlett, M.; and Taylor, E. F. The rise and fall of PSI in physics at MIT. *American Journal of Physics*, 1976, *3*, 204–211.

Fritz, M. R. *Survey of tv utilization in army training.* Instructional Film Research Report SDC 530-0100, Special Devices Center, Office of Naval Research, December 1952.

Gage, N. L. *Handbook of research on teaching.* Chicago: Rand McNally, 1963.

Gagne, R. M., and Rohwer, W. D., Jr. Instructional psychology. *Annual Review of Psychology*, 1969, *20*, 381–418.

Gamson, W. A. *SIMSOC: a manual for participants.* Ann Arbor: Campus Publishers, 1966.

Gates, A. I. Recitation as a factor in memorizing. *Archives of Psychology*, 1917, *6*, No. 40.

Gerberich, J. R., and Warner, K. O. Relative instructional efficiencies of the lecture and discussion methods in a university course in American national government. *Journal of Educational Research*, 1936, *29*, 574–579.

Gibb, C. A. Classroom behavior of the college teacher. *Educational and Psychological Measurement*, 1955, *15*, 254–263.

Gibb, J. R. The effects of group size and of threat reduction upon creativity in a problem-solving situation. *American Psychologist*, 1951, *6*, 324 (Abstract).

Gibb, L. M., and Gibb, J. R. The effects of the use of "participative action" groups in a course in general psychology. *American Psychologist*, 1952, 7, 247 (Abstract).

Goldschmid, B., and Goldschmid, M. L. Peer teaching in higher education: a review. *Higher Education*, 1976, *5*, 9–33.

Goldschmid, M. L. Instructional options: adapting the large university course to individual differences. *Learning and Development*, 1970, *1*(5), 1–2.

―――. The learning cell: an instructional innovation. *Learning and Development*, 1971, 2(5), 1–6.

―――. *When students teach students.* Paper presented at the International Conference on Improving University Teaching, Heidelberg, Germany, May 1975.

Goldschmid, M. L., and Shore, B. M. The learning cell: a field test of an educational innovation. In W. A. Verreck, ed., *Methodological problems in research and development in higher education.* Amsterdam: Swets and Zeitlinger, B. D., 1974, 218–236.

Goldstein, A. A controlled comparison of the project method with standard laboratory teaching in pharmacology. *Journal of Medical Education*, 1956, *31*, 365–375.

Goodhartz, A. S. Student attitudes and opinions relating to teaching at Brooklyn College. *School and Society*, 1948, *68*, 345–349.

Greene, E. B. Relative effectiveness of lecture and individual readings as methods of college teaching. *Genetic Psychology Monographs*, 1928, *4*, 457–563.

Greenhill, L. P. New direction for communication research. *Audio-Visual Communications Review*, 1959, 7, 245–253.

Greenlaw, P. S.; Herron, L. W.; and Rawdon, R. H. *Business simulation*. Englewood Cliffs, N.J.: Prentice Hall, 1962.

Greeno, J. G. *The structure of memory and the process of solving problems*. Technical Report 37. Ann Arbor: University of Michigan, Human Performance Center, 1972.

———. *Process of understanding in studying from text*. Paper prepared for the Symposium, "Information Processing Analyses of Instruction," presented at AERA, San Francisco, April 1976.

Grossman, L. I.; Ship, I. I.; and Romano, M. T. Evaluation of teaching and television vs. classroom demonstration. *Journal of Dental Education*, 1961, *25*, 330–337.

Grubb, R. E., and Sefridge, L. D. Computer tutoring in statistics. *Computer and Automation*, 1963, *13*(3).

Gruber, H. E., and Weitman, M. *Cognitive processes in higher education: curiosity and critical thinking*. Paper read at Western Psychological Association, San Jose, CA, April 1960.

———. *Self-directed study: experiments in higher education*, Report No. 19. Boulder: University of Colorado, Behavior Research Lab, April 1962.

Guetzkow, H. S.; Kelly, E. L.; and McKeachie, W. J. An experimental comparison of recitation, discussion, and tutorial methods in college teaching. *Journal of Educational Psychology*, 1954, *45*, 193–209.

Haigh, G. V., and Schmidt, W. The learning of subject matter in teacher-centered and group-centered classes. *Journal of Educational Psychology*, 1956, *47*, 295–301.

Haines, D. B., and McKeachie, W. J. Cooperative vs. competitive discussion methods in teaching introductory psychology. *Journal of Educational Psychology*, 1967, *58*, 386–390.

Hansen, W. L.; Kelley, A. C.; and Weisbrod, B. A. Economic efficiency and the distribution of benefits from college instruction. *American Economic Review*, May 1970, *60*(2), 364–369.

Harlow, H. F. Learning motivated by a manipulation drive. *Journal of Experimental Psychology*, 1950, *40*, 228–234.

Hartman, F. R. Recognition learning under multiple channel presentation and testing conditions. *Audio-Visual Communication Review*, 1961, *9*, 24–43.

Haythorn, W.; Couch, A.; Haefner, D.; Langham, P.; and Carter, L. The effects of varying combinations of authoritarian and equalitarian leaders and followers. *Journal of Abnormal Psychology*, 1956, *53*, 210–219.

Heath, R. W. *A study of achievement in high school chemistry: report to the chemical bond approach project*. Princeton, NJ: Educational Testing Service, 1962a.

———. *A study of achievement in high school chemistry: report to the chemical education material study*. Princeton, NJ: Educational Testing Service, 1962b.

———. Curriculum, cognition, and education measurement. *Educational and Psychological Measurement*, 1964, *24*, 239–254.

Hebb, D. O. *The organization of behavior*. New York: Wiley, 1949.

Heckhausen, H. *How to improve poor motivation in students*. Paper presented at the 18th International Congress of Applied Psychology, Montreal, August 1974.

Heilman, J. D., and Armentrout, W. D. The rating of college teachers on ten traits by their students. *Journal of Educational Psychology*, 1936, *27*, 197–216.

Henderson, W. T., and Wen, S. Effects of immediate positive reinforcement on undergraduates' course achievement. *Psychological Reports*, 1976, *39*, 568–570.

Hess, J. H. *A bibliography of operant instructional technology*. Unpublished manuscript, Eastern Mennonite College, P.S.I. Psychology Clearinghouse, Harrisonburg, VA, 1972.

Heyns, R. W. Conference leadership which stimulates teamwork. *Michigan Business Review*, 1952, *4*, 16–23.

Hiler, W., and McKeachie, W. J. The problem-oriented approach to teaching psychology. *Journal of Educational Psychology*, 1954, *45*, 224–232.

Hill, R. J. *A comparative study of lecture and discussion methods*. New York: Fund for Adult Education, 1960.

Hill, W. F. *Learning through discussion*. Beverly Hills, CA: Sage, 1969.

Hirsch, R. S., and Moncreiff, B. *A simulated chemistry lab*. Paper presented at the 56th National meeting of the American Institute of Chemical Engineers, San Francisco, CA, May 1965.

Hirschman, C. S. *An investigation of the small groups discussion classroom method on criteria of understanding, pleasantness, and self-confidence induced*. Unpublished master's thesis, University of Pittsburgh, 1952.

Hoban, C. F. The dilemma of adult ITV college courses. *Educational Broadcasting Review*, June 1968, 31–36.

Hoban, C. F., and Van Ormer, E. B. *Instructional film research 1918–1950*. Technical Report No. SDC 269-7-19, Special Devices Center, Office of Naval Research, December 1950.

Hockenberry-Boeding, C., and Vattano, F. J. *Undergraduates as teaching assistants: a comparison of two discussion methods*. Unpublished manuscript, 1975.

Hoffman, L. R. Homogeneity of member personality and its effect on group problem solving. *Journal of Abnormal Psychology*, 1959, *58*, 27–32.

Horner, M. S. *Sex differences in achievement motivation and performance in competitive and non-competitive situations*. Unpublished doctoral dissertation, University of Michigan, 1968.

Horwitz, M. The verdicality of liking and disliking. In R. Taguiri and L. Petrullo, eds. *Person perception and interpersonal behavior*. Stanford: Stanford University Press, 1958.

Hovland, C. I., ed. *The order of presentation in persuasion*. New Haven: Yale University Press, 1957.

Hovland, C. I.; Janis, I. L.; and Kelley, H. H. *Communication and persuasion*. New Haven: Yale University Press, 1953.

Hovland, C. I.; Lumsdaine, A. A.; and Sheffield, F. D. *Experiments in mass communication*. Princeton: Princeton University Press, 1949.

Hovland, C. I.; and Mandell, W. An experimental comparison of conclusion-drawing by the communicator and by the audience. *Journal of Abnormal and Social Psychology*, 1952, *47*, 581–588.

Hsiao, J. C. The learning effectiveness of microeconomic simulation. *Education*, 1975, *3*, 270–275.

Hudelson, E. *Class size at the college level*. Minneapolis: University of Minnesota Press, 1928.

Hunt, P. The case method of instruction. *Harvard Educational Review*, 1951, *3*, 1–19.

Hunter, B.; Kastner, C. S.; Rubin, M. L.; and Seidel, R. J. *Learning alternatives in U.S. education: where student and computer meet*. Englewood Cliffs, NJ: Educational Technology Publications, 1975.

Husband, R. W. A statistical comparison of the efficacy of large lecture vs. smaller recitation sections upon achievement in general psychology. *Journal of Psychology*, 1951, *31*, 297–300.

Inbar, M., and Stoll, C. *Simulation and gaming in social science*. New York: Free Press, 1972.

Isaacson, R. L.; McKeachie, W. J.; and Milholland, J. E. Correlation of teacher personality variables and student ratings. *Journal of Educational Psychology*, 1963, *2*, 110–117.

Isaacson, R. L.; McKeachie, W. J.; Milholland, J. E.; Lin, Y. G.; Ho-feller, M.; Baerwaldt, J. W.; and Zinn, K. L. The dimensions of student evaluations of teaching. In W. J. McKeachie; R. L. Isaacson; and J. E. Milholland. *Research on the characteristics of effective college teaching.* Cooperative Research Project No. OE850. Ann Arbor: University of Michigan, 1964.

Jamison, D.; Suppes, P.; and Wells, S. The effectiveness of alternative instructional media: a survey. *Review of Educational Research,* 1974, *44,* 1–67.

Jenkins, R. L. The relative effectiveness of two methods of teaching written and spoken English. Unpublished doctoral dissertation, Michigan State University, *Dissertation Abstracts,* 1952, *12,* 258.

Jensen, B. T. A comparison of student achievement under conditions of class attendance and nonattendance. *Colleges and Universities,* 1951, *26,* 399–404.

Johnson, D. M. Increasing originality on essay examinations in psychology. *Teaching of Psychology,* 1975, *2,* 99–102.

Johnson, D. M., and Smith, H. C. Democratic leadership in the college classroom. *Psychological Monographs,* 1953, *67,* no. 2 (Whole No. 361).

Johnson, K. R., and Ruskin, R. S. *Behavioral instruction: an evaluative review.* Washington, D.C.: American Psychological Association, 1977.

Johnston, J. J. Sticking with first responses on multiple-choice exams: for better or for worse? *Teaching of Psychology,* December 1975, *2*(4), 178–179.

Johnston, R. E., Jr. *Magnetic recordings and visual displays as aids in teaching introductory psychology to college students.* OE Grant No. 73056, Drexel Institute of Technology, Philadelphia, PA, May 1969.

Judd, W. A. Learner-controlled computer-assisted instruction. In K. Zinn; M. Refice; and A. Romano. *Computers in the instructional process: report of an instructional school.* Amsterdam: Elsevier, 1973.

Kaplan, S. Searching behavior in undergraduates. *Psychology in the Schools,* October 1964, *1*(4), 403–405.

Kapstein, F. F., and Roshal, S. M. Learning foreign vocabulary from pictures vs. words. *American Psychologist,* 1954, *9,* 407–408.

Kasten, D. V., and Seibert, W. F. *A study of televised military science instruction.* Purdue University, TVPR Report No. 9, 1959.

Katona, G. *Organizing and memorizing.* New York: Columbia University Press, 1940.

Katz, D. *Gestalt psychology.* New York: Ronald Press, 1950.

Kay, L. W. Role-playing as a teaching aid. *Sociometry,* 1946, *9,* 263–274.

———. Role-playing as a teaching aid—some theoretical considerations. *Sociometry*, 1947, *10*, 165–167.

Keller, F. S. Goodbye teacher.... *Journal of Applied Behavior Analysis*, 1968, *1*, 79–89.

Keller, F. S., and Sherman, J. G., eds. *The Keller Plan handbook*. Menlo Park, CA: W. A. Benjamin, Inc., 1974.

Kelley, A. C. An experiment with TIPS: a computer-aided instructional system for undergraduate education. *American Economic Review*, May 1968, *2*, 446–457.

———. The economics of teaching: The role of TIPS. In K. G. Lumsden, ed. *Recent research in economics education*, Englewood Cliffs, N.J.: Prentice-Hall, 1970, 44–66.

King, P. G. Development and evaluation of CAI lessons for use in macro economic theory. *CLCA Faculty Newsletter*, April 30, 1977.

Kishler, J. P. *The effects of prestige and identification factors on attitude restructuring and learning from sound films*. Port Washington, NY: U.S. Naval Research, Technical Report No. SDC 269-7-10, 1950.

Kitchener, K. G., and Hurst, J. C. *Education through student interaction manual*. Unpublished manuscript, Colorado State University, 1972.

———. Faculty consultation: changing role for the counseling psychologist. *Journal of Counseling Psychology*, 1974.

Klapper, H. L. *Closed-circuit television as a medium of instruction of N.Y. University*. New York: N.Y. University, 1958.

Koenig, K., and McKeachie, W. J. Personality and independent study. *Journal of Educational Psychology*, 1959, *50*, 132–134.

Krathwohl, D.; Bloom, B. S.; and Masia, B., eds. *Taxonomy of educational objectives: affective domain*. New York: David McKay, 1964.

Krauskopf, C. J. The use of written responses in the stimulated recall method. Unpublished doctoral dissertation, Ohio State University, *Dissertation Abstracts*, 1960, *21*, 1953.

Kruglak, H. Experimental outcomes of laboratory instruction in elementary college physics. *American Journal of Physics*, 1952, *20*, 136–141.

Krumboltz, J. D. The nature and importance of the required response in programmed instruction. *American Educational Research Journal*, 1964, *1*, 203–209.

Krumboltz, J. D., and Farquhar, W. W. The effect of three teaching methods on achievement and motivational outcomes in a how-to-study course. *Psychological Monographs*, 1957, *71*, no. 14 (Whole No. 443).

Kulik, J. A., and Jaksa, P. *A review of research on PSI and other educational technologies in college teaching*. Report No. 10, Center for Research on Learning and Teaching, Ann Arbor, MI, May 1977.

Kulik, J. A.; Kulik, C. L. C.; and Smith, B. B. Research on the personalized system of instruction. *Programmed Learning and Educational Technology,* February 1976, *13,* 23–30.

Kulick, J. A., and McKeachie, W. J. The evaluation of teachers in higher education. In Kerlinger, F. N., ed. *Review of research in education, vol. 3.* Itasca, IL: F. E. Peacock Publishers, 1975.

Lahti, A. M. The inductive-deductive method and the physical science laboratory. *Journal of Experimental Education,* 1956, *24,* 149–163.

Lancaster, O. E.; Manning, K. V.; White, M. W. et al. The relative merits of lectures and recitation in teaching college physics. *Journal of Engineering Education,* 1961, *51,* 425–433.

Landsman, T. *An experimental study of a student-centered learning* method. Unpublished doctoral dissertation, Syracuse University, 1950.

Lange, P. C. *Today's education.* National Education Association, 1972, *61,* 59.

Lee, C. B. T., ed. *Improving college teaching.* Washington, D.C.: American Council on Education, 1967.

Leith, G. O. M. Conflict and interference: Studies of the facilitating effects of reviews in learning sequences. *Programmed Learning and Educational Technology,* 1971, *8,* 41–50.

———. Individual differences in learning: interactions of personality and teaching methods. In Association of Educational Psychologists, *Personality and Academic Progress,* London, 1974a.

———. *Goals, methods and materials for a small-group, modular-instruction approach to teaching social psychology.* Paper presented for the Institute of Social Psychology, University of Utrecht, 1974b.

Lempert, R. Law school grading: an experiment with pass-fail. *Journal of Legal Education,* 1972, *24,* 251–308.

Lepore, A. R., and Wilson, J. D. *An experimental study of college instruction using broadcast television.* Instructional Television Research Project No. 2. San Francisco: San Francisco State, 1958.

Levien, R. E. *The emerging technology: instructional uses of the computer in higher education.* New York: McGraw-Hill, 1972.

Lewin, K. Group decision and social change. In G. E. Swanson; T. M. Newcomb; and E. L. Hartley, eds. *Readings in social psychology,* 2nd ed. New York: Holt, 1952, 330–344.

Lewin, K.; Lippitt, R.; and White, R. K. Patterns of aggressive behavior in experimentally created social climates. *Journal of Social Psychology,* 1939, *10,* 271–299.

Lifson, N.; Rempel, P.; and Johnson, J. A. A comparison between lecture and conference methods of teaching psychology. *Journal of Medical Education,* 1956, *31,* 376–382.

Long, K. K. Transfer from teaching to learning. *Journal of Educational Psychology*, 1971, *62*, 167–178.

Longstaff, H. P. Analysis of some factors conditioning learning in general psychology. *Journal of Applied Psychology*, 1932, *16*.

Lovell, G. D., and Haner, C. F. Forced choice applied to college faculty ratings. *Educational and Psychological Measurement*, 1955, *16*, 291–304.

Lublin, S. C. Reinforcement schedules, scholastic aptitude, autonomy need, and achievement in a programmed course. *Journal of Educational Psychology*, December 1965, *56*, 295–302.

Lumsdaine, A. A. Instruments and media of instruction. In N. L. Gage, ed. *Handbook of research on teaching*. Chicago: Rand McNally, 1963, 583–682.

Lumsdaine, A. A., and May, M. A. Mass communication and educational media. *Annual Review of Psychology*, 1965, *16*, 475–534.

Lumsden, E. A. Use of student feedback cards for diagnostic purposes during classroom lectures. *Improving College and University Teaching Yearbook 1976*, Oregon State University Press, 1976, *39*.

Lyle, E. An exploration in the teaching of critical thinking in general psychology. *Journal of Educational Research*, 1958, *52*, 129–133.

Macomber, F. G., and Siegel, L. Experimental study in instructional procedures. *Progress Report No. 1*. Oxford, OH: Miami University, 1956.

———. A study of large-group teaching procedures. *Educational Research*, 1957a, *38*, 220–229.

———. Experimental study in instructional procedures. *Progress Report No. 2*. Oxford, OH: Miami University, 1957b.

———. Experimental study in instructional procedures. *Final Report*. Oxford, OH: Miami University, 1960.

Mager, R. F. *Preparing instructional objectives*. Palo Alto: Fearon Publishers, 1962.

Maier, N. R. F. *Principles of human relations*. New York: Wiley, 1952.

———. *Problem-solving discussions and conferences*. New York: McGraw-Hill, 1963.

———. Innovation in education. *American Psychologist*, 1971, *26*(8), 722–725.

Maier, N. R. F., and Maier, L. A. An experimental test of the effects of "developmental" vs. "free" discussion of the quality of group decisions. *Journal of Applied Psychology*, 1957, *41*, 320–323.

Maier, N. R. F., and Solem, A. R. The contribution of a discussion leader to the quality of group thinking. *Human Relations*, 1952, *5*, 277–288.

Maier, N. R. F., and Zerfoss, L. F. MRP: A technique for training large groups of supervisors and its potential use in social research. *Human Relations*, 1952, *5*, 177–186.

Maloney, R. M. Group learning through group discussion: a group discussion implementation analysis. *Journal of Social Psychology*, 1956, *43*, 3–9.

Mann, R. D. *Interpersonal styles and group development*. New York: Wiley, 1967.

Mann, R. D. et al. *The college classroom*. New York: Wiley, 1970.

Mann, W. R. *Changes in the level of attitude sophistication of college students as a measure of teacher effectiveness*. Unpublished doctoral dissertation, University of Michigan, 1968.

Martin, J. R. Two-way closed-circuit educational television. *Research Report No. 941-1*, Cleveland: Case Institute of Technology, 1957.

Martin, J. R.; Adams, R. B.; and Baron, M. R. Studies in educational closed-circuit television. *Research Report No. 948-5*, Cleveland: Case Institute of Technology, 1958.

Marton, F., and Säljö, R. On qualitative differences in learning: I—outcome and process. *British Journal of Educational Psychology*, 1976a, *46*, 4–11.

———. On qualitative differences in learning: II—outcome as a function of the learner's conception of the task. *British Journal of Educational Psychology*, 1976b, *46*, 115–127.

May, M. A., and Lumsdaine, A. *Learning from films*. New Haven: Yale University Press, 1958.

Mayer, R. E. Acquisition processes and resilience under varying testing conditions for structurally different problem-solving procedures. *Journal of Educational Psychology*, 1974, *66*(5), 644–656.

Mayer, R. E., and Greeno, J. G. Structural differences between learning outcomes produced by different instructional methods. *Journal of Educational Psychology*, 1972, *63*, 165–173.

Mayer, R. E.; Stiehl, C. C.; and Greeno, J. G. Acquisition of understanding and skill in relation to subjects' preparation and meaningfulness of instruction. *Journal of Educational Psychology*, June 1975, *67*(3), 331–350.

McClelland, D. C.; Atkinson, J. W.; Clark, R. A.; and Lowell, E. L. *The achievement motive*. New York: Appleton-Century-Crofts, 1953.

McClusky, H. Y. An experimental comparison of two methods of correcting the outcomes of examination. *School and Society*, 1934, *40*, 566–568.

McCollough, C., and Van Atta, E. L. *Experimental evaluation of teaching programs utilizing a block of independent work*. Paper read at Symposium, "Experimental Studies in Learning Independently,"

American Psychological Association, Washington, D.C., September 1958.

McKeachie, W. J. Anxiety in the college classroom. *Journal of Educational Research*, 1951, *45*, 153–160.

———. Individual conformity to attitudes of classroom groups. *Journal of Abnormal and Social Psychology*, 1954, *49*, 282–289.

———. Students, groups, and teaching methods. *American Psychologist*, 1958, *13*, 580–584.

———. Appraising teaching effectiveness. In W. J. McKeachie, ed. *The appraisal of teaching in large universities*. Ann Arbor: University of Michigan Extension Services, 1959a, pp. 32–36.

———, ed. *The appraisal of teaching in large universities*. Ann Arbor: University of Michigan Extension Service, 1959b.

———. *Research on college teaching: a review*. Washington, D.C.: ERIC Clearinghouse on Higher Education, 1970.

McKeachie, W. J.; Forrin, B.; Lin, Y.; and Teevan, R. Individualized teaching in elementary psychology. *Journal of Educational Psychology*, 1960, *51*, 285–291.

McKeachie, W. J., and Kulik, J. A. Effective college teaching. In F. N. Kerlinger, ed. *Review of research in education*, vol. 3. Itasca, IL: Peacock, 1975.

McKeachie, W. J., and Lin, Y. G. *Use of standard ratings in evaluation of college teaching*. Ann Arbor: Dept. of Psychology, University of Michigan, 1975. Final Report to National Institute of Education, Grant NE-6-00-3-0110.

McKeachie, W. J.; Lin, Y.; and Mann, W. Student ratings of teacher effectiveness: validity studies. *American Educational Research Journal*, 1971, *8*, 435–445.

McKeachie, W. J.; Lin, Y.; Milholland, J.; and Isaacson, R. Student affiliation motives, teacher warmth, and academic achievement. *Journal of Personality and Social Psychology*, 1966, *4*, 457–461.

McKeachie, W. J.; Pollie, D.; and Speisman, J. Relieving anxiety in classroom examinations. *Journal of Abnormal Psychology*, 1955, *50*, 93–98.

McKeachie, W. J., and Solomon, D. Student ratings of instructors: a validity study. *Journal of Educational Research*, 1958, *51*, 379–382.

McMichael, J. S., and Corey, J. R. Contingency management in an introductory psychology course produces better learning. *Journal of Applied Behavior Analysis*, 1969, *2*, 79–83.

McTavish, C. L. *Effect of repetitive film showings on learning*. Instructional Film Research Report, SDC 269-7-12, Special Devices Center, Office of Naval Research, November 1949.

Means, G., and Means, R. Achievement as a function of the presence of prior information concerning aptitudes. *Journal of Educational Psychology*, 1971, *62*, 185–187.

Melton, A. W.; Feldman, N. G.; and Mason, C. N. *Experimental studies of the education of children in a museum of schools*. Washington, D.C.: Publications of the American Association of Museums, 1936, *15*, 1–106.

Mertens, M. S. *The effects of mental hygiene films on self-regarding attitudes*. Instructional Film Research Report SDC 269-7-22, Special Devices Center, Office of Naval Research, July 1951.

Michael, D. N., and Maccoby, N. Factors influencing the effects of student participation on verbal learning from films: motivation vs. practice effects, feedback, and overt vs. covert responding. In A. A. Lumsdaine, ed. *Student response in programmed instruction: a symposium*. Washington, D.C.: NAS-NRC, 1953, *943*, 18.

Miller, N. M. Scientific principles for maximum learning from motion pictures. *Audio-Visual Communication Review*, 1957, *5*, 61–113.

Mintz, J. J. The A-T approach 14 years later: a review of the research. *Journal of College Science Teaching*, 1975, *4*, 247–252.

Monaco, G. E. *Inferences as a function of test-expectancy in the classroom*. Kansas State University Psychology Series, KSU-HIPI Report 77-3, 1977.

Moore, J. W.; Hauck, W. E.; and Gagne, E. D. Acquisition, retention, and transfer in an individualized college physics course. *Journal of Educational Psychology*, 1973, *64*, 335–340.

Moore, J. W.; Smith, W. I.; and Teevan, R. *Motivational variables in programmed learning: The role of need achievement, fear of failure, and student estimate of achievement*. Final Report U.S.O.E., Title 7, Grant No. 7-48-0070-149, Lewisburg, PA: Bucknell University Press, 1965.

Moore, M. R., and Popham, W. J. *The role of extra-class student interviews in promoting student achievement*. Paper read at joint session of American Association for the Advancement of Science and American Educational Research Association, Chicago, December 1959.

Moreno, F. The learning process in nurse's training. *Sociatry*, 2001, *2*, 207–214.

Morris, C. J., and Kimbrell, G. McA. Performance and attitudinal effects of the Keller method in an introductory psychology course. *Psychological Record*, 1972, *22*, 523–530.

Morsh, J. E., and Wilder, E. W. Identifying the effective instructor: a review of the quantitative studies, 1900–1952. *Research Bulletin*,

ARPTRC-TR-54-44, Air Force Personnel and Training Research Center, 1954.

Mueller, A. D. Class size as a factor in normal school instruction. *Education*, 1924, *45*, 203–227.

Nachman, M., and Opochinsky, S. The effects of different teaching methods: a methodological study. *Journal of Educational Psychology*, 1958, *49*, 245–249.

Naftulin, D. H.; Ware, J. E.; and Donnelly, F. A. The Dr. Fox lecture: a paradigm of educational seduction. *Journal of Medical Education*, 1973, *48*, 630–635.

Nash, A. N.; Muczyk, J. P.; and Vettori, F. L. The relative practical effectiveness of programmed instruction. *Personnel Psychology*, 1971, *24*, 397–418.

Nelson, T. *Teaching and learning at Kalamazoo College.* Unpublished manuscript, Kalamazoo College, Kalamazoo, MI, 1970.

Newman, S. E., and Highland, R. W. *The effectiveness of four instructional methods at different stages of a course.* Lackland Air Force Base, TX: Air Force Personnel and Training Research Center, Technical Report AFPTRC-TN-56-88, June 1956.

Norman, D. *Teaching learning strategies.* Mimeo, University of Calif., San Diego, April 11, 1977.

Northrop, D. S. *Effects on learning of the prominence of organizational outlines in instructional films.* Pennsylvania State University Instructional Film Research Program, Port Washington, NY: U.S. Naval Training Device Center, Office of Naval Research, Technical Report No. SDC 269-7-33, 1952.

Novak, J. D. An experimental comparison of a conventional and a project centered method of teaching a college general botany course. *Journal of Experimental Education*, 1958, *26*, 217–230.

Olson, D. Toward a theory of instructional means. *Educational Psychologist*, 1976, *12*, 14–35.

Pambookian, H. S. *The effect of feedback from students to college instructors on their teaching behavior.* Unpublished doctoral dissertation, University of Michigan, 1972.

Parsons, T. S. A comparison of instruction by kinescope, correspondence study, and customary classroom procedures. *Journal of Educational Psychology*, 1957, *48*, 27–40.

Parsons, T. S.; Ketcham, W. A.; and Beach, L. R. *Effects of varying degrees of student interaction and student-teacher contact in college courses.* Paper read at American Sociological Society, Seattle, Washington, August 1958.

Pascal, C. E. Instructional options, option preference, and course outcomes. *Alberta Journal of Educational Research*, 1971, *17*, 1–11.

Pask, G. Conversational techniques in the study and practice of education. *British Journal of Educational Psychology*, 1976, *46*, 12–25.

Pask, G., and Scott, B. C. E. CASTE: a system for exhibiting learning strategies and regulating uncertainties. *International Journal of Man-Machine Studies*, 1973, *5*.

Patton, J. A. *A study of the effects of student acceptance of responsibility and motivation on course behavior.* Unpublished doctoral dissertation, University of Michigan, 1955.

Paul, J. B. The length of class periods. *Educational Research*, 1932, *13*, 58–75.

Paul, J., and Ogilvie, J. C. Mass media and retention. *Explorations*, 1955, *4*, 120–123.

Perkins, H. V. The effects of climate and curriculum on group learning. *Journal of Educational Research*, 1950, *44*, 269–286.

Perry, R. P.; Abrami, P. C.; and Leventhal, L. *Educational seduction: the validity of student ratings under simulated classroom conditions.* Paper presented at the annual meeting of the American Psychological Association, Washington, D.C., September 1976.

Peterson, H. J., and Peterson, J. C. The value of guidance in reading for information. *Transactions of the Kansas Academy of Science*, 1931, *34*, 291–296.

Peterson, P. L. *Interactive effects of student anxiety, achievement orientation, and teacher behavior on student achievement and attitude.* Unpublished doctoral dissertation, Stanford University, 1976.

Petrie, C. R., Jr. Informative speaking: a summary and bibliography of related research. *Speech Monographs*, 1963, *30*, 79–91.

Poppen, W. A., and Thompson, C. L. The effect of grade contracts on student performance. *Journal of Educational Research*, 1971, *64*, 420–424.

Postlethwait, S. N.; Novak, J.; and Murray, H. T., Jr. *The Audio-tutorial approach to learning: through independent study and integrated experiences*, 2nd ed. Minneapolis: Burgess, 1969.

Potter, S. *One-upmanship.* New York: Henry Holt, 1955.

Pressey, S. L. A simple apparatus which gives tests and scores—and teaches. *School and Society*, 1926, *23*, 373–376.

Rasmussen, G. R. Evaluation of a student-centered and instructor-centered method of conducting a graduate course in education. *Journal of Educational Psychology*, 1956, *47*, 449–461.

Remmers, H. H. Learning, effort, and attitudes as affected by three methods of instruction in elementary psychology. *Purdue University Studies in Higher Education*, 1933, *21*.

Remmers, H. H., and Brandenburg, G. C. Experimental data on the Purdue rating scale for instructors. *Educational Administration and Supervision*, 1927, *13*, 519–527.

Remmers, R. H., and Elliott, D. N. The Indiana college and university staff-evaluation program. *School and Society*, 1949, *70*, 168–171.

Riley, J. E.; Ryan, B. F.; and Lifshitz, M. *The student looks at his teacher.* New Brunswick, NJ: Rutgers University Press, 1950.

Ristenbatt, M. P. *A tutorial communication system—blackboard-by-wire picturephone.* Unpublished paper, University of Michigan, 1968.

Rockart, J. F., and Morton, M. S. S. *Computers and the learning process in higher education.* New York: McGraw-Hill, 1975.

Rohrer, J. H. Large and small sections in college classes. *Journal of Higher Education*, 1957, *28*, 275–279.

Romig, J. L. An evaluation of instruction by student-led discussion in the college classroom. *Dissertation Abstracts International*, 1972, *32*, 6816.

Rose, A. M. *Human information processing: an assessment and research battery.* Technical Report No. 46. Ann Arbor: University of Michigan, Human Performance Center, January 1974.

Rosenshine, B. *Teaching behaviors and student achievement.* London: National Foundation for Educational Research in England and Wales, 1971.

Ross, I. C. Role specialization in supervision. Unpublished doctoral dissertation, Columbia University, *Dissertation Abstracts*, 1957, *17*, 2701–2702.

Roth, C. H. *Continuing effectiveness of personalized self-paced instruction in digital systems engineering.* Paper presented at the meeting of the American Society for Engineering Education, Lubbock, TX, June 1972.

Rothkopf, E. Z. Variable adjunct question schedules, interpersonal interaction, and incidental learning from written material. *Journal of Educational Psychology*, 1972, *63*, 87–92.

Ruja, H. Outcomes of lecture and discussion procedures in three college courses. *Journal of Experimental Education*, 1954, *22*, 385–394.

Runkel, P. J. Cognitive similarity in facilitating communication. *Sociometry*, 1956, *19*, 178–191.

Russell, H. E. *Inter-relations of some indices of instructor effectiveness: an exploratory study.* Ph.D. dissertation, University of Pittsburgh, 1951.

Scheidemann, N. V. An experiment in teaching psychology. *Journal of Applied Psychology*, 1929, *13*, 188–191.

Schirmerhorn, S.; Goldschmid, M. L.; and Shore, B. S. Learning basic principles of probability in student dyads: a cross-age comparison. *Journal of Educational Psychology*, 1975, 67(4), 551–557.

Schramm, W. L. Learning from instructional television. *Review of Educational Research*, 1962, *32*, 156–157.

———. *The research on programmed instruction.* Washington, D.C.: U.S. Government Printing Office, 1964.

Schurdak, J. J. *An approach to the use of computers in the instructional process and an evaluation.* Research Report RC-1432, IBM Watson Research Center, Yorktown Heights, NY, July 1965.

Seashore, C. E. Elementary psychology: an outline of a course by the project method. *Aims and Progress Research*, No. 153, Iowa City: University of Iowa Studies, 1928.

Seashore, S. E. *Group cohesiveness in the industrial group.* University of Michigan Survey Research Center, Publication No. 14, 1954.

Seibert, W. F. *A brief report and evaluation of closed-circuit television instruction in the first semester calculus course.* Lafayette, IN: Purdue University Audio-Visual Center, 1957.

———. *An evaluation of televised instruction in college English composition.* TVPR Report No. 5, Lafayette, IN: Purdue University, 1958.

Seibert, W. F., and Honig, J. M. *A brief study of televised laboratory instruction.* Television Project Report 8, West Lafayette, IN: Purdue University, 1959.

Sharp, D., and Cole, M. Patterns of responding in the word associations of West African children. *Child Development*, 1972, *43*(1), 55–56.

Siegel, L.; Adams, J. F.; and Macomber, F. G. Retention of subject matter as a function of large-group instructional procedures. *Journal of Educational Psychology*, 1960, *51*, 9–13.

Siegel, L., and Siegel, L. C. The instructional gestalt: a conceptual framework and design for educational research. *Audio-Visual Communication Review*, 1964, *12*, 16–45.

———. *The instructional gestalt in televised courses.* Miami University, Oxford, OH, 1966.

Sime, M., and Boyce, G. Overt responses, knowledge and results of learning. *Programmed Learning and Educational Technology*, 1969, *6*(1), 12–19.

Skinner, B. F. Teaching machines. *Science*, 1958, *128*, 969–977.

Slomowitz, M. A comparison of personality changes and content achievement gains occurring in two modes of instruction. Unpublished doctoral dissertation, N. Y. University, *Dissertation Abstracts*, 1955, *15*, 1790.

Smalzreid, N. T., and Remmers, H. H. A factor analysis of the Purdue rating scale for instructors. *Journal of Educational Psychology*, 1943, *34*, 363–367.

Smith, B. O. On the anatomy of teaching. *Journal of Teacher Education*, 1956, 7, 339–346.

Smith, D. E. P. Application transfer and inhibition. *Journal of Educational Psychology*, 1954, *45*, 169–174.

Smith, D. E. P. et al. Reading improvement as a function of student personality and teaching methods. *Journal of Educational Psychology*, 1956, *47*, 47–58.

Smith, H. C. Team work in the college class. *Journal of Educational Psychology*, 1955, *46*, 274–286.

Smith, N. H. The teaching of elementary statistics by the conventional classroom method vs. the method of programmed instruction. *Journal of Educational Research*, 1962, *55*, 417–420.

Smith, W. F., and Rockett, F. C. Test performance as a function of anxiety, instructor and instructions. *Journal of Educational Research*, 1958, *52*, 138–141.

Snow, R. E. *Research on aptitudes: a progress report.* Technical Report No. 1, Aptitude Research Project, School of Education, Stanford University, September 1976.

Solomon, D.; Rosenberg, L.; and Bezdek, W. E. Teacher behavior and student learning. *Journal of Educational Psychology*, 1964, *55*, 23–30.

Spence, R. B. Lecture and class discussion in teaching educational psychology. *Journal of Educational Psychology*, 1928, *19*, 454–462.

Stanford, G., and Roark, A. E. *Human interaction in education.* Boston: Allyn and Bacon, 1974.

Stephan, F. F., and Mishler, E. C. The distribution of participation in small groups: An experimental approximation. *American Sociological Review*, 1952, *17*, 598–602.

Stephens, A. L. Certain special factors involved in the law of effect. *Abstracts of Doctoral Dissertations*, Ohio State University, 1953, *64*.

Stephens College. Courses to be taught over closed-circuit TV. *Stephens College New Reporter 14*, No. 4, 1955.

Stern, G. G. Congruence and dissonance in the ecology of college students. *Student Medicine*, 1960, *8*, 304–339.

————. Environments for learning. In N. Sanford, ed. *The American college*, New York: Wiley, 1962, 690–730.

Stuit, D. B.; Harshbarger, G. C.; Becker, S. L.; Bechtoldt, H. P.; and Hall, A. E. *An experiment in teaching.* Iowa City: State University of Iowa, Dept. of Speech, 1956.

Stuit, D. B., and Wilson, J. T. The effect of an increasingly well-defined criterion on the prediction of success at Naval Training School (Tactical Radar). *Journal of Applied Psychology*, 1946, *30*, 614–623.

Sturgis, H. W. The relationship of the teacher's knowledge of the student's background to the effectiveness of teaching: a study of the extent to which the effectiveness of teaching is related to the teacher's knowledge of the student's background. Unpublished doctoral dissertation, New York University, *Dissertation Abstracts*, 1959, *19*, No. 11.

Sullivan, A. M., and Skanes, G. R. Validity of student evaluation of teaching and the characteristics of successful instructors. *Journal of Educational Psychology*, 1974, *66*, 584–590.

Svensson, L. *Study skill and learning.* Goteborg, Sweden: Acta Universitates Gothoburgensis, 1976.

Taylor, S. H. An experiment in classification of students in mathematics. *Mathematics Teacher*, 1931, *23*, 414–423.

Tharp, J. B. Sectioning in romance language classes at the University of Illinois. In E. W. Bagster-Collins et al. *Studies in modern language teaching.* New York: Macmillan, 1930, pp. 367–432.

Thistlethwaite, D. L. College environments and the development of talent. *Science*, 1959, *130*, 71–76.

———. *College press and changes in study plans of talented students.* Evanston, IL: National Merit Scholarship Corporation, 1960.

Thomas, E. J., and Fink, C. F. The effects of group size. *Psychological Bulletin*, 1963, *60*, 371–385.

Thompson, W. N. *Quantitative research in public address and communication.* New York: Random House, 1967.

Throop, J. F.; Assini, L. T.; and Boguslavsky, G. W. *The effectiveness of laboratory instruction in strength of materials by closed-circuit television.* Troy, NY: Rensselaer Polytechnic Institute, 1958.

Timmel, G. B. A study of the relationship between method of teaching a college course in mental hygiene and change in student adjustment status. Unpublished doctoral dissertation, Cornell University, *Dissertation Abstracts*, 1955, *15*, 90.

Travers, R. M. W. Appraisal of the teaching of the college faculty. *Journal of Higher Education*, 1950, *21*, 41–42.

Trotter, V. Y. *A comparison of the laboratory and the lecture demonstration methods of teaching survey of food preparation for freshman home economics at the University of Vermont.* Unpublished paper, Ohio State University, 1960.

Trowbridge, N. *An approach to teaching a large undergraduate class.* Unpublished manuscript, Drake University, Des Moines, IA, 1969.

Ullrich, O. A. *An experimental study in ability grouping.* Unpublished doctoral dissertation, University of Texas, 1926.

Vandermeer, A. W. *Relative effectiveness of instruction by films exclusively, films plus study guides, and standard lecture methods.* Instructional Film Research Report SDC 269-7-12, Special Devices Center, Office of Naval Research, July 1950.

———. *Effect of film-viewing practice on learning from instructional films.* Instructional Film Research Report SDC 269-7-20, Special Devices Center, Office of Naval Research, November 1951.

Vattano, E. J.; Hockenberry, C.; Grider, W.; Jacobson, L.; and Hamilton, S. Employing undergraduate students in the teaching of psychology. *Teaching of Psychology Newsletter*, March 1973, 9–12.

Vinacke, E. W. Some variables in buzz sessions. *Journal of Social Psychology*, 1957, *45*, 25–33.

Voeks, V. Ridicule and other detriments to effective teaching. *AAUP Bulletin*, 1954, *40*, 621–630.

Wakely, J. H.; Marr, J. N.; Plath, D. W.; and Wilkins, D. M. *Lecturing and test performance in introductory psychology.* Paper read at Michigan Academy, Ann Arbor, Michigan, March 1960.

Ward, J. Group-study vs. lecture-demonstration method in physical science instruction for general education college students. *Journal of Experimental Education*, 1956, *24*, 197–210.

Ware, J. E., and Williams, R. G. The Dr. Fox effect: A study of lecture effectiveness and ratings of instruction. *Journal of Medical Education*, 1975, *50*, 149–156.

Warren, R. A comparison of two plans of study in engineering physics. Unpublished doctoral dissertation, Purdue University, *Dissertation Abstracts*, 1954, *14*, 1648–1649.

Waterhouse, I. L., and Child, I. L. Frustration and the quality of performance. *Journal of Personality*, 1953, *21*, 298–311.

Watson, R. P. *The relationship between selected personality variables, satisfaction, and academic achievement in defined classroom atmospheres.* Unpublished doctoral dissertation, University of Michigan, 1956.

Webb, N. J. Student preparation and tape recording of course lectures as a method of instruction. *Psychological Reports*, 1965, *16*, 67–72.

Webb, N. J., and Grib, T. F. *Teaching as a learning experience.* (Technical Progress Report, 5-0923-2-10-1), West DePere, WI: St. Norbert College, June 1966.

———. *Teaching process as a learning experience: the experimental use of student-led groups.* Final Report, HE-000-882. Washington, D.C.: Department of Health, Education, and Welfare, October 1967.

Wells, S.; Whelchel, B.; and Jamison, D. The impact of varying levels of computer-assisted instruction on the academic performance of disadvantaged students. *Research Bulletin*, Princeton, NJ: Educational Testing Service, June 1974.

Wells, W. D. Instructor's manual for Hilgard's *Introduction to psychology*. New York: Harcourt, Brace and Company, 1952.

White, J. R. A comparison of the group-laboratory and the lecture-demonstration methods in engineering instruction. *Journal of Engineering Education*, 1945, *36*, 50–54.

Wieder, G. S. Group procedures modifying attitudes of prejudice in the college classroom. *Journal of Educational Psychology*, 1959, *45*, 332–334.

Wilke, W. H. An experimental comparison of the speech, the radio, and the printed page as propaganda devices. *Archives of Psychology*, 1934, *25*.

Williams, J. Comparison of several response modes in a review program. *Journal of Educational Psychology*, 1963, *54*, 253–260.

Williams, R. G., and Ware, J. E. Validity of student ratings of instruction under different incentive conditions: a further study of the Dr. Fox effect. *Journal of Educational Psychology*, 1976, *68*, 48–56.

Wilson, W. R. Students rate teachers. *Journal of Higher Education*, 1932, *3*, 75–82.

Wish, M. An unfolding analysis of cognitive preferences. *ETS Research Bulletin*, 1964, 64–67.

Wispe, L. G. Evaluative section teaching methods in the introductory course. *Journal of Educational Research*, 1951, *45*, 161–168.

Witters, D. R., and Kent, G. W. Teaching without lecturing: evidence in the case for individualized instruction. *Psychological Record*, 1972, *22*, 169–175.

Wolfle, D. The relative efficacy of constant and varied stimulation during learning. *Journal of Comparative Psychology*, 1935, *19*, 5–27.

Wrigley, C. Undergraduate students as teachers: apprenticeship in the university classroom. *Teaching of Psychology Newsletter*, March 1973, 5–7.

Zander, A., and Lippitt, R. Reality practice as educational method. *Sociometry*, 1944, 129–151.

Zeleny, L. D. Experimental appraisal of a group learning plan. *Journal of Educational Research*, 1940, *34*, 37–42.

Zuckerman, D. W., and Horn, R. E. *The guide to simulations/games for education and training*. Lexington, Mass.: Information Resources, Inc., 1973.

INDEX

Books. *See also* Textbooks
  goals of, 296
  vs. lecture, 26
  "managed," 9
  paperback, 8, 102
Boredom, 107
Bork, A., 109
Born, D. G., 114
Bovard, E. E., Jr., 59, 60
Boyce, G., 106
Bradley, R. L., 84
Breland, N. S., 116
Briggs, L. J., 65
Broadcast television courses, 127. *See also* Television
Bronfenbrenner, U. A., 185
Bulletin boards, 297
Burke, H. R., 57
Burkhardt, S. M., 85
Burtt, H. E., 65
Buzz groups, 13
  in developmental discussions, 42, 63
  and film viewing, 130
  goals of, 297
  and lecturing, 23

CAI, 235. *See* Computer-assisted instruction
Calhoun, J. F., 113
California Psychological Inventory, achievement scales of, 248
Calvin, A. D., 245, 251
Carlton, B. J., 131
Carpenter, C. R., 89, 95, 121
Carrier, N. A., 251
Carroll, J. B., 133
Case method, 149
Casey, 27, 28
Cassette recorders, 132–133
CASTE (Course Assembly System and Tutorial Environment), 240
Categories, and semantic memory, 235
Centra, J. A., 269
Chance, C. W., 133
Chassel, L. M., 65
Cheating, 163–167. *See also* Tests
  handling, 165–167
  prevention of, 164
Cheydleur, F. D., 203
Child, I. L., 185
Child development course, independent study in, 90–91
Churchill, R., 88, 97
Class, first, 15–16
  introduction of teacher in, 19–20
  introduction of text in, 20–21

outline distributed during, 18–19
problem posting in, 18
questions in, 21
Classes
  group-centered, 59
  lack of preparation for, 194
  large, 210–214
  preparing for, 193–194 (*see also* Course preparation)
  television in, 124
Classroom. *See also* Discussions; Lectures
  authority in, 72
  games in, 146–148
  learning process in, 242–243
  order in, 188–193
  role playing in, 137
  student-centered vs. instructor-centered, 52–54
  two-column method used in, 47
  visiting, 13
Class size
  and educational goals, 206–207
  for group discussions, 66
  multi-section courses, 208–209
  optimum, 202
  research on, 203–205, 208
  small classes, 205–206
  and student intelligence, 245–246
  theory, 204
  and transfer of learning, 242
Coats, W. D., 24
Code of Ethics, of APA, 218–220
Cognition, 232–243
  retrieval, 234
  semantic memory, 232–233
  storage, 233–234
Cognitive style, of students, 247
Cole, M., 235
College
  definition of, 253
  independent study in, 87–89
  individualized teaching in, 201
  pre-professionalism of, 74
  programmed instruction in, 107–108
  as subculture, 2–3, 263
Collins, A. M., 233
Communication
  in classroom, 16
  persuasiveness of, 32
Compartmentalization, 254
Competence, 231. *See also* Achievement; Motivation
  and motivation, 223–224
Computer
  influence on education, 101

of tests, 169
Graduate Record Examination, 95
Graduate school, encouragement for, 74
Graduate students
    proctoring by, 166
    ratings of, 267
    as teachers, 94
Greene, E. B., 30, 103
Greenhill, L. P., 121, 259
Greeno, James G., 236, 239, 246
Greenough, W. T., 267
Grib, T. F., 96
Gripe sessions, 68
Grossman, L. I., 126
Group dynamics, problems in, 18
Group participation. *See also* Discussion
    in developmental discussion, 37, 39
    and group size, 66
    importance of, 54
    and individual sensitivity, 48
    in large classes, 211
    and nonparticipants, 41–43
    in test construction, 153
Grubb, R. E., 110
Gruber, H. E., 89, 95
Guessing. *See also* Tests
    correction for, 169
    methods of, 162
Guest lecturer, goals of, 297
Guetzkow, H. S., 56, 61
Guilford Inventory of Factors, 249
Guilford-Zimmerman Temperament
    survey, 65

Haigh, G. V., 55, 59
Haines, D. B., 48, 184, 185, 253
Haner, C. F., 268
Hansen, W. L., 246
Harden, E. L., 245
Harlow, H. F., 29, 230
Hartman, F. R., 103
Hatch, E. M., 65
Hauck, W. E., 116
Hawthorne effect, 258
Haythorn, W., 262
Heath, R. W., 247
Hebb, D. O., 29
Heckhausen, H., 226
Hedley, R. H., 127
Heilman, J. D., 268
Henderson, W. T., 117
Hess, J. H., 113
Heyns, Roger W., 64, 253
Highland, R. W., 132
Hiler, W., 104
Hill, R. J., 28

Hirsch, R. S., 109
Hirschman, C. S., 27
Hoban, C. F., 127, 131
Hockenberry-Boeding, C., 97
Hoffman, F. K., 245
Hoffman, L. R., 65
Holidays, and course preparation, 11
Homework, 193
Honig, J. M., 124
Honor system, 164
Horner, M. S., 224
Horrocks-Troyer test, for class atti-
    tudes, 57
Horwitz, M., 54
Hovland, C. I., 32, 33, 46, 131
Hsiao, J. C., 147
Hudelson, E., 205
Humor, in lecture, 24
Hunt, P., 149
Hurst, J. C., 97
Husband, R. W., 27, 28

Independence, of students, 247
Independent study programs, 87
    pyramid plan, 89–90, 95
    variety of, 90–91
Individual instruction, 145, 200–201
Individualization, in education, 254
Industry, implications of research in,
    283
Information, presentation of new, 35–36
Information-processing approach, to
    psychology of learning, 232,
    236–238
Innovations, barriers to, 277
Instruction. *See also* Teaching
    adaptation to individual differences,
    239
    individual, 144, 145, 200–201
    programmed, 104–109
    PSI, 30, 98, 108, 112–117, 296
    student evaluation of, 268–272
    test, 160–163
Instructors, 253. *See also* Teachers
    and achievement motivation in class,
    266
    counseling of students by, 194–195
    in discussion groups, 49
    feedback from, 230–231
    and personalized education, 253
    role, 2, 238
    role playing, 137–138
    student ratings of, 267–268
    and university personnel, 215–217
Intelligence, and class size, 246
Introversion, 251

Inventory of Academic Adjustment, 59
Isaacson, R. L., 24

Jaksa, P., 134
Jamison, D., 110
Janitors, 216
Jenkins, R. L., 58
Jenson, B. T., 90
John, P., 97
Johnson, D. M., 57, 242
Johnston, J. J., 162
Johnston, R. E, Jr., 133, 134
Judd, W. A., 110

Kaplan, S., 104
Kapstein, F. F., 131
Kasten, D. V., 125
Katona, G., 25, 53, 228
Katz, David, 228
Keller, Fred, 112
Keller, F. S., 114
Keller courses, 114–117
Keller Plan, 30, 95, 99, 112–117, 154,
        171. *See also* Personalized Sys-
        tem of Instruction
    basic features of, 113
    evaluation of, 117, 261
    fixed sequence of, 119
Kelly, Allan C., 117, 246
Kelly, B. L., 60
Kelly, E. L., 56, 61
Kent, G. W., 115
Ketcham, W. A., 90, 91, 123, 260
Kimbrell, G. McA., 115
King, P. G., 110
Kintsch, 233
Kishler, J. P., 131
Kitchener, K. G., 97
Klapper, H. L., 29
Knowledge, and course objectives, 289
Koenig, K., 249
Krathwohl, D., 7
Krauskopf, C. J., 51
Kruglak, H., 84, 85
Krumboltz, J. D., 58, 107
Kulik, C. L. C., 116, 117
Kulik, J. A., 116, 117, 134, 238, 267

Laboratory, teaching in, 83–85, 297
Lahti, A. M., 33, 85
Lamphear, 94
Lancaster, O. E., 28
Landsman, T., 57
Lange, P. C., 106
Language laboratories, 132–133
Leadership, in discussion, 37–49, 63–64.

See also Group participation
Learning
    active vs. passive, 230
    complex, 233
    computer uses in, 109–111
    content, 117
    contract, 118
    course preparation for, 7
    deep-level vs. surface processing,
        237–238
    through discussion, 47–49
    by "doing," 229
    field experience, 145
    and grades, 177
    influence of textbooks on, 9
    information-processing approach to,
        232, 236–238
    in lecture process, 25
    and motivation, 221–227
    organization in, 102
    in pairs, 98–99
    programmed, 30
    from reading, 103–104
    resistance to, 51
    strategies for, 241
    student perceptions of, 291–295
    and teaching machines, 105
    transfer of, 239
Learning cell, 98–99, 251
Learning groups, media-activated, 134–
        135. *See also* Group participation
Learning theory, changes in, 232
Lecture. *See also* Teaching
    authenticity of, 267
    and automated learning, 29–32
    vs. automation, 29–32
    by cassette recorder, 133
    vs. discussion, 26–29
    discussion supplement for, 97
    dynamics of, 24
    goals of, 296
    methods, 32–34
    organization of, 25
    preparation of, 13
    role of, 31
    vs. television instruction, 125
    theory, 25–26
Lecturer, role of, 34. *See also* Instruc-
        tors; Teachers
Leith, G. O. M., 99, 119, 229, 240, 242,
        251
Lempert, R., 185
Lepore, A. R., 122, 127
Lessons, microlesson, 140. *See also*
        Course
Leventhal, L., 24

Mueller, A. D., 203
Mulder, F. J., 203
Multiple-choice tests, 155, 157–160. *See also* Tests
answer sheets, 167–168, 171
Multi-section courses, 208–209. *See also* Courses
coordinating, 209–211
Murray, H. T., 134

Nachman, M., 203, 260
Naftulin, D. H., 267
Nash, A. N., 106
National Defense Education Act, 132
National Merit Scholars, 52, 223, 281
Nelson, T. T., 95
Newman, S. E., 132
Nonparticipants, problem of, 41–43. *See also* Discussion techniques
Norman, Donald, 233, 237, 243
Norms
influence of instructor on, 253
for research and teaching, 4
Northrop, D. S., 131
Novak, J. D., 85, 87, 134

Objectives. *See also* Goals
in course preparation, 6–7
in independent study programs, 91
O'Connor, P. A., 226, 227
Ogilvie, J. C., 131
Olson, D., 238, 242
Opochinsky, S., 203, 260
Organization. *See also* Course preparation
in learning, 102
in lecture process, 33–34
and motivation, 227–229
and student intelligence, 246
Otis Test of Mental Ability, 153
Outline, course, 12, 18–19
Overview, in discussion, 97

Pambookian, H. S., 269
Paperback books, 8, 102
Parents, and achievement motivation, 231
Parsons, T. S., 90, 91, 123, 260
Participation. *See* Group participation
Pascal, C. E., 240
Pask, G., 109, 110, 111, 240
Pass-fail grading, 185
Patton, J. A., 59, 60, 248
Paul, J. B., 92, 131
Pep meetings, 68
Periodicals, 297
Perry, R. P., 24
Personality, teacher's, and student

ratings, 266–267
Personalized System of Instruction (PSI), 30, 108, 112–117. *See also* Keller Plan
goals of, 296
and learning cell, 98
Peterson, H. J., 105
Peterson, J. C., 105
Peterson, P. L., 250
Petrie, C. R., 25
Photographs, 133–135
Physical Science Study Committee's course (PSSC), 247
Physics course
content of, 191–192
independent study in, 89
"Picture-phone," 132
Plath, D. W., 91
Pollie, D., 163, 168, 250
Popham, W. J., 59
Poppen, W. A., 118
Postlethwait, S. N., 133, 134
Potter, Stephen, 224
Practice, 230
Pressey, S. L., 105
Pretesting, 159–160
Print media and revolution in education, 102. *See also* Books
Problem-centered approach, to teaching, 25
Problem posting, 17–18, 38, 194
Problem solving. *See also* Tests
and anxiety, 250
and authoritarianism, 262
in developmental discussions, 47
and discussion techniques, 36–37
in laboratory method, 85
in multiple-choice tests, 159
serialist vs. holist strategies for, 240
subproblems, 43–44
Proctoring, by graduate students, 165
Professional schools, overcrowding of, 3
Professors. *See also* Instructors; Teachers
characteristics of, 253
and grades, 176
Programmed instruction, 104–109
Programmed texts, goals of, 297
Program planning, 198–199
Project method, of teaching, 87
PSI. *See* Personalized System of Instruction
Psychology. *See also* Motivation
cognitive, 103, 104, 232, 237
of students as teachers, 95–96
Psychology course
audiovisual techniques for, 134

code of ethics for, 218–220
content of, 191–192
goals of, 153
grading for, 178
objectives of, 285–290
role playing in, 138
small-group discussion in, 95
Pyramid plan, of independent study, 89–90. *See also* Independent study programs

Questionnaire, for student evaluation, 291–295
Questions
in developmental discussions, 38–40
essay, 168–169
in first class, 21
and motivation of students, 223
multiple-choice, 157–160
number on tests, 160
and order in classroom, 190–191
short-answer, 155
study, 274–275
value, 104
Quillian, M. R., 233
Quizzes, scheduling of, 12

Radio, for educational instruction, 131
Rasmussen, G. R., 58
Reading
learning from, 103–104
materials, 31
outside, 213
Reading list, preparation for, 12
Reading log, 8
Registrar's office, 216
Regulations, college, 217. *See also* Norms
Reinforcement, 232
Remedial work, 199–200
Remmers, H. H., 26, 28, 29, 245, 266, 267
Repetitive drill, 229
Reports, student, 143–144, 296
Reprint series, 8, 102
Research
on achievement motivation, 226
on authoritarianism, 248–249
on class size, 203–205, 208
on contract plans, 118
on discussion methods, 50–63
on essay vs. objective tests, 241
evaluation of, 261–263
on grading, 184–185
on independent study, 87–92
on instructional films, 130–131

on laboratory teaching, 84–85
on learning from reading, 103–104
on lecture vs. discussion, 26–28
student intelligence and class size, 245
on teaching, 280–281
vs. teaching, 3–4
on television in education, 121–122, 123–124
Resources. *See also* Course preparation
advance work for, 13
choosing of, 7–9
Responsibility, of students, 247
Restructuring, 233
Reviews, purpose of, 240
Riley, J. E., 268
Rockett, F. C., 163, 251
Rohwer, W. D., 95
Role playing, 136–139
goals of, 297
in large classes, 211
techniques, 13
Romano, M. T., 126
Romig, J. L., 96
Roney, H., 127
Rorschach tests, for class attitudes, 57
Rosenberg, L., 27, 38, 61
Roshal, S. M., 131
Ross, I. C., 184
Roth, C. H., 115
Rothkopf, E. Z., 104
Ruja, H., 26, 28
Runkel, P. J., 247
Russell, H. E., 266
Russian History course, game used in, 147–148

Säljö, R., 34, 104, 153, 237, 241
Sampling, biased, 258
Satisfaction. *See also* Student ratings
in teaching, 281, 283
testing of student, 248–249
Schedule, college, and course preparation, 11
Scheidermann, N. V., 87
Schirmerhorn, S., 99
Schmidt, W., 55, 59
Schramm, W. L., 106, 127
Schumer, H., 250
Schurdak, J. J., 110
Scores, standard, 169–170. *See also* Grades
Scott, B. C. E., 110, 111, 240
Seashore, C. E., 87
Seashore, S. E., 54
Seating charts, 16